BOOKS BY
Tay Thomas

Only in Alaska
Follow the North Star
Our Flight to Adventure
(with Lowell Thomas, Jr.)

ONLY IN ALASKA

ONLY IN ALASKA

by TAY THOMAS

DOUBLEDAY & COMPANY, INC.
Garden City, New York   1969

Most of Chapter VIII, *Earthquake!*, appeared in the July, 1964 issue of National Geographic, © 1964, National Geographic Society.

Lines of "The Spell of the Yukon" from *The Collected Poems of Robert Service*. Reprinted by permission of Dodd, Mead & Company, The Ryerson Press, and Ernest Benn Limited.

Letter from Eugene D. Smith which appeared in the *Inlet Courier Weekly*, Homer, Alaska, May 4, 1962. Reprinted by permission.

Excerpts from *The Milepost*, reprinted by permission of Robert A. Henning, Editor and Publisher.

Excerpts from the 1967 Centennial Edition of *The Alaska Travel Guide*, reprinted by permission of Lake Advertising, Inc.

Contents

I

But I Don't Live
in an Igloo

I was still struggling to put up the tent when the sun set with what seemed incredible speed. My fingers were already stiff from cold, despite my heavy gloves, and I could feel that peculiar sensation in my nostrils which comes when the temperature starts down well below zero.

I yelled to Lowell to hurry and come help me, but all I heard in return was a few muttered cuss words, drifting over the fifty yards between us. He was still out on the lake ice, working with his little "fire pot" heater, which, when placed beneath the engine of our airplane, would hopefully guarantee its starting the next morning. Otherwise we could be marooned hundreds of miles from nowhere.

I stopped struggling and clapped my hands for a few moments, to start the circulation again. At least the two children seemed content, running about in the deep snow, their hooded fur parkas and knee-high mukluks keeping them warm while they filled our tin pots with snow to melt for water. But the light was fading fast, and the great snowy peak of Mount McKinley, towering above the head of the little lake, was becoming a shadowy hint of its majestic self.

I glanced at the spruce-lined shore. We still had to cut boughs for the tent floor and firewood for a cooking fire. And just what was I going to do with our frozen cans of food to make some supper? Actually, just what in the world was I doing there anyway! Me, a girl born and brought up in a luxurious suburb of New York City (my parents always took us to Florida during the winters, to escape the worst of the cold weather). I know, I should have expected anything when I married Lowell.

After ten years of maintaining a home in Princeton, New Jersey (most of the first five were spent wandering all over the globe), it was our decision to move up to Alaska and make the brand new forty-ninth state our permanent home. It was no sudden impulse but a conclusion carefully reached over a two-year period and after a three-month-long visit all over the Far North. We had both become increasingly fed up with Eastern suburban living, with the long hours of travel necessary in order to go skiing or get to camping areas, and with a general feeling of inadequacy and frustration with regard to making any meaningful contribution to society and our fellow neighbors. As we tossed our decision back and forth, we kept thinking of the truly important and exciting challenge of actively taking a part in the development of a new state. And to be able to enjoy the great, unspoiled wilderness of Alaska just beyond one's front yard was a temptation for both of us. The added lure, for Lowell, was the fact that the forty-ninth state was the "land of the light plane," and Lowell no longer enjoyed flying his Cessna in the smog-ridden, crowded air lanes of the East.

While we were making our big decision, we lugged out our atlas and studied other parts of the country: northern New England, the Southwest, the Rockies, and the Northwest. But no matter where our eyes roamed, they always went back to that new state which is twice as large as Texas and Indiana put together. To decide to move, lock, stock, and barrel, over five thousand miles away from where one was born and brought up, away from all family and friends, was difficult enough, but we knew that as the years went on and our five-year-old Anne and three-year-old David became more involved with school and playmates, it would become tougher. It was really now or never, and when in early 1960, we finally agreed IT WAS NOW, we felt a vast sense of relief and a conviction that what we were doing was absolutely right.

Now we ran headlong into the next obstacle: explaining the big decision to family and friends. Actually, our parents were the easiest to sell: all being globe-trotters, distance meant nothing but a few hours by jet, and anyway, I think they were conditioned to expect anything from us. With friends and acquaintances it was another story. It was the outward "yes, we understand" but the silent "they're nuts" reaction. Several of my neighbors nodded in agreement, but with pitying looks, and sealed their approval with, "Well, as long as you don't mind hauling your water from the well and going out hunting for your meat . . ." As a final gesture to help us face the unknown wilds, one of our "bon voyage" gifts was a miniature brass kerosene lantern, which now sits high on a shelf like a cherished antique in our electrically lit house. We knew we were headed for a home in a small city with all the conveniences to be found anywhere (our winter camping episode was one of Lowell's adventuresome schemes, but more about that later!); however, no one else seemed to want to believe us. We finally decided to keep quiet and instead devote our energies to the big move.

For a long while after we had become confirmed Alaskans, completely sold on our new home, we continued to try to explain why we lived in the Far North, always to get the same response. It seems that no matter what Alaska does to sell itself to its sister states, through magazine stories, TV films, or Lowell's many illustrated lectures, other Americans seem to have a built-in, conditioned response: Alaska is their last great frontier, a still untamed vast wilderness of snow and ice and rugged individuals. They are proud that there is a place like this left within the United States, and remain convinced that this dream will never change. So be it, I have given up, but my enthusiasm for our new life here is so great that I want to tell of some of the adventures and experiences since our big move, and the reader can decide for himself whether we are nuts or to be envied!

How does one get to Alaska? A glance at the map graphically points out how far north one has to travel (a fact we find easy to forget while living here) and how a vast stretch of Canada separates the forty-ninth state from its neighboring states. The easiest way is to fly. We could jet it from Chicago to Anchorage in five hours or from Seattle in three. But we wanted to take our International Travelall, a roomy, four-wheel-drive vehicle, with us, and although a heavily loaded moving van was carrying most of our possessions northward, the car (and a small baggage trailer) would be loaded with mounds of leftovers, including Bozie, our over-sized German shepherd dog.

Obviously we would have to drive, and while there is no easiest way to tackle the great distance from New York to Seattle (especially with children under six!), the Alaskan ferry system, begun in 1963, has been a big boon to motorists at the western end of the route. The traveler can relax and enjoy magnificent coastal scenery and let the ship do the driving between Prince Rupert, British Columbia, and Haines, Alaska, a distance of some five hundred miles. Haines, at the head of the Lynn Canal in southeast Alaska, is just a two-day drive to Anchorage, in South-central Alaska, or Fairbanks, in the interior. But in 1960 the ferry system was not yet in existence, and we were faced with no other choice except the much maligned Alaska Highway. In earlier days called the Alcan, this road was a tremendous feat of engineering, spanning 1523 miles from Dawson Creek, Canada, to Fairbanks. All but three hundred miles of the highway lies in Canada, and virtually all still remains a gravel roadway, despite constant pressure, pleas, and plans for its paving.

The highway was begun in 1942 when the United States became concerned over a possible Japanese threat to Alaskan sea lanes. Over ten thousand U. S. Army engineers and six thousand American and Canadian civilians completed the work in an unbelievable eight months' time, blazing the twenty-four-foot-wide roadbed through muskeg, mud, thick forests, rugged mountains, and over two hundred glacial streams. The men lived under extreme conditions, with temperatures ranging from 90 degrees above zero to 70 degrees below, and with constant dust or mud, and rain or ice and snow. They learned to live with the bears and moose—virtually the only inhabitants of the entire area—but the hordes of mosquitoes almost succeeded in sabotaging the whole venture.

As we approached Dawson Creek via Glacier National Park and Edmonton, we were thinking only of all the stories we'd heard for so long: of car breakdowns, innumerable flat tires, ghastly mud, rocks, and boulders, and even more horrible dust. Perhaps because we were expecting the worst, we were almost pleasantly surprised by the smooth, hard-packed surface of the road, and we never encountered one mechanical problem, including a flat tire, along the entire route. We made no effort to maintain normal U.S. highway speeds, only averaging about forty miles per hour, and we decided that this was the secret to keeping the car in good shape. Actually, the only incident of the entire journey occurred while we were still on a super highway crossing North Dakota: Lowell's suitcase flew off the roof of the car and spread its contents all over the pavement and adjacent fields.

We did encounter clouds of dust whenever cars or trucks sped by, but we introduced a "dust patrol game," which was not only an effective dust controller but also provided great amusement for two bored youngsters. They took turns at guard duty, rushing for open windows at the first sign of a gray cloud up ahead. In between alerts, Anne and David sprawled on a mattress in the back, alternately sleeping or playing with toys, and when they lost interest in these activities, they could always turn to the big, good-natured dog, Bozie, who, somehow or other, found space to sprawl beside them and was good for at least fifteen minutes of petting and ear pulling.

The ride up the Alaska Highway was made immeasurably easier and more enjoyable by the beautiful scenery along its entire length. What a great joy to gaze on mile after mile of virgin pine forests, with breathtakingly beautiful mountains for a backdrop and ever-present swift glacial streams beside us—and not a single billboard to remind us of the ugliness of the urbanization we were leaving behind! In fact, the only signs we ever saw were discreet small ones which announced the approach of gas stations, campgrounds, or motel facilities, a welcome sight after a thirty- or forty-mile stretch of total wilderness. Signs also marked the mileage all along the way, and we found that a little Alaska Highway guidebook (several are published annually) was an indispensable accompaniment. For instance, at "mile 195 panoramic views of Northern Rockies and car pullout spaces; 222.7—spring

water, west side of highway (delicious!); 232—St. Paul's Roman
Catholic Mission and School; 242—Prophet River Esso Service,
cafe and cabins."[1] The book also describes historical landmarks
and gives such helpful details with regard to lodgings as available
laundry facilities, the number of rooms, phone service, and even
children's play areas.

We spent an occasional night at a motel along the way and
found them unpretentious but clean and comfortable. The rest of
the time we camped out at some of the many excellent campgrounds. It gave the children and Bozie a much better chance to
burn off excess energy, and Lowell loved to hike about or just sit
and fully enjoy the wilderness scenery. My enjoyment of the wilds
was tempered by the practical problems of cooking over a camp-
fire and washing nighttime diapers. My appreciation was further
dampened by a steady chilly rain during the two nights before we
reached the Alaskan border. It was impossible to keep the children from getting wet and cold, and as a result, when we pulled
up to the customs station, David was running a temperature of
103 degrees, with a raw sore throat. There was no doctor available there or for many miles in any direction. So we harnessed
our concern and kept him filled with aspirin until we reached
Glennallen, about two hundred miles to the west. A doctor at the
small but excellent Faith Hospital there diagnosed the problem
as tonsillitis and prescribed an antibiotic, plus some warm, dry
surroundings! With Anchorage, our ultimate goal, less than a
day away, the latter could be easily rectified.

I wish I could describe our arrival in Anchorage, our long
sought-after new home, in terms of Jason finding the Golden
Fleece or Marco Polo reaching China. I can't because dark clouds
hovered above the treetops and we could hardly find our way in a
heavy downpour through a maze of unfamiliar streets. However,
since that rainy day in 1960, I have been constantly awed by the
beauty of Anchorage's natural surroundings. With my Eastern
background, lovely scenery meant to me streets lined with tall,
stately elms and maple trees, their luxuriant foliage so thick that
one could just catch glimpses of the sky above. New England

[1] "The Milepost," 19th annual edition, Juneau, Alaska, Alaska Northwest
Publishing Co., page 73.

fields and meadows carefully bordered by old stone walls were my idea of "open space."

Now, after these years in Anchorage, I am continually aware of the great openness around me. Only an occasional birch or spruce tree intrudes between me and the vast expanse of sky. And as I look east from almost anywhere in the city, which has been built on a high bluff above Cook Inlet (a bay of the Pacific Ocean), I can see the ten-thousand-foot Chugach Mountains. They are always breathtakingly beautiful, whether they are covered with snow or simply wear the soft greens and browns of summer. Some of the taller peaks are craggy and sharp, in contrast to the lower, more softly rounded Talkeetna Mountains lying to the northeast. To the west, about eighty miles away, eleven-thousand-foot Mount Spur (a live volcano), twelve-thousand-foot Mount Gerdine, and other ten-thousand-foot peaks, extensions of the Alaska Range, are always a spectacular sight. Snow-covered year round, they often can be mistaken for a mass of fluffy white clouds on the horizon. The most awe-inspiring and majestic mountain view, however, is to our north: 20,320-foot Mount McKinley, highest point in North America, almost 140 miles away but still a commanding sight. One can see such a great distance here (on a clear day the weather bureau frequently reports a visibility of 110 miles) because of the clarity of the air—Alaska is undoubtedly one of the few states left which does not know the meaning of the word smog.

My favorite mountain within our sweeping view is not very high (4397 feet), but she rises alone from the flat plain and is covered with at least some snow for ten months of the year. She is called Susitna, or the "Sleeping Lady," and one can clearly see the outline of her long, flowing hair, her face, and her body as she lies in sleep. Local Indian legend tells of two giants in days long gone who were very much in love. They had to part when the boy went off to war. The girl promised to wait for him beside the water but grew tired and lay down to sleep. The boy was killed, and rather than break the news to the young girl, the gods took pity on her and put her to sleep forever beneath a warm blanket of pure white snow. It is so easy for me to see, whenever I look toward Susitna, the beautiful Indian girl eternally waiting for her young lover.

There is a more "down to earth" story about Susitna, a mountain that although not high, has on several sides a virtually straight sheer drop from the summit to the plain. A privately owned communications system maintained a radiotelephone relay station on the top at the time we arrived in Anchorage. A man and his wife were living there, and a small Super Cub airplane kept them in regular touch with the city. One morning in early spring, the man stepped out of their little house on the summit to empty the garbage, but while in the process of performing what is a routine chore for many husbands, he fell straight down the entire west side of Mount Susitna! When his wife finally went outside to see what was keeping him, she heard faint cries from far down the mountainside. She was able to summon a helicopter for help, and her husband was rescued unharmed, thanks to the deep powder snow which helped to break his fall. These are the perils of emptying the garbage in the Far North!

If one ever tires of looking at our mountains, there is always the water, the deep blue waters of Cook Inlet that divide before the city's bluffs: Knik Arm continues northeast until it becomes Knik River, and eventually Knik Glacier, an icy wedge between peaks of the Chugach. To the south, Turnagain Arm, like a Norwegian fiord, winds among the mountains to Portage Glacier. Just before his tragic death in Hawaii, Captain Cook sailed into Cook Inlet, hoping to find that illusive Northwest Passage. Twice the gigantic tides turned him back, and one of his young seamen, historian for the voyage and later to win fame as the captain of the ill-fated *Bounty,* wrote, "we turn again." So Seaman Bligh played a role in the naming of Turnagain Arm.

Just what kind of city lies between these two arms? Anchorage, born only fifty-four years ago, claims to be the fastest growing metropolitan area in the United States, with the nation's highest birth rate, with the most boats, airplanes, and cars per capita, the highest average income, the second highest educational level, with more business and cultural activity than most cities twice her size, and the busy residents make more telephone calls, man for man, than the people of any other American city!

Anchorage did not start with a gold rush like many other Alaskan towns. When the federal government decided to build a 741-mile railroad from the port of Seward to Fairbanks, deep in the interior, they chose the flat land stretching from the Chugach Mountains to Cook Inlet as their base of construction operations. A tent city of over two thousand people sprang up almost overnight during the summer of 1915. The streets were two feet of dust, one well supplied everyone with water at five cents a bucket, and several eating houses served meals at fifty cents each. Conditions quickly became chaotic, so since the construction work was being carried out by the federal government, local citizens petitioned Washington to lay out an adequate town on the higher land behind the tents. Thus, the Anchorage of today was carefully staked out just over fifty years ago. On executive order directly from the President, land was wisely set aside for schools and parks and for federal and municipal purposes, and wide streets connected all in an orderly pattern. The name Anchorage was chosen in a similar orderly fashion: An election was held, and the people were asked to vote on Anchorage (evolved from the many supply ships anchoring in nearby Ship Creek), Matanuska, Alaska City, and Ship Creek.

The little town had many lean years during the 1920s and 1930s. Once the railroad construction work had ended (President Harding came up in 1923 to help drive the golden spike), the population of six thousand fell to around twenty-seven hundred, and only the undaunted spirit and vitality of the local citizens kept their city from becoming a ghost town. All during that time Anchorage was under the control of the Alaska Engineering Commission and faraway Washington, D.C. Congress had no interest in their distant Arctic Railroad, and the lack of funds and poor management were a constant source of problems for the city.

One bit of help came their way in 1935 when the government sent up farmers to settle in nearby Matanuska Valley. Although most of these people did not stay, some did, and gave farming a good start close to the markets of Anchorage. (Matanuska provides us with most of our milk, eggs, and summer produce. Everything else has to be shipped, flown, or trucked in over 1500 miles.)

In 1939, the military arrived to select land for an air base, and boom days began again. After war was declared and construction was begun on a huge army base and airfield, another tent city sprang up and the dirt streets and stores of the town were crowded again. There was such a housing shortage that garages and backyard shacks were turned into homes. Although things were booming, life was difficult during the war years because Alaska was considered a combat zone. Many men were away fighting, supplies were hard to get, travel was almost impossible, and blackout rules were strict. But once the Japanese were ousted from the Aleutians, restrictions were eased and the post-war boom was on.

The Anchorage population has soared to 45,000 now, but Anchorage serves an area of over 121,000 people, so the old railroad town has become a modern city practically overnight, home for half the population of the entire state. Besides the huge International Airport, a major stop for seven international airlines, we have two other airfields; brand new year-round port facilities equipped to handle the largest ships afloat; five AM and two FM radio stations; three television stations; two newspapers; four hospitals; over ninety churches; three high schools; a university; a community college (a branch of the University of Alaska); and an endless variety of shops, sprawling suburbs, and enough skyscrapers to compete with the mountains encircling us!

In one way it is surprising that we picked Anchorage for our new home, for we did not know a single person living there (although we were acquainted with some people in other parts of the state). However, from all we had read and heard, this city seemed best suited for us, and so Lowell flew our Cessna up in the spring of 1960 to rent a house through real estate man Muktuk Marston, in what was then the newest residential area: Turnagain-by-the-Sea. He also found himself a job for the year (making a film on the Alaskan king crab) through public relations man and author Herb Hilscher. A WORD OF ADVICE to anyone planning to move to Alaska with family in tow: Be sure you have a place to stay and a job lined up before you come!

So we had at least two contacts when we arrived in town that rainy August first, and the two men happened to be together at the Hilscher home in Turnagain, along with other neighbors, half-expecting us on that particular day. However, they were not at all prepared for our mode of arrival, or so we learned later. After weeks on the road, our Travelall was covered with dust and grime, and to varying degrees, so were we. We were all dressed in an odd assortment of clothing, whatever still remained clean. Lowell and David were in great need of haircuts, and we girls could certainly have used shampoos. But the crowning touch was something I gave no thought to at all at the time. I had been sitting barefoot on the mattress, trying to help the children through those last long hours. When we arrived at the Hilscher home, I could not find my shoes. I can't bother with them, I thought, so excited over finally reaching our destination. We rushed as we were through the rain, into the warmest of Alaskan greetings. It wasn't until many weeks later that we learned we had inadvertently made a sensational arrival. Not only had bets been lost over no Cadillac, furs, or jewels, but also, although many people have reached Alaska penniless, I was considered the only person to ever arrive barefoot!

We faced many surprises during the first few weeks after our arrival, most of them happy. We had expected the beautiful scenery all around us and the outdoor way of life enjoyed by virtually everyone, but we were unprepared for the tremendous friendliness and sincerity of the Alaskan people. There is something special about the feeling between people here. It isn't just the friendliness and warmth: despite the beauty and livability of the countryside and all the enmities of civilized city life, we do live in a harsh and sometimes hostile climate. We need our neighbor, and he needs us, regardless of who he is and where he comes from. Natural disaster can strike anyone at any time, and most of us are far from immediate families or long-time friends. We live in a state which covers a tremendous area and yet has few people. So we must frequently shoulder burdens few of us knew existed when we lived in other more populous areas. Fires, earthquakes, floods pull us together—all help one another in a wholehearted, selfless way that is seldom found any more.

Because Alaskans must face hardship together, because they share, to some extent, a different way of living and are more separated from sister states who have common borders, Alaskans do consider themselves a special kind of people. A certain element of pride creeps into the voice when saying, "I have to make a trip 'outside.'" And anyone who is not an Alaskan is an "outsider." Old-time Alaskans used to call newcomers to their territory "Cheechako," and the word is still widely used today. One story says the word originated with natives along the Yukon River during the gold-rush days. The Indians watched a couple of bungling gold seekers from Chicago and then began calling any incompetent newcomer "Cheechaker"—that being as close to Chicago as the native tongue could come.[2]

The word "Sourdough" has a double meaning: It is used to refer to the old-time Alaskan and also is the name of the fermented dough used in making pancakes—the staple food for early Alaskan prospectors. After living here for a while, we wanted to shed the label of Cheechakoes and set about determining just when this became possible. I finally stumbled upon the technical definition of the word "Sourdough," which involves a polar bear, a squaw, a bottle of whisky, and the Yukon River. After considerable blushing on my part, coupled with the knowledge that it simply could not be printed in a book such as this, I decided I will have to leave it to the reader to discover for himself when he comes to visit Alaska. Anyway, everyone seems to have a different idea as to the length of time it takes to become a Sourdough. Among the old-timers, one just doesn't have a chance—if you weren't born here, forget about it—you will always be a newcomer, and watch your p's and q's! Just about everyone else has come since the end of World War II (at least one third of Anchorage's residents have come since 1960), so in some ways we do feel like Sourdoughs now.

Another big and very pleasant surprise for us upon our arrival in Anchorage was the masses of beautiful flowers in front of our rented house (tall, blue delphiniums, pink and red poppies, yellow daisies and marigolds, pink and white carnations and fuchsias, mammoth begonias, and pansies of all colors) and a large vegetable garden and greenhouse in the rear. Even the house itself was a most delightful surprise to me in that Lowell rented it on his own and he is one of those men who would be perfectly content living in a half-furnished tent. Needless to say, I was prepared to expect anything and was virtually overwhelmed by the spacious living room and three bedrooms, the large, sunny kitchen, and a basement that included a laundry, pine-paneled

[2] *An Alaskan Dictionary*, Robert O. Bowen, Spenard, Alaska, Nooshnik Press, 1965, p. 11.

study, workshop, and ample storage space. A far cry from a tent or log cabin!

The flowers could simply be looked at or sniffed to be appreciated, but the vegetables were another story. Before we had even explored the house, Muktuk Marston (who is not just a real estate agent but a tremendous story in himself) roared in with, "You have to help the cucumbers mate before you even unpack a suitcase." We did not know what a cucumber plant looked like, much less anything about its sex life, but before we knew it, we were both standing in the greenhouse, surrounded by a jungle of green foliage, while Muktuk showed us all about the pollen and the male and female flowers. Lowell became quite fascinated with the entire pollination process, but I found it so time consuming that I finally sneaked out to open doors and windows for a few hours to let bees do the work for me.

The effort was certainly rewarding—in Alaska cucumbers can grow to the size of one's forearm and are delicious as well. The greenhouse was also crammed with tomato plants—that first day I found at least a dozen large tomatoes on each vine. Both these vegetables are usually grown indoors here in the North because there is not quite enough summer warmth to ripen the fruit. Through constant experimentation, however, different strains are being developed which will stand cooler climates.

While the greenhouse alone kept us busy, the large vegetable garden beside it almost turned us into full-time farmers. (In the early spring, when snow was still on the ground, Lowell didn't know he was renting this house from a pair of avid horticulturists!) There were three rows each of giant cabbages, broccoli, cauliflower, potatoes, beans, peas, carrots, lettuce, onions, radishes, and enough strawberries, raspberries, and currants to supply the entire Turnagain area. I hoed and weeded and picked, and then canned and froze until I truly felt like an Alaskan homesteader.

At least I learned quite a bit about gardening in the North in a great hurry and have become addicted to the challenge ever since. In order to grow anything out-of-doors here one must first accept the fact that nothing is safe from frost until after the first of June, so even the most eager gardener is forced to face a very short growing season. There are ways of getting around this relatively firm and sensible rule, however. Many Alaskans start with seeds inside the house or in greenhouses early in the spring. Then by the first of June they have good-sized plants to put out-of-doors. Milk and egg cartons and two-pound coffee cans are in great demand among avid gardeners because they make perfect containers for begonias, dahlias, tomatoes, and many annuals started indoors. In fact, it is a common sight, when visiting a home in April or May, to find every available window sill crammed with plants of all kinds. Such gardening in our home faces an extraordinary hazard, however—five cats, who usually decide in the spring of the year that their diet lacks something green. I have yet to solve this problem, although Lowell insists he knows the perfect solution. The less said the better about this family disagreement, but I'm sure the Society for the Prevention of Cruelty to Animals would be shocked.

One year our family (not the cats) grew pretty tired of walking, eating, and even washing among myriad boxes of small plants, to say nothing of the hours it took me to transplant them from container to container and finally into the ground. I decided there must be an easier way. There was—subsequently I learned about the large group of perennials (delphiniums, peonies, and columbines are my favorites) which will winter over successfully here. There is another way, too—we have a number of excellent local nurseries where one can buy almost anything, but buying a large amount can be expensive, and besides, I always feel as though I'm cheating on my gardening neighbors.

Another sensible gardening rule of the Far North is to stick to those plants which grow best in cool weather, but this can also be circumvented, I've discovered. One summer I became homesick for those delicious ears of New England corn that ripen so quickly during the kind of heat virtually unknown to Anchorage. (I do remember six or eight days in eight years when the thermometer rose into the high eighties, and Anchoragites nearly collapsed from heat exhaustion.) I was determined to at least try growing my own corn, so the following spring I planted a particularly hardy variety in peat pots in my greenhouse. By June first the plants were healthy and ankle-high, so I transplanted them to a sunny, protected spot near the house. This activity brought on some violent reactions from one of our neighbors. He was from

Iowa, and you just can't transplant corn!!! I can't say that my plants were knee-high by the Fourth, but they looked like corn, and by August first, there were a few ears. The family was highly excited the day I finally harvested my rewards, but they were very good about watching their remarks when we shucked ears that were about the size of that miniature corn sold for hors d'oeuvres and could be eaten cob and all.

Since then others have had greater success with corn, and I might just try again one of these years. Others have also been most successful with orchids and other tropical plants, using lights of various kinds indoors and maintaining tropical temperatures in greenhouses during the summers. I recently visited our large new city greenhouse and was astounded to find lemon and banana trees, hibiscus, and bird of paradise all thriving among the more traditional Alaskan growth. The city of Anchorage, through its able head gardener, Mann Leiser, has achieved miracles in planting flowers and shrubbery. The project has had tremendous impact on the summer tourists, who come expecting a barren northland.

One tremendous help to the Alaskan gardener, almost making up for the short, cool summer season, is that famous midnight sun. Everyone has heard about this phenomenon, but I'm sure few realize just what it is like unless they actually experience it. We were unprepared and even today find it hard to sleep well or long in the summertime. It isn't just that the sun stays up late (in June and July we have good daylight until close to midnight)— the infernal thing rises again almost immediately. It is almost impossible to distinguish between a sunset and sunrise—pink spreads right across the horizon from west to east. By 3 A.M. the sun has the brightness of midmorning, and so not only is it hard to go to bed early at night, it's almost impossible to sleep late. Everyone takes advantage of the long evening hours of daylight, a special boon to those who work indoors in offices during the day. While gardeners can keep going until ten or eleven o'clock and the product of their efforts grows to supersize (our cabbages average thirty pounds, and radishes look like "outside" tomatoes), the sports-minded are even more active.

I'm sure it is obvious from what I have said that one of my few disappointments has been the cool summer weather. But once I

stopped comparing our Alaskan summer activities with the more
languid ones of the East, I felt better. Many Alaskans would
disagree with me—some have come North just to escape heat. But
the midnight sun makes a big difference to the sun worshipper,
and it is surprising how quickly one adjusts and feels warm at
50- and 60-degree temperatures. Summer clothing is a must (for
morale purposes especially) in June, July, and August, and many
are the days when the children and I have gone barefoot and
sweaterless and the thermometer has read 58 or 60 degrees. In
fact, since most Alaskans dress in similar fashion, it is easy to
spot the tourists in the summertime—they are invariably dressed
in wool suits and topcoats.

Summer is the time to enjoy the great out-of-doors, and the entire life of the community changes pace; all work and social activities are geared to allow the maximum of free time during
evenings and over weekends. In fact, on a clear day there are always a number of unexplained "sick leave" business absences.
Once, shortly after our arrival here, we had no mail delivery for
several days. When I asked a neighbor what might be going on,
her casual reply was, "Oh, the silver salmon are running, and it
doesn't last long, you know." We, too, have learned over the
years: On a good summer's day, drop everything and go. Beds,
dishes, and other work can wait; that kind of weather won't.

So much of an Alaskan's summer time is spent camping, flying, and fishing that I'll save all these activities for following chap-
ters. However, an increasing number of Alaskans also head for
the beaches and boats. The Greater Anchorage area has an abundance of small lakes, and the water warms up rapidly under the
nineteen hours of sun. Several lakes within the city itself are
crowded on good days, and the coarse sand beaches swarm with
hundreds of bathers. Cook Inlet is not good for swimming because of its mud and silt and extraordinarily treacherous tides. A
few brave sailors dare the currents with small boats, but most
head for some of the larger lakes, within an hour or two of Anchorage, either for the day or longer. Shorelines are dotted with
weekend cabins, almost a commonplace acquisition for many
Alaskan families these days. Regattas are held frequently, and
sailboat races are becoming very popular. Water skiing has also
caught on in a big way, and it is not surprising to find zealous

young people zipping about behind the latest model speedboats any time from early evening until two or three in the morning.

Most Alaskan children find summer months a totally happy time. Ours have usually vanished from the house early in the morning and do not reappear until dinnertime. If I'm lucky, I can corral a thoroughly dirty child or two for lunch, but usually the easiest thing is to make sandwiches for the whole neighborhood gang and feed them out-of-doors while they are on the run. We have been fortunate in that our homes here have been in or near wooded areas and in the midst of a plentiful supply of playmates. When we first arrived and I watched the children playing in the woods for hours at a time, I was pleased to see that they could be content with leaves and sticks and stones, instead of the toys and play gimmicks deemed so indispensable these days. We were also relieved to find that free time for young children was not especially carefully planned and regimented here. But as our son has grown older, the fun and adventures of Boy Scouting have fit in well with the homemade tree houses and tents in the woods, and as our daughter reaches her teens, we begin to see the need for additional city tennis courts and a new golf course. Most older teen-agers work hard at jobs all summer, so Anchorage's juvenile delinquency problems have not been as great as those in other urban areas.

Days of fun-filled leisure for Alaskan youngsters, as for those who live "outside," come to an end with Labor Day and the reopening of schools. The Alaskan school system is acknowledged in education circles to be one of the finest in all fifty states. This factor had a lot to do with our final decision to move here, and it seems to have influenced other residents as well. Because of the newness of the community, it has been possible to set aside land for schools in potential residential areas before suburbs become built up. Therefore, the majority of primary school children live within a mile of their classrooms and can walk with relative ease. The five junior high and three high schools also have been placed in geographically strategic sections of town, and an elaborate bus system solves transportation problems for everyone.

Most of the school buildings have been built within the last twenty years, and so are the latest in design and good planning. In fact the junior-senior high complex that our Anne attends was built in 1967, and while I'm sure that there is nothing quite like it in all of Alaska, I doubt that there are many finer institutions in all of the "outside." There are of necessity some frills which will have to wait until later: Swimming pools are sadly lacking— at the moment there is no public pool in all of Anchorage, and Alaskan children are notoriously poor swimmers. (Our lakes can be used for a very short time of the year, and the cool air is more conducive to a big splash than to a long swim.) With the growing popularity of boating and fishing activities, the rate of drownings rises alarmingly each year.

Another program only recently introduced was kindergartens. Anchorage educators have had to face such tremendous enrollment increases (from 2400 pupils in 1949 to more than 19,000 in 1965 and 23,500 in 1967, and school authorities now know they will need 134 more classrooms by 1976) that some innovations have had to take a back seat in order to insure enough uncrowded classrooms for everyone. A practical means of keeping pace with this great increase has been the relocatable classroom. Some schools have six or eight of these highly satisfactory "portables" at one time, and the rooms can be moved as the enrollment fluctuates from year to year.

Of course, facilities alone don't make good schools, and I think there are a number of reasons behind the good quality of ours. I would start with the high caliber of the administration and the excellent teachers. While many states are suffering from a severe teacher shortage, only 8 per cent of those who apply to teach here (from all over the United States) can be accepted. The lure of challenge and adventure in the Far North seems to be the main reason, and while many may not settle down here as permanently as in other states, this transiency does not affect the quality of the teaching.

I can't help but feel that another reason for the good educational system is the fact that virtually every child attends public schools here, whereas in many other areas of the United States private schools siphon off the brighter or more ambitious students. In Anchorage, we parents who might have sent children to private schools while living in the East, now do whatever we can as parents and taxpayers to insure continued excellent public schooling. A large percentage of high school seniors here go on to good colleges "outside." Many also go on to the rapidly expanding University of Alaska at Fairbanks (an Anchorage branch will be opened in 1969) or to the excellent local Alaska Methodist University. First begun in 1960 under the direction of the Methodist Division of National Missions and now a fully accredited four-year college, AMU's 1967–68 enrollment was 576 students.

School for Anne, on our arrival in 1960, meant kindergarten at a nearby Baptist Church, while David, at three, was still free to pursue the usual active and mischievous preschool life—peddling his tricycle up and down our quiet street and thoroughly enjoying every mud puddle in sight. He was really very little trouble, except at night, when he suddenly decided it would be fun to wander about the house around 3 or 4 A.M. I didn't worry when he helped himself to food in the refrigerator, but when he started letting the perfectly willing Bozie out the front door, I panicked. We were sure the next step would be David on the street at four in the morning, so we beat him to it by installing a lock on his door.

(In retrospect, I suspect David was really walking in his sleep during those nocturnal wanderings. As he grew older, he did this whenever there were periods of stress in our lives. His most adventuresome walk took place the winter after the earthquake, when we were living in the Windemere subdivision. It was 20 degrees below zero with snow on the ground, and he was in cotton pajamas and barefoot. He let himself out of the house around 11 P.M., walked to the home next to us, knocked on our neighbors' door, and asked them if he could borrow some paper. The rather startled couple carried him right back, and he was still sound asleep! I was so frightened by the experience that I barricaded the front door with a chair for many weeks afterward, but Dave's only concern was that the kids at school might hear about his midnight escapade.)

With the children occupied and happy, I had my hands full that first fall with the harvesting of the last of the garden crops. Faced with the chore of digging up mounds of potatoes, I found an easy way out—David and his little friends could think of nothing more fun than digging into dirt to see who could find the biggest and most spuds. While standing about in my new role as supervisor, I took stock of what was left in the garden and wondered just what several rows of large-leafed plants were. We suspected a kind of cabbage, but the leaves were not coming to a head. One evening while on his "gentleman farmer's inspection tour," Lowell looked beneath some of the large leaves and discovered many little sprouts growing on the stems. What a feast of Brussels sprouts we had that night—and now we know how sprouts sprout!

While working in the garden one day in early October, we heard a great commotion in the sky above us and looked up to see hundreds of honking geese winging their way southward in perfect V formations. An exciting and unmistakable sign that winter was on its way. The thermometer also began to warn us, dipping a bit lower each week. When the temperature slid into the thirties at night, we looked for our first frost, but the timing of the frosts themselves is highly unpredictable. For many years there has been a slight freeze in early September, but one not hard enough to kill much growth. I have often had flowers blooming into the first week in October, while my mother loses most of hers in Connecticut in mid-September. But it is possible to have an early killing frost, and the yearly lament of the gardener is, "Now that my flowers have just begun to bloom, we'll have an August frost."

One doesn't mind the loss of the flowers, however, when the trees and undergrowth begin to change their color. Accustomed as I was to the brilliance of New England falls, the bright, intense splash of colors here still leaves me breathless. Autumn is far too brief in the Far North—it lasts two or three weeks at the most— but nature seems determined to make up for the brevity by supplying the hues of yellows and reds in double strength. The small wild dogwood, lingonberry, and strawberry plants closest to the ground turn a deep red first, followed by the taller fireweed, wild rose, wild red currant, and rusty menziesia. Amid this bright red wild growth, the large leaves of the devil's-club turn a vivid yellow. Then the leaves of the birch and aspen become such a rich and brilliant gold that on clear days even the most unartistic person is highly tempted to reach for a paintbrush and try to capture the scene. And it isn't just the yellows and reds of the leaves—the waters of the lakes and the inlet turn an extra-deep blue, the birch bark seems whiter, and the mountains take on soft, gentle hues of red, beneath violet-colored peaks.

It is no wonder, with such surroundings, that everyone makes a headlong dash for the out-of-doors. The less athletic will simply sit in a park or meadow, but many families find berry-picking one of the most delightful fall pastimes. The woods around Anchorage are filled with cranberry bushes, and I had never known until I came North what fun it is to make one's own cranberry sauce or delicious cranberry bread. Blueberry picking is just as popular and involves invigorating walks up into the nearby hills. On a good weekend hundreds of Anchorage families head for these slopes of the Chugach, either to pick blueberries or just to hike. Within a half hour from the heart of the city, we can find ourselves in high wild valleys, surrounded by craggy stone peaks, with no human being in sight.

One recent sunny Labor Day weekend, we loaded our International Travelall with children, dog, and camping equipment and followed a power-line track up into a Chugach valley. We set up our tent on a warm gravel patch beside a small, azure-blue pond, and while Lowell climbed to the top of several shale-covered slopes, the kids and I looked for berries nearby. I felt as if we were in the heart of a vast wilderness, as there was no sign of any other living thing. Actually, I was very comforted to have the dog nearby—although it seemed that we were totally alone, I knew that where there were berries, there could also be bears! The fall is the berrypicking season for them, too. But bears don't like dogs, and anyway, more about them later in my story.

Many local people of all ages enjoy climbing the mountains behind us, as Lowell did that weekend. Fortunately, there is an infinite variety of climbs available, from the toughest, sheer, rock-walled peaks to relatively simple hikes up "flat-top," where Anchorage youngsters get their start in mountaineering. But any outing among the Chugach is not the same as a similar excursion in most other parts of the country. Just beyond the mountains lies Prince William Sound, spawning ground for bad weather. Storms can develop with frightful suddenness and can spell disaster for those who are unprepared. Violent weather means snowstorms at almost any time of the year which can rage on for days. At least two or three parties of people have perished in this way in the years since we moved here. Whether they were on the higher slopes, on or near the glaciers, or in the more protected valleys, all died from overexposure—freezing to death because of inadequate supplies or preparation in the face of unexpected weather.

While all mountain outings should be carefully planned, other fall activities, such as biking and horseback riding, can be taken more casually. As a family, the four of us often take off on our bikes for an hour or two, or even a whole day, and explore the many dirt roads in the area. While we curse such potholed, dusty roads (of which Alaska has far more than her share) when driving a car, they are perfect for biking off into outlying areas. They also are ready-made trails for horseback riding, a sport which has greatly increased in popularity in the last five years. While only those few people who lived on farms or homesteads owned horses in earlier years, now we have a number of active stables, with stalls where many may keep their horses, large indoor rings for riding in the winter, and besides the dirt roads, there are bridle paths among the nearby parks and foothills.

Our Anne took riding lessons for several years, so the Diamond H Ranch became a familiar place to us. Although only Anne did the riding, we all enjoyed going out to see the horses and the many cats and dogs belonging to Sammye and Howard Taplin, owners of the ranch. Of far greater interest, however, was the pet we encountered in the Taplin living room on our first visit there —Oley the seal. Oley was napping by the fireplace, totally unaware that he has made history as the only hair seal ever raised in domestic captivity in Alaska. He may even think he is just another feline, because he sleeps among the many Taplin cats, occasionally rousing himself long enough to chase one of them about—a rather difficult feat in that kitty is a fast four-footed creature, while Oley must depend upon his more awkward flippers and fat tummy to "flip-flop" about. He has even been known to pick up a cat by the scruff of her neck, doing it so gently that he undoubtedly thinks he's her guardian or related to her in some way.

Oley and the cats also share a love for fish—the only difference being that Oley eats pounds of salmon fillets at one meal. In fact, he can stash away so much fish that the Taplins have to issue frequent pleas for help through the local newspapers to fishermen who may have more fish in the freezer than they can eat. When Oley decides he is hungry, his begging is far more raucous than the meows of Taplin cats. He flops about the house, following Sammye wherever she goes, gently poking her with a flipper, all the while barking in a sharp, guttural way, as any seal should.

Also in true seal fashion (and this is where he loses his cat friends), Oley loves water. To solve the dilemma, the Taplins showed him the way to the ground-floor bathtub. They taught him so well that now Oley flops in all by himself and turns on the cold-water tap. The only trouble is that he has never learned to turn it off (or does not want to), and after coping with numerous flooded bathrooms, the Taplins are forced to regulate bath time by closing the door. This hasn't been too successful, either, because the smart seal has learned to flip-flop up their stairs and use the second-floor bathtub.

Summers are much less frustrating for Oley and the Taplins because each morning he "hops" into a little red express wagon and is pulled out to a small pond in the back yard. There he can spend the entire day almost totally immersed, happy to be a real seal for a little while, anyway. When I went down to visit him there, one warm July day, I called his name, and almost immediately a little black nose appeared on the water's surface, followed by two beady eyes which seemed to say, "What do you want now? Can't you see I'm busy!"

As if the Taplins weren't involved enough already, they became the parents of another rather unusual pet several years ago. Jack Snyder, the owner of a local food store, won a contest and for his prize had the choice of three thousand dollars in cash or a baby elephant. At that particular moment Anchorage happened to be in the midst of plans for a zoo, so, of course, he chose the elephant. No sooner had Annabelle, the pachyderm, arrived, than Anchorage voters turned down the whole proposition. Poor Annabelle—poor Mr. Snyder! Of course, he immediately thought of the Taplins and Diamond H Ranch, and Annabelle has been there ever since. The baby elephant's dietary needs are even more complicated than Oley's—four half-gallon bottles of milk, five pounds of apples, one pound of carrots, two heads of lettuce, twenty pounds of horse pellets, and six pounds of horse grain in one day! But the biggest problem facing the Taplins in the care of Annabelle is "winterizing." Apparently chilly weather doesn't necessarily bother elephants, but they do get cold feet. When I last visited the stables, many of the women among the riders and spectators were knitting and sewing elephant-sized booties, preferably with leather soles. My one disappointment during that visit was that I did not have the chance to see Annabelle and Oley together. I had wondered just how a seal would react to an elephant, but the Taplins are quite wary about the development of such a friendship. . . . The cats romp all over Oley, but one five-hundred-pound elephant foot on a fat seal tummy might have more serious consequences!

Animals, but not elephants, play a big role in the lives of many Alaskans during the fall season. Hunting, to a number of people in the North, means meat for the winter. To some it is vital to existence; to others it is a great help in combating high food prices. For the local hunter moose are relatively easy to find. A day or weekend is usually sufficient time to shoot a good-sized animal, which will supply a large family with enough meat for the whole winter. Caribou, the game meat especially important to the people of the Far North, migrate in great herds, moving up to the higher hills in the springtime and back to the lower plains in the fall. Anchorage hunters must travel farther afield to find their caribou, but many do, and both caribou and moose meat are delicious if properly handled and prepared. (In fact, I have served moose meat in stews and roasts to people who would swear it was beef. One lady visitor from "outside" vowed she could never eat moose but happily devoured what she thought was my beef pot roast.)

The gourmet food among meats, I think, is the Dall sheep; it is far more tender and delicately flavored than lamb. Unfortunately, we seldom get much sheep meat, mainly because sheep hunting is a more rigorous, time-consuming, and expensive project. The Dall sheep is rather the target of the avid sportsman or trophy hunter, another type of hunting which is also popular with many Alaskans. Eighteen species of big game can be hunted in this state, including moose, caribou, deer, elk, mountain goat, sheep, the brown, grizzly, black, and polar bear, wolf, walrus, seal, sea lion, and whale.

Big-game hunting in Alaska is second only to that of Africa in variety and quantity of animals. Each year more and more sportsmen from all over the world come to hunt and thereby contribute to the state's economy. Fortunately for Alaskans, in terms of conservation, game harvest tags are expensive, ranging from ten dollars for deer in the southeast to one hundred-fifty dollars for polar bears up north. Guides, camps, and outfits are far more expensive. Although I am glad to see revenue come to the state and to the many excellent guides we have, still, I would hate to see the animals depleted here, as they have been virtually everywhere else. On the whole we have had excellent wildlife management: careful regulating of the seasons, close watch over the numbers of animals and possible infringements of the laws. However, there are some aspects which still have to be rectified. Hunting by small airplane has so greatly increased in popularity that the animal's chances of losing himself in the wilderness have considerably lessened. The polar and brown bear have suffered especially, and so have the Dall sheep. It is very easy for us Alaskans to blow our stacks when we hear the stories of "bigwigged" officials who fly in from "outside" for two days, hop a light plane to some remote area, spot a bear, land, walk a few hundred yards and shoot him, then return to the "lower 48" to boast of a great Alaskan visit, with a trophy as the proof. This happens far too often, and while in one way it helps Alaska, in the long run it can be nothing but detrimental.

I cannot say much about big-game hunting because neither Lowell nor I are hunters. In fact, if either of us had to shoot anything other than an inanimate target, we'd both dissolve into tears. We (and most Alaskans), however, have had a much closer (sometimes closer than we'd like) association with Mr. Moose. The poor guy could never win a beauty contest. His great bulbous nose, small beady eyes, gangling, skinny legs, and ungainly over-all bulk are a truly comical sight, but Mr. Moose is by no means a silly sorry clown. He is large (the Kenai moose is the largest in the world, the bulls often weighing more than fourteen hundred pounds), powerful, surprisingly fast and graceful, and he has a tremendous air of dignity about him, especially if he is carrying massive antlers, which could spread as much as six feet from tip to tip. And unfortunately for us, unlike the bear, he is not afraid of anything, including people or dogs.

Unlike the caribou, the moose does not travel in herds, but in much smaller groups or even alone. In the spring, he heads for the high hills and more distant meadows where somehow he can fill his vast bulk with a simple diet of scrub willow, birch, and aspen leaves. He is especially fond of the greenery which grows beneath the water of ponds, and it is a not uncommon sight to come upon a moose with his head totally submerged in a lake, munching away at his favorite delicacies. I have heard that the moose needs forty or fifty pounds of leafy material in one day, so no wonder he can become quite desperate in the winter months—hungry enough to march down the streets of Anchorage, ignoring cars, dogs, people, and even police sirens, while he searches out succulent hedges and vines or any greens in sight. Many an astonished Anchoragite has watched Mr. Moose amble slowly and deliberately down a main thoroughfare while police cars with flashing lights trail behind him quite help-lessly. Many more of us have come close to totally demolishing automobiles when the unconcerned critters wander out onto the highways. And an encounter with a moose in one's back yard is an annual event.

One day, during our first September in Anchorage, we were eating breakfast in front of a big window which looked out on the back-yard garden. Suddenly the children both yelled that someone's "horse" was crossing the yard. I simply could not believe my eyes. The sight of a huge wild moose ambling through cultivated gardens within a few feet of the windows of homes, mailboxes, and cars was just too incongruous to comprehend. We had a similar visit while we lived in the Windemere subdivision: the clatter of the moose's hoofs on the paved street added considerably to the incongruity of the scene.

The encounter that I will never forget, however, took place one snowy winter when we lived on the more isolated Chilligan Drive. It was about 7:30 in the morning, still dark, and we had just gotten up. I opened the front door to let Bozie out, and there, standing less than five yards away, was a large mama moose with her young one beside her. For a moment I was too surprised to move. She reacted faster than I, starting to paw the ground and snort. At that point it dawned on me that she would very likely charge right through the open door. It was also beginning to dawn on Bozie that he was faced with a rather unusual policing situation. He started to growl, so I grabbed his collar, pulled him inside and slammed the door in one split-second Gargantuan effort. Then both dog and I totally lost any courage we had had . . . he headed for the bedroom and hid beneath the bed for the rest of the morning, while I collapsed in the nearest chair, shaking from head to foot. When I finally recovered enough to peek out a window, mama was still there, but she had obviously decided not to attack the closed door, and the two ambled down the front path, nibbled at a few long-dead sweet-pea vines at the corner of the house, and then wandered into the back yard. She was definitely in no hurry to leave, and after a rather distracted family breakfast, we finally decided we simply could not let the children walk through our woods to school that day. They were driven, and it was many days before I stopped worrying each time the kids went out the front door.

My neighbor across the street on Chilligan Drive, Vee Bashaw, was far braver than I when she encountered what was probably the same moose a few weeks later. We watched the great brown creature wander into Vee's yard and nibble at several small mountain-ash and crab trees on which my neighbor had lavished many hours of tender loving care. Thinking about nothing but her priceless shrubs, Vee burst out of the house, waving a broom and shouting horrid unladylike things. The moose was obviously quite surprised and turned to run on down the street. Although we onlookers had been frightened up until this moment, we now had to roar with laughter. There was Vee, dressed only in a filmy white negligee and pink satin slippers, chasing a moose with a broom down a snow-covered street. Only in Alaska!

II

I Just Sit
by the Fire

"I'm sure you will need these far more than any of the rest of us," wrote my mother on a note enclosed with a box of long johns, heavy wool dresses, and sweaters and sent to me when we first moved to Anchorage. Yet, during our winters in the North we have frequently heard our families in the East complain of being battered by raging blizzards and arctic cold while we ourselves were enjoying mild and sunny weather. Our Anchorage winter is without a doubt the most maligned and misunderstood aspect of living in Alaska! Of course, I do wear a pair of long johns for skiing and other winter outdoor activities, but my greatest desire, when offered a gift of clothing, is for a formal evening gown or dressy, short-sleeved, thin cocktail dress. Our homes are for the most part draft-free and well heated, and rather than hibernating in front of a fire, we carry on extraordinarily busy lives, indoors and out, all winter long.

In early October each year, when the temperature starts to fall and early morning frosts leave the grass with a sparkling touch of white, all eyes turn to the Chugach Mountains behind us. At the end of each rainstorm, as the clouds lift from the

peaks, there is one collective holding of breath as we wait to
see whether snow fell on the slopes. At first we usually find
a very slight dusting of the highest peaks, but as the weeks go
by, the covering becomes thicker and begins to creep slowly but
inexorably down the mountainsides.

Old-timers had a name for this first Chugach snow—Termination Dust—meaning it was time for virtually all work to come to
a halt and for the men to head, via the next steamer, for the
warmer climes of the "lower 48." Of course some hardy souls
remained, readying their cabins for the long winter months ahead
and laying in supplies for at least the next six months. After the
last boat of the fall, there would be no contact with the "outside" until late the following spring. One old-timer's definition of
winter preparedness was when they had "got the wood up, the
cabin chinked, the moose butchered, and this year's baby here."[1]

Today, in this modern age of technology, we still call the first
signs of snow Termination Dust, but now, instead of thinking
about leaving or holing in for the winter, we suddenly remember
all the routine chores we should complete before the snow
reaches the city: the digging up of begonia and dahlia bulbs,
new boots and mittens for the younger generation, the finishing
off of the back-porch steps, studded tires and more antifreeze
for the family car. Just the same winter chores facing anybody
living in the temperate areas of the rest of the United States.
But there is more of a sense of urgency here, in that once the
snow comes, it stays, and the procrastinator has no reprieve until
spring breakup the following March. In other words, if David
has left his football or camping gear out in the back yard, there
they will remain for a good six months.

This sense of urgency is felt particularly by the construction
industry and road- and utilities-maintenance people. Until 1964
practically all building activity came to a halt with the arrival of
winter. After our great earthquake, when much reconstruction
work simply had to continue into fall and winter, it was discovered that by enveloping an entire project in visqueen (a new,
tough, see-through plastic material) and using heaters inside,
men could continue working even if temperatures plummeted to

[1] *Anchorage Daily Times,* October 25, 1967.

20 degrees below zero. Also, thanks to a new use of chemicals, it is now even possible to pour concrete under these conditions. Since 1964 a number of businesses and homes have been built during the winter months, providing jobs for men who would otherwise have been laid off. The only drawback to cold weather construction is an approximate 30 per cent increase in costs. We can attest to this personally because we had just begun to build our present home when we were caught by an early October snow, and we watched bricks being laid and siding nailed on beneath a "balloon" of visqueen.

It is the road- and utilities-maintenance people who really panic at the first sign of Termination Dust. They rush all their heavy equipment to every part of the city at once, and then the fun begins. We never know from one day to the next which major street will be closed off. Part of the game is for the frustrated motorist, already late for an uptown appointment, to guess just which of the main thoroughfares is blocked off that day and where the detour might lead him. Every fall some irate driver comes up with the inevitable story: "I was driving down Spenard Road, discovered it was blocked, turned to go back, and darned if they didn't block off the other end, too!" Of course, sewer and water lines cannot be laid in midwinter because of the deeply frozen ground, but the long-suffering driver sometimes feels that all such projects are deliberately postponed until September.

Another element which provides suspense is the uncertainty over just when that first snow will fall. Like the frosts, its coming varies greatly every year. I suppose a good "average" date would be October 15, but our first winter in Anchorage was one we will never forget—we had a green Christmas! All children, skiers, and dog mushers (sled-dog racers in Anchorage are few in number but with a large, enthusiastic following) began to weep and wail by mid-November. By the first of December, when we continued to have mild weather, the editorial in one of our local papers, noting that icy cold had hit Arizona and other southern states with a vengeance, pleaded with Old Man Winter to please come back where he belonged.

However, no amount of pleading from anyone could change our luck that winter—for the first time in recorded history, Anchorage had a green Christmas. The weather remained sunny with temperatures in the thirties, and when Santa Claus visited the children of Turnagain, he was forced to add wheels to the runners of his sleigh. The frustrated weatherman tried to explain that a high-pressure ridge, lying over the Pacific Ocean south of Alaska, was forcing cold arctic air down through the Central States, while the warmer storms from the South Pacific were bombarding us. Shortly after Christmas that year, matters went from bad to worse—I checked our outdoor thermometer at 7:30 one morning and was shocked to discover it read 48 degrees! By noon it had risen to 58 degrees, setting a thirty-year record, and the children cavorted outdoors on the grass in thin summer sweaters. That same day, the temperature in Des Moines, Iowa, was 7 degrees, in Chicago 23 degrees, 38 degrees in Philadelphia, minus 2 degrees in Salt Lake City, 38 degrees in San Francisco, and 25 degrees in Southern California!

This miserable performance on the part of Old Man Winter has not been repeated since 1960 (although we frequently have warmer temperatures and less snow than many other parts of the country). In fact, I think he decided to seek revenge the following Christmas when our temperatures remained at minus 30 degrees for over fourteen days straight. This was equally unusual weather for this area, and although the ground had a good covering of snow, neither the children nor the skiers could brave that severe cold long enough to enjoy winter sports. Whenever the thermometer plummets well below zero (perhaps a once-a-winter occurrence in the Anchorage area), frostbite of the feet, hands, and face is something to think about when going out-of-doors for any length of time. Parents and teachers must check younger children to and from school (lost mittens could mean frozen fingers), outdoor recesses are called off, windows in homes ice up in fragile lacy patterns, pipes not properly laid at deep depths will freeze up, and the smoke from chimneys and cars lies heavily in the air.

The use of a car at these coldest temperatures poses all sorts of problems: Tires feel square and flip-flop when they first turn, windows are so thickly coated with frost that it takes a lot of work and ingenuity on the part of the driver to keep the windshield clear enough to see through, and the starting of the engine can be a major challenge. Batteries become sluggish at below-zero temperatures, but head-bolt heaters, an item unknown in more southern states, virtually guarantee a car's starting on a sub-zero morning. In Fairbanks, to the north of us, where minus-30-degree temperatures are a normal occurrence, these heaters are as common as parking meters and must be used whenever a car engine is stopped for any length of time. Here in Anchorage some home and apartment owners who must leave their cars parked out-of-doors overnight will plug electric cords into small heaters in their engines. However, the more common practice for Anchorage men and women headed for work at an early hour is to run outside in various stages of dress, start the car, leave it running, rush back inside for another ten minutes to continue dressing or eating breakfast, then drive off in a warm car with the windows frost-free. Expensive in terms of using gas but a practical and easy solution to a cold car on an early morning!

Ordinarily winter does not hit Anchorage with these weather extremes—to me and to many Alaskans, it is the most delightful and beautiful time of the year. I have always felt the eagerness of a child when looking for a snowfall, and I remember so clearly my deep disappointment when the snows of southern New England turned to the almost inevitable drizzle, slush, and mud. I hated the rain, wind, and dampness which typify winter in the New York area. In Anchorage, I love the dryness, the still air, the many days of blue sky and sunshine, and especially the snow-storms (Anchorage has a 63-inch annual snowfall), which continually build up a white ground covering that stays. We may experience one or two slight thaws with rainy spells during the four months of deep winter, but often we will not see a raindrop from mid-October until mid-March.

Also, it does not feel as cold as it should—with the stillness and dryness of the air one does not become chilled as readily as in a damp, windy climate. And while nighttime temperatures can drop to minus 10 or minus 15, daytime readings seldom fall below zero. (In December, considered our coldest month, the weather bureau says the thermometer average is plus 13 degrees). A typical winter's day is crisp and clear, the temperature at about 15 degrees, with crunchy white snow underfoot and incredibly blue sky overhead. The snow has such a magical way of covering all the ugliness on the ground: Dirt roads become carpets of white (even the potholes are filled in); the inevitable roadside litter is hidden beneath giant snowbanks; fences, mailboxes, hydrants all become decoratively draped in white. The wires and street lights overhead are similarly disguised, and the roofs of our houses look like traditional gingerbread huts with a topping of thick white icing. Long icicles hang from the eaves like crystal candy. The trees are the most beautiful sight of all—each branch and twig is daintily coated with white, altogether forming a patchwork of fragile lace against the blue sky.

This winter covering on the trees and on the wires and other man-made objects builds up with each snowfall or ice fog, with seldom a wind to blow it away, and there are many times when one must stop everything and just admire the fairyland beauty of the winter's scene. Frequently at sunset, when the low sun bathes all of the white world in soft, rosy hues, even the busiest or most hardened individual will step out-of-doors or pull the car over to the side of the road and take time to watch the glorious pinks of the mountains, the trees, and the sky fade slowly into the blackness of the arctic night. In the days when we lived on Chilligan Drive and looked out over Cook Inlet to Mount McKinley, sunset on any clear day was a special treat.

Old Man Winter has an extra spectacular surprise for those living in the arctic—the aurora borealis (or northern lights), a phenomenon which I have heard scientifically explained as the bombardment of the earth's upper atmosphere by electrons shot from the sun. These particles are directed toward the earth's magnetic poles and seem to be most frequent during periods of greatest sunspot activity. I doubt that I will ever fully understand this scientific explanation, but I'm sure I will always be awed by any display of the aurora. Occasionally the sky is swept by frosty white beams and arcs of light: streaks of brightness which move at incredible speed over the northern horizon. At other times we are dazzled by a fireworks-like display of reds and greens—curtains moving rapidly up and down, back and forth, all over the sky. Scientists say the aurora makes no sound, but many a long-time Alaskan who has watched this ghostly display in the midst of the wilderness of the North claims to have heard crackling sounds of varying intensity as the lights moved across the sky. In the early days of Anchorage, when the police force consisted of one man, he had a list of telephone numbers he called at any hour of the night to awaken people just to see the aurora borealis.

When nature surrounds us with such a winter fairyland, it is no wonder that many Alaskans again head for the great out-of-doors. The key to the fullest enjoyment of our winter playground is adequate clothing and an interest (active or passive) in any one of the many winter sports available. Not only is it important to have warm gloves, boots, and coats but also to have spares and an organized place to keep them. A "mud room" is ideal, but even a boot and coat rack by the door does the trick, and I hang wet mittens and socks from a pegboard—our children can go through several pairs of each in one morning's romp in deep snow.

Young people of junior high and high school age have an entirely different attitude toward winter preparedness, however—they ignore it altogether. The girls continue to wear short, short skirts, with sneakers and nylons to school, while boys stick to their usual summer attire, with perhaps a light jacket added just for the heck of it. When I try to argue with our eighth grader, her reply is that the bus is warm and the school is warm. My plea that the bus might break down goes unheeded, and each year I tell Anne the story of the high school girl, wearing sneakers, who missed her bus, walked to school, and froze most of her toes on the way. Anne's usual reply is that this occurred way back in the "Dark Ages" of 1961, and nothing like it has happened since. (Unfortunately for my cause, this is true.) Yet, these same teen-agers, especially the boys, will spend a great amount of the money they have earned on large quantities of ski equipment —one son of friends of ours owns six pairs of racing skis and three pairs of ski boots.

Downhill skiing has become an increasingly popular way of enjoying winter in Alaska, and in recent years the state has seen the development of a number of small rope-tow and T-bar facilities, from Fairbanks in the north to Juneau in the southeast. Eight of these ski areas are located in and around Anchorage, including one at an old gold mine in the Matanuska Valley and several on the Kenai Peninsula. Closer to the city is Arctic Valley, a lovely snow bowl in the Chugach Mountains, just forty-five minutes from our doorstep. The terrain is treeless—a joy to someone used to New England narrow-trail skiing, and the slope has a good 990-

foot vertical drop. The facilities are not extensive—a T-bar, three rope tows, and a small warming hut—but we have spent many a delightful day skiing there. The big advantage to Arctic Valley is its proximity—frequently one can go up for just a brief afternoon's outing. Also, the slopes are gentle enough so that many families, from fathers down to smallest child, can begin to learn the sport there. Although Lowell and I have skied at more elegant resorts, nothing can match the late spring day at Arctic, dashing over the abundant corn snow, with a hot sun beating down on the bowl, and the spectacular view of the city and Cook Inlet just below.

Alyeska (an Aleut word meaning "Great Land of White to the East," the same origin for the word Alaska) is the closest our state comes to the sophisticated ski resorts of the "lower 48." First opened in 1960, and financed by the unusual combination of wealthy Frenchman François de Gunsburg and some Texas oil tycoons, Alyeska offers the combination of a high snow bowl and wooded trails, with a total two-thousand-foot vertical drop. We reach the higher slopes via the fifty-eight-hundred-foot double-chair lift, while several rope tows and a pomalift provide good skiing for beginners farther down the mountain. A large restaurant at the base is a good warm place for those just watching, and within the last few years over two hundred cabins have been built in the surrounding Girdwood Valley by Anchorage families who wish to spend the whole weekend on or near the ski slopes.

Alyeska is just an hour's drive from our home, so we find it an easy excursion, and we also find it a great relief not to have to face the one- and two-hour lift lines so prevalent at many areas "outside." And for an average skier like me, a run down the entire mountain at Alyeska is quite an undertaking. Lowell, the expert, can handle it virtually nonstop and usually passes me at least three times before I finally reach the bottom.

The descent from the top of the lift down into the bowl is precipitous (Lowell calls it a little pitch), and I frequently take twenty minutes to sideslip my way down, while keeping a constant watch over my shoulder for the fast skiers who barrel on past me. Once I reach the bowl, I am so overcome by my awesome surroundings—vast, empty white slopes rising all about me to peaks way above—that I make frequent stops just to admire the scenery. By now Lowell has already passed me twice, occasionally stopping to ask if I'm all right but usually just muttering something about cautious skiers as he swishes by. (Last year our Anne was right at his heels, and this I found harder to take. Next year, Dave will probably be there, too, and I'll either have to sign up for a new series of lessons in the latest technique or retire to a chair in the restaurant.) Beneath the bowl, the rest of the mountain consists of a number of steep, narrow trails carved from the wooded slopes, and the less said the better about the technique I use in getting down them. Fortunately for those of us who take frequent pauses, the view, from the slopes, of Turnagain Arm and the mountains beyond could hardly be surpassed anywhere.

While Alyeska can qualify for internationally sanctioned competition under Olympic and FIS standards (the 1963 U. S. National Ski Championships were held there), it will be a long while before it can match any of the big "lower 48" ski resorts—those with a number of chair lifts and wide choice of ski slopes, plus larger facilities at the foot of the mountain. However, most of these ski developments lie near urban areas with population figures in the millions. Alyeska can only count on the Southcentral Alaska population, with an occasional wealthy skier flying in from the "outside" just for kicks. We are all convinced, however, that Alyeska will grow, and in the meantime we are close to a most delightful spot for good downhill skiing.

The caliber of the young Alaskan skiers also continues to rise. Ten years ago organized skiing for boys and girls was almost unknown. Now eight-, nine-, and ten-year-olds whiz down the slopes in crash helmets, displaying the latest in equipment and techniques, and races and training sessions are held regularly. The young people we send out to race in national competition still don't do very well, despite the fact that they have more months in which to ski. The feeling among skiers is that these youngsters have not had sufficient racing training or experience. It would be financially prohibitive for them to travel the race circuit, the way many in the lower states do.

Alaskan youngsters fare far better in cross-country competition. (Few states can compete with us in the length of time we have snow on the ground!) Our schools, from elementary to high, have begun cross-country programs for physical education. Most of the schools have ample space outdoors, and cross-country boots and skis, unlike downhill equipment, are relatively inexpensive. In fact, the equipment is often purchased at surplus stores by school PTA's. This program has caught on rapidly, and some of our young cross-country racers (especially the girls) have already made remarkable performances in national competition.

Alaskans could dominate this particular sport, and undoubtedly will before too long. Not only are the schools promoting it, but more and more families are taking an active part. Even a mediocre skier like me can quickly learn to enjoy a cross-country jaunt, and little ones can join in almost as soon as they learn how to walk. What fun it is to keep the family skis lined up near the front door and just hop into them and take off on the spur of the moment! While we can ski along paths in our woods, there are plenty of trails available to those who live in the more built-up areas, and the active local Nordic Ski Club promotes races and training sessions.

Another popular winter activity which is ideally suited to Alaska involves the use of snowmobiles. First introduced just a few years ago, these little buggies on skis have become so popular that as a household machine in the Anchorage area they rank fourth only to washers, television sets, and freezers. Snowmobiles are used for hunting trips, racing, skijoring, or just plain flitting about the countryside. In fact, these motorized sleds have become so popular all over the state that the traditional dog-sled teams of the northern Alaskan Indians and Eskimos may totally disappear within a few years. The Alaskan native has discovered that he can check his trap lines in half the usual time, and hunting in inaccessible areas is far handier by snowmobile. Thirty of the machines were shipped to Barrow alone last winter, and the number will undoubtedly increase this year.

Other popular winter sports in the Anchorage area are skating, curling, and ice fishing, but undoubtedly the most colorful sport and the one which originated in arctic regions is dog-sled racing. The dogs and sleds were once the only means of travel in most of wintertime Alaska. The rugged and tireless Malemute was the dog used by coastal Eskimos. He is large (seventy-five to ninety pounds), and therefore not the best racing dog, with a thick gray coat, sharp nose, slant eyes, and short legs which are well suited to the hard, compacted snow of the coast. The blue-eyed Siberian husky, the other distinctive breed of the North, was imported about 1902 from across the Bering Strait for racing purposes. Other strains, mainly mixtures of all kinds, were used by the Indian peoples of the interior. Today most racing dogs do not look like the magnificent specimens one sees in pictures of the past but rather like scrawny mongrels bred primarily for speed.

The earliest missionaries found the dogs a superior means of winter transportation, and many traveled hundreds of miles all over the Far North in this fashion. In the early 1900s, Bishop Peter Trimble Rowe of the Episcopal Church made a 350-mile solo trek from Fairbanks to Valdez in the dead of winter at minus-60-degree temperatures. Episcopal Archdeacon Hudson Stuck made a series of winter journeys covering from fifteen hundred to two thousand miles a year, and one of the best-known Alaskan books, written about a Moravian missionary, Dr. Joseph Romig, is called "Dog Team Doctor." The first gold seekers to come to Alaska also used dogs and sleds, and the first mail routes were run with dogs.

Most of the larger communities in Northern, Central, and Southcentral Alaska hold annual dog-sled races. The big week for Anchorage followers of this sport is in February, over Washington's birthday. Called the Fur Rendezvous, our gigantic winter carnival first began in 1917 as a three-day affair for fur auctions. The name came from the old-time rendezvous held by the French-Canadian and Indian fur trappers of northern Canada. The auction was dropped for a while in the late '20s and early '30s, but an athletic-minded group of young men revived it in 1935 and added basketball and hockey games to the traditional fur auction. Incidentally, there were quantities of pelts in those early days, and of high quality, too. Silver fox sold for three hundred to twelve hundred dollars a pelt, and buyers came from as far away as London. A Fur Rendezvous queen was also chosen, and crowned at a coronation ball, and some family-fun dog-sled races were held, the beginnings of the present-day world championship event.

The Fur Rendezvous came back bigger than ever after a halt during the war years, with over seven thousand dollars in prize winnings for the champion dog racers, glittering balls, and large parades. The fur auction has become a very minor part of the big celebration now: the few small rows of rather insignificant pelts half-hidden among the merry-go-round, ferris wheel, and food booths, favorite hangouts for the children during the week-long carnival.

We will long remember our first Fur Rendezvous in 1961, especially the dog races because they provide a rare opportunity for newcomers (and many other residents who do not have the chance to travel about the state) to catch a glimpse of the peoples and cultures of the Far North. Each year a number of Indians and Eskimos bring their teams in to race—local businesses sponsor the individuals, absorbing travel costs involved. The dogs have to be flown in, and this is quite an undertaking in itself! Since it is difficult for any of these individuals to raise and maintain a prize race dog team, many of the northern villages pool all of their dogs, and the racer, chosen to represent that village, has his choice. Some of the men from the North have returned to race year after year, occasionally winning, always putting in a good performance. A great rivalry has developed among these northern communities, which adds tremendously to the excitement and interest of the race. The tiny village of Huslia, on the Koyukuk River just south of the Arctic Circle, has been a frequent winner: represented by Jimmy Huntington, brothers Alfred and George Attla, and Bergman Sam (who later moved to Hughes and then represented that community). Isaac Okleasick has been a three-time contender from Teller (which has also sent Chester Topkok), Koyukuk has been represented by Leo Kriska, and Galena has sent half brothers Jimmie Malamute and Raymond Paul.

Native dog mushers from the North by no means dominate the races, however; Fairbanks, which holds its own State Championship Dog Races each winter, has sent—among others—top contender Gareth Wright; and a number of Anchorage racers, including Joey Reddington, Billy Sullivan, Orville Lake, and Earl Norris have also led the field. However, the top winner for three years in a row, from 1963 to 1966, was Dr. Roland Lombard, a

New Englander from Weyland, Massachusetts! In the last few years he has been joined by fellow veterinarian Dr. Charles Belford from Deerfield, Massachusetts. Dog-sled racing has by no means been limited to Alaska—one reason why the word "world" was added to the championship race title. Lombard and Belford represent an active New England racing group, and there are two more race centers in Idaho and northern California. Although also a popular sport in Canada, no Canadians have come here to race, other than Andy Smith from Whitehorse in 1947.

Because race officials use the title "world," I suppose they hope to lure dog racers from other parts of the globe. Dog teams are used in all arctic-rim countries: Norwegian cross-country skiers use dogs and sleds to carry their gear on long runs, the peoples of Siberia have their own winter gatherings centered about dog races, and the Eskimos of Greenland hold impromptu races to and from their hunting grounds. However, no one has ever appeared to represent any area other than North America, with the sole exception of an Englishman, "Fox" Ramsey, who ran in the Nome All-American Sweepstakes in 1908. (I wonder if he did his training on the moors of Scotland!) Rumor has it that an invitation has been sent repeatedly to the Russians, but presumably the Soviets are still searching for an unbeatable Siberian team.

While these contestants enjoy the thrill of such competition each year, it is especially fun for the spectator. The races are run three days in a row, twenty-five miles each day, and they start and finish on Fourth Avenue, in the heart of the city. One might think that only in the Far North could a main street have enough snow covering for sleds—actually almost every year snow has had to be trucked in from the mountains and spread out by plows and graders before the start of each race. The rest of the course covers outlying areas: trails in the woods and swamps well covered with snow. But as each year goes by, racers have to cross more and more main thoroughfares which must also be coated with trucked-in snow.

Most spectators crowd the downtown area to watch the starts and finishes and to enjoy other Rendezvous activities. We followed suit for several years, fascinated by the sight of the dogs being harnessed, straining and jumping in their eagerness to be off. The tense racers stand on the runners, occasionally stopping to untangle an overanxious dog at the start. Once off down the street, a racer can lose precious time, as a lead dog, distracted by something in the crowd (usually a dog spectator), veers off to investigate. The finishes are always exciting: the weary men running behind their sleds, the equally weary dogs, their long tongues hanging almost to the ground, still going for all their worth. Sometimes a racer may have one or even two dogs "in the basket" (riding in the sled): the rule being that one must finish with the same number of dogs that started, so that any dog who has injured a paw or become totally exhausted gets a free ride back.

After our first few races, we decided it might be more fun to watch from along a trail farther out in the countryside. There one can see the men and dogs racing in more natural surroundings, and it is most exciting to watch teams pass each other on the narrow wooded trails. After hiking through the woods on skis, we stand half-hidden at the edge of a trail, with few other people in sight. A native musher flies past, snapping his whip over the heads of his ten or twelve speeding dogs, and it is easy to imagine oneself transplanted to the distant arctic wilderness. But a couple of jarring features of our modern life bring us quickly back to reality. A helicopter circles constantly overhead, keeping track of the teams, reporting in by radio and TV on the progress of every contestant. The 'copter also reports the inevitable spectator dog (a great distracting hazard to the musher) or equally distracting people walking on the trails, and occasionally it even tries to herd away a curious moose or two. TV and radio play a big role in carrying all details of the races to the house or office-bound audience. At checkpoints along the trail TV cameras follow every racer, and those racing fans unwilling or unable to stand out-of-doors to watch the races can relax in warmth before a TV set and see all the goings on.

Radios, we discovered with great surprise, are important to the racers, too—most contestants carry small pocket transistors with ear plugs, and as they mush along, they can keep tabs on the times and positions of their opponents. I wonder what the Nome contestants of 1904 would have thought of these modern innovations! And things may go from bad to worse: A visitor from Huslia was heard to remark last year that there just aren't many racing dogs being raised in the villages any more. He said there were already fourteen snowmobiles in his village alone, and that represented fourteen dog teams. Perhaps the dog races will go the way of the fur auction, but I fervently hope not.

For those not interested in the sports activities of Fur Rendezvous, there are any number of indoor events, including art exhibits, homemade fur-hat-judging contests, Indian dancers, an Eskimo blanket toss, a Coronation Pageant, a Queen's Ball, and a Miners' and Trappers' Ball. The latter event is especially fun because old-time costumes are worn, and the highlight of the evening is the beard-judging contest. Many Anchorage men use Fur Rendezvous as a good excuse to grow a beard. For weeks beforehand prominent bankers, storekeepers, lawyers, and an occasional doctor start sporting whiskers. They never have a chance, though, when they meet face to face (or beard to beard) at the judging with old-time sourdoughs who have grown belt-long, bushy beards for years and come in from the sticks each year just to carry off the Mr. Fur Face awards.

As with Fur Rendezvous, our many winter activities are by no means strictly geared to the sports-minded or outdoors enthusiast. In fact, so much goes on indoors during the winter months that the relatively quiet and less hectic summertime is always a welcome respite. There are clubs and organizations for everyone, and it is not uncommon to be going to one activity or another six nights a week. Besides the many national service clubs (Rotary, Lions, Kiwanis, Zonta, Soroptimists, etc.) and the Women's Club, the League of Women Voters, the World Affairs Council, garden clubs, and university, business and professional groups, there are also such diverse organizations as the Newcomers' Club, African Violet Club, Parents Without Partners, Alaskan Prospectors' Society, the Chugach Gem & Mineral Society, Toastmistress Club, and many more. The list of civic and social welfare groups is even longer, and when one adds related activities of the ninety-some odd churches, our community calendar becomes more than full.

It is quite easy for an Anchorage newcomer to find a special interest out of such a variety—the problem for many people is how to avoid becoming too heavily involved. There is the feeling in such a new community that there is so much to be done—so much to be accomplished by a relatively few (most Anchorage women either work or are tied down by small children, and few retired people, with time on their hands, remain in Alaska).

Lowell and I both had a few years of such frantic activity that it seemed the only time we ever saw each other was when we'd pass on the road. We still have to face such periods of hectic pace (the kind we had thought we left back East), but we have learned to direct our efforts to those few endeavors which have interested us the most. St. Mary's Episcopal Church, our friends there, the many activities related to it and to the Episcopal Missionary District of Alaska, have meant a great deal to both of us in our new life in the North. The Alaska Crippled Children's Treatment Center here in Anchorage has been the other project to which I have devoted many hours. One visit to the center is enough to convince anyone of the importance of this private organization. Highly trained physical therapists care for physically handicapped children, a teacher of the deaf and three speech and hearing specialists treat the hard-of-hearing, and four diagnostic nurseries and kindergartens help care for the multi-handicapped. The ACCA gives hope for normal life to over seven hundred children a year.

All of these activities are good, a New Yorker or San Franciscan might say, but what about the symphony, the opera, or museums, and art galleries? While it is true that our cultural attractions could never hope to match those of large urban areas "outside," the arts resources which are available to us may surprise many non-Alaskans. Not only do we have the opportunity to attend concerts given by the Anchorage Symphony Orchestra and Community Chorus, but we can also enjoy listening to the music of many visiting artists. To be at the crossroads of air traffic from the United States to the Orient or over the pole to Europe is a great advantage—we can snare en-route performers for one- or two-day layovers here. In past years enthralled Anchorage audiences have heard the New York Philharmonic, the Boston Symphony Orchestra, Van Cliburn, the Viennese Boys Choir, and other world-renowned musicians. Last year the Anchorage Concert Association winter program included the Vienna Symphony Orchestra, Polish pianist Wojciech Matuszewski, English guitarist Julian Bream, and Janos Starker, famed cellist.

The grand climax to our musical year comes each June, with the Alaska Festival of Music. For two weeks Anchorage reverberates with music to match her mountains, and the many talented local musicians are joined by artists from elsewhere in Alaska and all over the United States. The visitors not only take part in orchestral and vocal recitals but also conduct seminars on various musical subjects. Over the years guest artists from "outside" have included the Interlochen Arts Quintet, tenor Blake Stern, contralto Florence Kopleff, music master Julius Herford, and conductor Robert Shaw, who has directed the festival for many seasons.

Music from a different tradition is brought to the festival each year through seminars conducted by Lorraine Koranda, who has made extensive studies and recordings of Eskimo music. And thanks to an annual Sears Roebuck scholarship, twelve young people representing distant Eskimo, Indian, and Aleut communities also come into Anchorage for the many musical events. Other Alaskans come in from some of the state's larger communities, and Fairbanks, Juneau, and Ketchikan have active cultural programs of their own. The Alaska State Council on the Arts, formed in 1966, has done much to promote many of these statewide activities and to enable artistic programs to travel and perform in more isolated areas. Ballet, art, and theater groups are also active in Anchorage and the other towns. Music and other arts have come a long way in the Far North!

When first faced with such a full calendar of winter activities, I used to worry about the weather and poor driving conditions. Surely a heavy snowstorm or icy streets would cut down attendance at concerts or leave meetings poorly attended. While living in the East, I stayed home at the first sign of a snowflake and seldom drove alone at night, anyway. It didn't take me long to discover that Alaskans always go, regardless of weather. We have seen every seat filled in our largest auditorium in the midst of a blizzard. We have attended all kinds of gatherings during the worst weather imaginable and have found that everyone else is there, too. And I drive over many dark, often isolated roads at night now, still amazed at the great amount of nighttime traffic—all Anchorage en route to one meeting or another.

I suppose one reason Alaskans do drive in the worst of winter weather is because our road-maintenance people do such a wonderful job. While twelve inches of snow can cripple Chicago or

Washington or most areas in the "lower 48," here in Alaska we have yet to see city living come to a halt because of any amount of snow or ice. I can remember as a child feeling great joy and excitement when a winter storm closed our schools—an experience our kids may never face! We have seen much snow and ice during our winters here, but never once have the children not been able to get to school. Our own driveways may occasionally pose problems, but nonsleeping highway crews work around the clock to keep roads passable, and the Alaskan motorist develops a pretty sound technique for winter driving. Whenever I find myself behind a particularly cautious driver on a snowy or icy road, I can almost guess that he or she has just moved up from some southern state.

Even the Alaskan driver can become a little rusty over the summer months, though, and the first day of snow each winter could also be called the annual "bump the other car, or into the ditch we go" day. We forget that we must slow down considerably earlier at intersections, and the inevitable result is a rash of accidents all over the city. It is enough to keep the more timorous driver home for the rest of the winter. Eventually, however, we all regain our skill, and I frequently wonder at my newly acquired bravado as I cruise down streets closely resembling skating rinks. (In fact, kids know that the quickest and easiest way to reach the neighborhood ice rink is to skate there!)

December is invariably our snowiest and coldest month, and it is also our time of greatest darkness. I think most "outsiders" believe that the arctic winter brings us interminable night, a belief perpetuated by occasional articles in national magazines containing pictures dwelling on life going on during a twenty-four-hour night. This would be an apt description of the land north of the Arctic Circle, where the sun never rises for six weeks in midwinter. But over three fourths of the Alaskan population lives from three to six hundred miles south of the circle, and this distance makes a big difference in terms of hours of daylight. We in Anchorage have five hours and twenty-eight minutes of sun on December 21, the shortest day of the year. This means that during the six weeks around that time, the sun rises about nine o'clock and sets around three. Some people do find the added darkness most depressing, and it is especially hard on the office worker, who leaves home in the dark and returns when it is the same way. But for many more of us, this season of the year, over Christmas, is the busiest time of all. We are so involved with the many holiday activities that the time rushes by, and when New Year's Day is over, we suddenly realize the days are growing longer again. It is amazing what a psychological impact can come from three additional minutes of sunlight each day—spring is just around the corner!

There is something especially exciting about Christmas in Alaska—perhaps because it comes closest to the old-fashioned holiday depicted on Christmas cards of any I have ever known. People actually do go on sleigh rides here, carolers walk from house to house in many neighborhoods, and popcorn balls and cranberry strands are hung on outdoor Christmas trees (ostensibly for the birds and squirrels but inevitably for the children who helped string them). And of course it is especially festive with the deep snow cover and crisp cold air.

I think, too, that there is an abundance of holiday spirit here because most of us must celebrate Christmas without relatives and so peace and good will toward all men has more depth of meaning to us. We are more aware of distances at this time, especially when it comes to buying and mailing gifts to the "lower 48." Since mail deadlines come the first part of December, we must shop early—much to the joy of local merchants, who begin their Christmas displays two weeks before Thanksgiving. The penalty for procrastinating can be high—if one does not mail packages and cards by December 10, the only alternative is airmail postage, and this can make a big difference in dollars and cents. (Actually, the U. S. Post Office does very well by Alaskans: Most first-class mail travels to Seattle by air anyway, and a letter mailed here on Monday will reach New York City by Wednesday morning.)

Christmas shopping in Alaska is especially fun when the streets are lined with lighted candy canes and giant spruce trees, and while in earlier days shopping here meant lengthy perusal of the Montgomery Ward and Sears Roebuck catalogues, Anchorage now has a great variety of stores, and virtually anything can be bought locally. Prices are high, but they are not outrageous, another common misconception about Alaska. The cost of living in

Anchorage is about 25 per cent higher than in the Pacific Northwest, but most incomes are that much higher, too. People moving here from some of the larger cities see little difference in the costs, while visitors from Hawaii find some of our food and rental prices lower. Although we pay a few cents more for meat, only the highest quality meat is brought in, and the more expensive vegetables and fruit are flown up in refrigerated planes, just one day away from California and Pacific Northwest farms. There is a great variety of produce here—pineapples and papayas from Hawaii, a number of Japanese foods, and gourmet canned goods from Europe are an everyday sight in Anchorage markets.

While shopping centers and downtown streets are well lit over the Christmas period, they are far outshone by the homes of Anchorage. Electricity bills may be high in midwinter, but that does not seem to deter people at all. If a house has no outdoor spruce tree to be lit, the owner will go ahead and put lights all over any old tree or hang strings of colored bulbs from the eaves or around the doorway. A whole neighborhood can get carried away, and the streets will be one great blaze of many-colored lights.

Some families go even further, using floodlights to illuminate crèche scenes—some large enough to cover the front lawn. One home puts Santa with his sleigh and reindeer on top of the roof each year; another modern-thinking family puts Santa in a rocket by their chimney; and in another Anchorage yard, old Mr. Claus rides in an ancient Model T. Ice sculptures used to be another popular way to decorate lawns for the holiday season, but the green Christmas of 1960 seemed to discourage this particular activity.

Our homes indoors are just as gay and festive—the focus being on a large Alaskan Christmas tree. Our children still know the joy of tramping into the woods as a family, selecting and chopping down the tree. But even here it becomes harder each year to find a tree nearby, and the store-bought variety is taking over. With the tree up and the yule log in the fireplace, the family is ready for the many festivities of the season. Most entertaining in Anchorage takes place in the homes, although for a city its size, we have an exceptional number of good restaurants of infinite variety. There are also many dances and balls, usually held in one of the two hotels uptown, which frequently call for formal clothing.

Although dress is for the most part casual in Anchorage, a number of women here dress most stylishly and I have often had a need for long evening gowns.

While all these parties and decorations make this season sound very gay, there are also people here, as elsewhere, who find the holidays a terribly lonely and depressing time. Our isolation does make it difficult for those without families and friends and also for low-income families who simply cannot afford anything beyond the bare necessities of life. In fact, while many of us love living in Alaska, there are others who, because of finances or other reasons, are miserable. Frequently families will come North, spending their last pennies on transportation, looking for the last frontier of opportunity, and then find themselves facing a long, dark, dreary winter with no job or money for anything.

Life here can be very difficult for some women, especially those with many young children. Living in a small home or trailer with two or three little ones is hard anyway, but when they have to be bundled up to play out-of-doors or when they can't get out at all, the difficult situation is compounded. To make it even harder on the women, daytime sitters and household help are extremely scarce in this area, and Anchorage is still without any kind of day-care center, something desperately needed by many local working mothers.

To make it even more difficult for some women, Alaska is definitely a "man's land." Faced with unlimited opportunities for hunting, fishing, camping, flying, or climbing, a man can just take off in his free time and, with plenty of male companionship, have a ball! This leaves the little woman even more alone and unhappy, with the inevitable result that either the marriage breaks up or the woman wins out and they return to more normal life in the "lower 48."

I think it is true that many of these unhappy women did not want to come here in the first place, and this makes a difference in one's attitude toward the problems of winter or the activities of the man's world. I have also known many women, living on small incomes, with little children, who cheerfully put a baby on their backs, papoose-style, with one or more children at their sides, and trudge right along with their husbands, whether going hunting, camping, or any other outdoor activity. I know one Negro couple who take all their seven children on outings every weekend: in the spring it is clamming, in the summer they all love to go fishing, and in the fall it is berrying. In the winter they go back to fishing, through the ice.

Almost everyone is tired of winter by the end of February—six months of snow is a long time for all but the most avid skier, like my husband. Lowell hates to see the snow go because it ruins late spring skiing. In fact, on every sunny weekend during the summer he flies his plane up to the Chugach glaciers so he can get in a little more skiing. But for the rest of us, spring can hardly get here quickly enough. If we could just close our eyes and jump from winter to summer. The trouble is that all that snow accumulation has to melt, and the ground has to thaw out, too. So we are faced with spring breakup, and the less said about it the better.

Just as the snow covered up ugliness, all is again revealed with its melting. Once more we can see last fall's roadside trash, but many unexpected items reappear, too—like a lost mitten or David's football or the long-forgotten garden hose. The biggest discovery of what lies under the snow was made by a close friend of ours a few years ago. In the late fall she married a local doctor, also a good friend, and they moved into a cute little house near the hospital, where he had to spend so much time. It was surrounded by woods and a snow-covered field with a number of gentle rises—just perfect for some cross-country skiing. Came the spring, and the snow melting from the "rises" revealed a back yard loaded with old abandoned cars.

Puddles is another apt word for breakup—there are lots of them everywhere. Each year one formed at a particularly low section of Northern Lights Boulevard. It was so deep that cars were invariably swamped when navigating it. The highway people must have gotten tired of the yearly reference to the Northern Lights lake—an extensive road project finally dried this one up. Other "lakes" at breakup time are harder to get rid of, especially in uneven, poorly drained yards. One year one of our neighbors found his "pond" so large he launched his rowboat on it. The neighborhood children thought this was great fun, but then all the children feel that way about every puddle, and so at least somebody enjoys Alaska's spring breakup. Fortunately for the rest of us, it doesn't last long—just during the month of April. May and June are warm and dry, filled with the light of the midnight sun.

III

Lowell and His
Flying Machine

"Alaska in the supersonic jet age will be the geopolitical center of the world, serving as the hub of a vast wheel of great circle routes to four continents." So spoke an aviation official at an Anchorage Chamber of Commerce banquet in 1965. The speaker happened to be my dad, Sam Pryor, then vice-president of Pan American World Airways. Ever since the days of Billy Mitchell, Alaska has been talked of as an important crossroads in world aviation. General and Mrs. Charles Lindbergh proved it was the shortest way to the Orient in 1931. Today seven international airlines stop in Anchorage, en route to Europe or the Far East— together with charter flights and Alaskan airlines—making over 150,000 landings and take-offs at Anchorage International Airport in 1968. Just a few miles away, the two military bases chalked up over 111,000 planes in and out in the same year.

However, we don't need statistics to tell us of the busy goings on at our international airport. While our new home is tucked away in the woods, twenty minutes by car from the heart of the city, it is within a mile of the airport runways. Fortunately we are not in the approach paths at either end, but we can look out our windows and watch planes landing and taking off. Perhaps it's the old wanderlust in us, but both Lowell and I always feel a thrill as we see a giant Boeing 707 or DC-8 climb into the sky, headed for Europe or the Orient. Lufthansa, SAS, Air France, KLM, Japan Air Lines, Pan Am, and Northwest—take your pick, and you can be in Tokyo in seven hours or any one of many European cities in eight.

At least three or four jets are usually parked in front of the terminal at the same time while passengers of many nationalities crowd into the airport gift shop to buy native artifacts or stare at the large stuffed polar bear in a nearby waiting room. One is always seeing Japanese or European crews at the local hotels during their layovers, and many of them take advantage of their free days to go skiing. Once a year Alyeska holds an international airlines ski race, and while twenty-eight companies, representing fourteen countries, send in their best skiing crews, the captains and stewardesses from Scandinavia invariably walk off with all the honors.

I have already mentioned one of the advantages of living at an international air crossroads—we frequently have the opportunity to hear world-renowned musicians. Many other well-known personalities also pass through, either just spending an hour or two between flights or laying over several days to visit or entertain. Three U. S. Presidents head the list—Eisenhower, Kennedy, and Johnson. The King and Queen of Nepal came in 1967 for an extensive hunting trip, the Japanese Foreign Minister, the British Prime Minister, Hubert Humphrey, Richard Nixon, a number of congressmen, cabinet officers, and many other distinguished persons have stepped onto the red carpet rolled out by our Chamber of Commerce. I wonder what that great stuffed bear was thinking about when Twiggy strolled by him recently. I do know that one of our most popular visitors was Louis "Satchmo" Armstrong, who, with his trumpet, packed our auditorium for two nights straight. The Turtles and the Grass Roots drew equal crowds of young people, while the littlest ones were thrilled over a visit by Lassie.

Perhaps the greatest furor was caused by a group who had to spend the night somewhat unexpectedly—their plane was delayed by a typhoon. Who else but the Beatles could come in at night with no advance publicity, secrete themselves at the hotel, and sneak out the next morning, leaving all young people in a total uproar. Somehow the word spread the moment the Beatles stepped off the plane, and hundreds of cars followed their limousine uptown. Crowds of youngsters kept watch beneath hotel windows all night long, rewarded only by one feeble wave of a hand. After the famous group had departed, certain hotel towels, dishes, and ash trays disappeared mysteriously, and one enterprising local group made money auctioning off items "touched by the Beatles."

Many more people pass through Anchorage daily who may not cause as much furor, but who are at the same time important, interesting and representative of all parts of the world. I sometimes feel we should hang out a hotel sign because we feed and put up so many travelers. But the constant comings and goings are all a part of the fun of living here, an opportunity for us to show others a bit of life in Alaska.

Fortunately, we have a study-guest room and a freezer well stocked with Alaskan king crab and moose meat. Also, I enjoy entertaining at a moment's notice, although I have no help. The only problem that ever upsets the household is the occasional guest who is allergic to cats! During a fairly typical week last spring, I barely had time to change sheets after the departure of a young college student from New Zealand before we welcomed the Anglican archbishop of Zambia, a small country in Central Africa. A few days later, Lowell gave me thirty minutes' advance notice that two Austrians would be coming to lunch—businessmen from Salzburg on a hunting vacation.

During the summer months tourists pour into the forty-ninth state, at a greater rate every year. There are times when we are tempted to take the phone off the hook because we average about three or four calls a day from visitors passing through—"your great-aunt Tillie told us to look you up . . ." We are also discovering that folks "outside" have begun to realize what a great place Alaska is for their young boys. Last summer we sent one nephew back home to Hawaii (he went most reluctantly) the day before two more arrived. And Lowell receives many letters a year from boys asking about summer-job opportunities. This poses a problem because while we are most eager to have these youngsters see the state (after one visit, there are always some who decide to come back later to stay), there are never enough summer jobs for local young people, and they certainly should come first. Lowell's advice to these queries by mail is for the writer to contact the State Department of Fish and Game, the U. S. Forest Service, or the Alaska Railroad.

Although national and international air travel has had a big impact on our lives, it is only a part of the aviation picture in Alaska. Airplanes, of necessity, have played a vital and unique role in this state—they have created modern highways in the skies over a vast land which may not see a network of land roads for many years to come. Flying is not only important to the economy of the state through the operation of state-wide airlines and the legendary bush pilots, but also more residents, in proportion to population, fly for pleasure than in any other state in the union. One out of every fifty Alaskans is a licensed pilot. All sizes and shapes of small planes are used for hunting, fishing, camping, or sight-seeing—just the way families in other states use the family car. When Lowell was elected to the state legislature in 1966, he was amazed to discover that out of a total of twenty state senators, thirteen had been or still were licensed pilots. I doubt that any other state can come close to matching that ratio.

Here in Anchorage hundreds of float planes are parked along the shores of Lake Hood, the site of the only seaplane control tower in the world. Families use these planes to visit the many lakes in this Southcentral area—either for a one-day outing to fish, hunt, or swim, or to spend the weekend at cabins built along the remote shore lines. Light planes on wheels rather than floats operate mainly from Merrill Field, a small city-owned airport just east of town. Perhaps small is not the right word—the runways are not long and facilities are not extensive, but in 1966 Merrill Field was ranked as the sixty-fifth busiest airport in the nation, and small planes accounted for over 268,000 landings and take-offs in 1968.

Our Cessna 180, nicknamed "Charlie" for the "C" in its registration, is the same plane Lowell and I flew around Africa and the Middle East in 1954, and we also used it while filming for television in Alaska in 1958. Our original plan had been to sell the plane while abroad, but "Charlie" became such a part of the family that we have never been able to part with it. Cessna 180's don't grow old, the way cars do, and it is an especially good airplane for the uses Lowell puts it to. ("Charlie" has a ski-wheel combination—the skis can be cranked up or down, and so are instantly available summer or winter.) Most of Lowell's landings and take-offs are from short bush strips, beaches, or sand bars, and high, snow-covered mountain slopes. According to Lowell, the 180 has the power and the short-field performance necessary for such operations. I take his word for it—I'm just the automatic pilot, the guy who steers it straight for hours on end, eight thousand feet up in the air.

I am often asked if I worry over our plane's having just one engine. My reply is, "not really," because I know Lowell will not push weather with only one engine and I also know that he could set "Charlie" down in just about any clearing or sand bar, or in the winter on frozen lakes or any snow-covered open area. And we have learned that the 180 engine is highly reliable, if cared for properly. In his years of flying in Alaska, Lowell has had to make only one emergency landing. Fortunately I was not aboard at the time, but it is still a day I will never forget.

It was in early November of 1964—Lowell had just been defeated in the race for Congress (a Republican in a Democratic landslide year), but the defeat was by such a narrow margin that it looked as if the absentee ballots would settle the outcome. In Alaska these ballots are not counted until ten days after the election—ten days of nerve-racking suspense for us. Lowell decided to get away from it all for a short while, so he and his Fairbanks campaign manager, Jim Binkley, took off for the northern wilds. He had been gone for three days when I decided that it would help me to pass the time by attending a ladies' luncheon. When I walked in the door of my hostess's home, one of her guests said, "I'm so glad Lowell is all right; you must be relieved." I couldn't imagine what she was talking about, and she, in great consternation, stammered that she had just heard over the radio something about a forced landing.

Needless to say, I did not really enjoy my lunch but rushed home as soon as I could. Of course it was impossible to reach Lowell anywhere, but two-inch headlines in the afternoon newspaper and hourly radio reports told of the congressional candidate making a forced landing on a road outside Fairbanks. A rather chagrined Lowell appeared at dinnertime—he had not called me because he hadn't wanted to frighten me unduly. By then I was a total wreck!

I finally did hear the story firsthand that evening—he and Jim were flying back to Fairbanks from the Yukon River after sunset the day before. It was almost dark, but they were within fifteen or twenty minutes of the airport, flying over the heavily wooded hills west of Fairbanks. Suddenly the engine coughed and quit with no warning at all (an air-intake valve on the gas cap froze, and so all the gas was siphoned from the one full tank). Of course they had to land immediately, and the only possibility, in such forested, hilly terrain, was the narrow, twisting road just beneath them. To make matters more difficult it was quite dark then and Lowell had to approach over tall trees, land on a short straight uphill stretch, maneuver past a roadsign, and then around a corner. Thanks to able piloting, "Charlie" was unscratched and the men were simply shaken. They pushed the plane off the road, hitched a ride to town, drove back later with a mechanic, and flew "Charlie" off again at daylight the next morning. All in a day's flying but certainly not an ideal way to calm one's election-frazzled nerves!

Flying in Alaska can be a very tricky operation—it is not like hopping into a plane in the "lower 48," tuning in one's radio omni and following the needle all the way, with innumerable airports beneath one at virtually all times. Alaskan pilots fly over hundreds of miles of wilderness on almost any flight, with no airstrips, few radio navigational aids, and only isolated towns and roads beneath them. In fact many areas are so wild and mountainous that maps cannot show the terrain in sufficient detail and in some cases even show total blank spots. Any pilot flying in or near mountainous areas must watch the map and the weather very carefully. A number of people have been lost while groping in poor visibility through mountain valleys which all too often end abruptly at a mountain wall.

Even when one is away from hilly terrain (almost an impossibility in Alaska), it is easy to get lost over hundreds of miles of tundra or forests, with countless streams and ponds, and no other distinguishing landmarks. Lowell and I went the wrong way when we first flew the well-traveled route between Anchorage and Fairbanks—the only route marked by a road and railroad—we followed a winter dog-sled trail instead!

Even if the pilot does not get lost, if he ever should have to sit down because of bad weather or mechanical failure, he may have a long wait before he is found. Our state has a highly effective search and rescue operation—a co-ordination of the very active Civil Air Patrol, the military Rescue Coordination Center, and the Coast Guard. However, no matter how able the group, they can face many enormous search tasks. Hampered by the size of the area involved and bad weather, it could be and often is weeks before the tiny speck of a plane is spotted in the midst of a vast wilderness. The pilots themselves can make it far more difficult for rescuers by failing to file a flight plan—if they do, it certainly helps to narrow the search area. Lowell files a plan each time he goes anywhere.

Because fliers might have to sit down in the midst of nowhere for a length of time, it is mandatory that pilots in Alaska carry emergency supplies: sleeping bag, tent, snowshoes, and enough food for one person for two weeks. Such a law, however, is hard to enforce, and it is surprising how many people blithely take off on a day's outing in midwinter, carrying nothing other than themselves and the clothes (usually inappropriate) on their backs. Most people will recall the story of the young couple who crashed in the Yukon wilderness, with no food for survival other than toothpaste.

When Lowell was faced with his first winter of flying in Alaska, he not only carefully selected survival gear to take along but also decided that it would be silly to carry all that equipment without actually testing it out first. That was why we decided, in January of 1961, to fly up to an isolated lake in the Mount McKinley area and camp out overnight, using our survival knowledge and gear. We decided to camp out as a family, dressing the children in fur parkas and mukluks. This part of the venture was highly successful, but other preparations left something to be desired. I did not yet realize that canned goods can readily freeze, so I had quite a time trying to thaw out food for dinner—we ended up with baked beans and hot chocolate. (Now we carry a good variety of dehydrated foods—they weigh less and there is no freezing problem.) Another mistake was to use a large tent. It had plenty of room for four people, plus a cooking area and a Yukon stove (a metal box, with a stovepipe going out a hole in the tent roof). The ideal way to stay alive in the arctic cold is to use a very small tent (or better still, a snow shelter or igloo), with people crammed together—there is less space to keep warm, and bodies wedged together give off surprising warmth. We also erred in forgetting some kind of gas or oil lantern. The early winter darkness caught us in the midst of our preparations, and there was much fumbling to find things inside the tent. Our two flashlights grew dim unbelievably fast—cold temperatures affect batteries, too.

We did make one right move in preparing sleeping accommodations—we used a tent with no floor, and cut and laid spruce boughs right on the snow. We covered them with a couple of caribou skins, widely used by native peoples in the Far North. However, we only had one light sleeping bag apiece, not nearly enough warmth for minus-20-degree temperatures. (Each of us should have had at least two, or better yet, shared bags with the children, further utilizing body warmth.) Lowell and I became so cold (kids never do!) that he spent most of the night chopping wood, under the dim glow of the northern lights, so that we could keep the Yukon stove going. This was a further mistake, we learned later: I singed my bag on the stove during one wiggly period while trying to get warm, and people have burned to death in just such a manner. No one camping out in our northern winter should try to keep a stove or fire going in a tent while sleeping— one should have enough warm sleep gear to survive even the coldest temperatures.

Needless to say, we did not linger in our arctic paradise but broke camp at first daylight the next morning and, thanks to "firepotting" the engine, were able to start the plane and take right off. As we passed over Talkeetna, on our way back to Anchorage, Lowell reported in to the radio facility there. The operator acknowledged our call and then added, "By the way, what were you doing on the lake overnight—ice fishing?" "Roger" was Lowell's curt reply.

While we have had many family excursions in "Charlie," not all as adventuresome as our midwinter camp out, much of Lowell's flying in the Cessna has been done by himself or with fellow skiing, climbing, and fishing companions. Fishing is one of my favorite pastimes, but Lowell and I are at opposite poles on the definition of this sport. My idea of going fishing is to find a quiet stream or lake amid beautiful natural surroundings, relax on some warm, sunny rocks with my trusty bamboo pole, and watch my little red bobber float on the placid waters. I use salmon eggs for bait because wiggly worms and horrid night crawlers would only destroy my peace and contentment. If I should be lucky enough to catch a fish, and much to Lowell's great surprise, I sometimes do, then I have to yell for help to get it off the hook (I usually take along a child or two just for this purpose). And of course, I always throw the poor creature back, relying on Lowell to keep our freezer filled.

Lowell's fishing excursions are high adventure in the fullest sense. They always start with a flight in "Charlie," and he usually lands on a sandy beach far down the inlet or at a small FAA airstrip somewhere off in the wilds but near a good fishing stream. One day last summer he and a friend landed on a deserted oil-company road down on the Kenai Peninsula. They parked the plane and walked through about a mile of dense woods to a small stream. Returning to "Charlie" after a few hours of successful casting, they discovered that the plane had had a thorough going over from another fisherman—a large black bear. Mr. Bear apparently stood on his hind legs, put his large muddy paws on all the windows, but didn't try to break in when he could detect no fish inside. As he ambled around the plane, he must have acquired a sudden itch, because Lowell found a few strands of black hair caught in the horizontal stabilizer. Fortunately the airplane tail didn't appear damaged, but we shudder to think what might have happened if Mr. Bear had decided to sit on it.

On another day a few summers ago, Lowell planned a fishing expedition with two ministers, the Reverend Sandy Zabriskie from our church and the visiting Reverend Peter Yoshimura from Japan. I decided he couldn't be in better hands, and drove to a nearby lake where I watched my bobber in great contentment. When the men had not returned by seven that night, I became a bit concerned. Not that I always expect Lowell in time for dinner, but there was to be an important function at the church that evening, and both ministers planned to be there without fail. Ten minutes before the church service was to begin, in walked a thoroughly wet and muddy Sandy and Peter but no Lowell. They hastily explained that although they had landed on a broad sand beach, the tide had come in while they were busy fishing and had completely wiped out their runway. Fortunately the plane could be moved above high-water line, but since there was no hope of taking off for many hours, Lowell radioed the Anchorage tower to ask if a seaplane operator could come to pick up the two ministers. Left alone to wait out the tide, Lowell built a fire and cooked himself a dinner of salmon and dehydrated potatoes. He still wonders why I can't cook fish that will taste as good as that one did that night!

While we continue to "discuss" whether I will go along with Lowell to fish according to his methods, there is never any disagreement over my participating in Lowell's mountain-climbing sorties—I stay home. In the years since we've come to Alaska, Lowell has joined the very small and elite group of glacier pilots, and I really feel that he is prouder and happier with this accomplishment than almost any other. To land high on a mountainside, selecting the right slope, weighing snow, wind, and weather conditions, is a highly exacting science, but Lowell has mastered it to such a degree that while I may be a proud wife, I still feel he is one of the best.

That doesn't mean I never worry! A number of unpredictable factors, such as a sudden change in weather, the breaking of a ski on landing, or a host of other more horrible obstacles like crevasses or avalanches, could greatly delay any mountain expedition. Just plain fun can also postpone the return home: One summer Saturday, Lowell and Dr. George Wichman, a frequent companion on these excursions, took off to spend the day among the glaciers of the Chugach. They parked the plane (Lowell is always careful to tie it down in case of unexpected winds) and, carrying skis on their shoulders and lunch in knapsacks on their backs, hiked high up a mountainside. After a pause to sun-bathe and enjoy the view, they had a tremendously exhilarating ski run back down to the plane.

The weather was still perfect and the surroundings so beautiful that the two decided to spend the night and take another run the next morning. While they could reach the FAA in Anchorage, thanks to Lowell's long-range radio, they were not able to transmit any private message, such as, "Dear, we would like to spend the night," or, "Honey, don't wait dinner [and we had planned a dinner party], have decided not to come home." Instead, the truants notified the FAA that they were having minor ski trouble with the plane and would have to spend the night while making repairs. Would they pass that message on to the wives? The wives, Peggy Wichman and I, did not believe one word, knowing full well what the boys were up to.

At least we had been notified that the men were not coming home. There have been a few times when I've waited many hours, wondering just what might have gone wrong on the mountaintop. While Lowell's most frequent excursions have been to nearby glaciers for a day's summer skiing, he has also participated in a number of mountain climbing expeditions: either just to fly the party in and out, or to park the plane and climb to the summit, too. He took on one of his first ferrying jobs over Memorial Day weekend of 1961. It also happened to be the weekend that we moved from the rented Turnagain house into our newly purchased home on Chilligan Drive. Of course there was no coincidence—the climbers needed him badly, and there was no reason why I couldn't carry the heavy cartons into the house and supervise the movers with the larger furniture.

So off he went, on a perfectly clear, calm day, ferrying the five climbers in in two trips, landing on ideal snow conditions on a broad, fairly flat glacier—the whole venture to be a lark over the holiday weekend. That was Friday, May 26. On Saturday clouds from nowhere began to pour down over the mountains, and by Monday morning, when Lowell was to return for the party, a virtual cyclone was howling over the whole Chugach range. When Lowell tried to follow a glacier up into the area, he encountered low clouds and severe turbulence (he estimated winds at seventy miles per hour). There was just no way he could get in to keep his rendezvous, and to make matters worse, the weather forecaster expected no improvement for the next forty-eight hours.

While I worried about Lowell, he worried about the climbers, and he tried morning and evening for those next two days to grope his way in. On Wednesday, the weather pattern remained the same, but Lowell was becoming desperate because he knew the party would be out of food. He decided to search the relatively sunny Lake George area, in the Matanuska Valley, in case they had tried to walk out, and he also shifted his base of operations to the Palmer airport, in the valley, where he would be closer to the mountain.

He took off at nine in the morning, planning to return to Anchorage by 3 P.M. By four o'clock I began to worry and called the Palmer airport. The manager there knew Lowell but had not seen him all day. He added that the clouds around the mountains still looked awfully low. Now in a grand panic, I called the Cessna distributors, where we park "Charlie" when he's not out flying. I tried not to sound like a distraught wife, but they were concerned, too, and decided to send out one of their pilots, Max Johnson, to scout the situation. After another two hours of frantic waiting, the search plane returned, unable to penetrate the mountains at all, but with the report that the Anchorage tower had just picked up a "mayday" message from Lowell—he had succeeded in finding the climbers and had landed safely but would have to wait for another break in the weather before flying them out.

With that relatively comforting word, although it was only seven o'clock, I went straight to bed along with the children. We were all awakened by Bozie's barking at midnight, and we found a profoundly tired Lowell waiting outside the front door. He told us he had joined the climbers during a brief lull in the weather that morning, making a harrowing landing on the glacier in a white-out. The party had been weathered in their small tent for two days—vicious winds of sixty and seventy miles an hour collapsing the tent a number of times and blowing away some of their clothing. Their food had run out, and they had had nothing to eat but tea since the morning before.

While they were desperately anxious to get out of there, the wind picked up again, gusting to over fifty miles per hour, and Lowell decided it would be foolhardy to try a down-glacier, down-wind take-off. They tied "Charlie" down securely to ice axes and snowshoes stuck in the snow. During their ten-hour wait, huddled in a badly shredded tent, the wind blew so hard that Lowell fully expected to see "Charlie" pull out the axes and take off of his own accord. By early evening, after a much-appreciated dinner from Lowell's emergency supply, the weather began to break, and Lowell was able to ferry everyone out by 10 P.M. (What would we do without that midnight sun!)

Something good can come from anything, and everyone learned much from that experience. The climbers realized they had not been adequately prepared for bad weather; Lowell gained more knowledge and a greater respect for mountains and glaciers under adverse conditions; and I decided to do a little less worrying in a future which undoubtedly would be filled with much more of the same kind of activity.

In the years since this first eventful experience, Lowell has participated in a number of mountain climbs, flying the whole party in to some relatively flat lower slope, staking "Charlie" down, and making a two- or three-day ascent to the peak above. Although all of the highest mountains in Alaska have now been conquered, there are many more in the ten- to twelve-thousand-foot range which remain unclimbed, and as long as there are any left, my mountaineering husband and his cohorts will be fretting to tackle each and every one. And don't ask them for an explanation of why they do it—I have never been given a satisfactory reason for their hours of physical toil, laden down with fifty- and sixty-pound packs and skis, climbing steep, icy, crevasse-crossed slopes. They toss me words, such as challenge, accomplishment, fun, peace, beauty—and the usual "because it is there."

Several of their goals have been in that part of the Alaska Range which we can see to the west of Anchorage. These mountains are high (from nine to twelve thousand feet), rising virtually from sea level, almost all unclimbed, and totally inaccessible except by plane. This is too much of a temptation for Lowell and his frequent climbing companions: Paul Crews, a consulting engineer, Jon Gardey, a Weather Bureau man, and doctors Rod Wilson and George Wichman. Early in 1963 they set out to climb the highest peak in this area—twelve-thousand-foot Mount Gerdine. Although they did not quite reach the top, they returned full of enthusiasm for this particular area, determined to go back just as soon as possible. They subsequently climbed and were the first to conquer Gerdine, only to discover, that due to an error in the original survey, nearby Mount Torbert was actually a few hundred feet higher! So off they went in May of the following year and made the first successful ascent of Mount Torbert on skis, within three gloriously sunny days.

Although I said that I have not accompanied Lowell on these mountain outings, there is one exception: a family visit to Don Sheldon's Mount McKinley cabin. Don is Alaska's best-known present-day glacier and bush pilot, with enough flying adventures behind him to gather into a thrilling and hair-raising best seller. He and his wife, Roberta (who is the daughter of Bob Reeve, Alaska's original glacier pilot), live in Talkeetna beside his own airstrip and hangar. While he flies almost twenty-four hours a day during the summer, Roberta keeps in touch by radio, running the business end of the bush operation from their living room.

Much of Don's summer flying is centered on Mount McKinley, ferrying most of the climbing parties in and out. (The climbers carry radios which they use to keep in regular touch with Roberta.) Don air drops or lands near camps with further supplies and keeps a constant aerial watch over the parties—like a mother hen checking on the progress of her chicks. Occasionally he has had to fly a body out, and frequently he, and the climbers as well, have had to wait out days of the worst imaginable weather. While Mount McKinley is not considered a difficult climb in the technical sense, the sudden weather changes, tornado-force winds, and well-below-zero temperatures pose the severest challenge to climbers, especially those who have had little experience beyond the mountains of the "lower 48."

As Don grew familiar with every nook and cranny of that majestic mountain, he became most excited over the idea of building a chalet somewhere on its slopes—after all, weren't many other people building ski cabins in the mountains these days? He selected a site about six thousand feet up: a rock outcropping in the middle of the vast Ruth Amphitheatre—a large, relatively flat glacial basin completely surrounded by other mountains and the southeast face of McKinley.

However, unlike owners of other ski chalets, he could not drive in all the building materials. While any ordinary person would not even consider such a project, Don is not an ordinary guy, and somehow he flew in ten thousand pounds of materials for the 16-by 16-foot hexagonal cabin all by himself. (We never ask how because FAA authorities might not appreciate such a feat.) Once the cabin was finished, complete with large windows, five benches, a central wood-burning stove, and men's and women's outhouses out back, Don decided he must have a house warming.

Whenever the phone rings and Lowell answers with, "Hi, Don, what's up?" I hold my breath. The two are off and running, planning some sort of new flying adventure around the slopes of Mount McKinley. On this particular day in early May of 1966, Don said, "Let's have a party." When Lowell asked where, it was "on the slopes of Mount McKinley, and let's you and me fly in everybody from Anchorage to have a real blast." While Lowell was slightly stunned by the size of the guest list Don reeled off, he readily agreed to help with "ferry operations." Don called the party a Hawaiian-style luau, with a day of skiing at his new home.

After flying in several loads of steaks and salad mixings, the appointed day dawned bright and clear, and the two started shuttling in the thirty-one guests—three per planeload. I was unable to go for that particular party but gathered that all were in high spirits, thoroughly enjoying every moment. Just as Lowell deposited his last passengers, after four flights back and forth between Talkeetna and Anchorage, he detected wisps of clouds spilling over the southern mountain wall. He was debating whether to stop to enjoy a much needed steak, when more clouds boiled into sight. After checking by radio with the weatherman, it was obvious that the beautiful day was deteriorating rapidly and that the shuttle service had better get back into operation immediately! On their third trip back up the Ruth Glacier, Lowell and Don were both stopped by impenetrable snow squalls and had to face the fact that nineteen guests would remain stranded.

While accommodations were slightly crowded, to say the least, the grounded party-goers made the most of an uncomfortable situation. Luckily, there were enough steaks for dinner, too, and while the women crowded into the hut to try to get a little sleep, others took sleeping bags, which the host had thoughtfully left behind, and crawled into quickly dug snow caves. Fortunately for everyone involved, the bad weather was mild and broke up enough for Lowell and Don to fly in the next morning. Considering the usual wild McKinley storms, those nineteen guests could very easily have been marooned in that 16 by 16 cabin for two weeks—a delightful ending to a Hawaiian luau!

Don's next house party, in late July of 1967, included thirty-two people and a dog, but the weather was not as co-operative as before, and we waited for two weeks until the big celebration could actually take place. This time the children and I were going along, accompanied by a group of Anchorage skiers and a large National Geographic Society TV film crew. It was they who had the dog in tow—no problem at all if the animal had been lap-dog size. Unfortunately, Brandy was an over-sized St. Bernard, and Lowell had trouble even squeezing him into the empty back-seat area. No sooner had he stuffed the ever-phlegmatic Brandy through one door, barely shutting it, than the other would pop open. Brandy finally made it up to the mountain house, but he could make no positive contribution to the party because he had neglected to bring his cask!

This time Don put me in charge of the food, quite a sizable undertaking. Most women will agree that it is no easy task to feed thirty-two people in one's own home. My problem was compounded by the constant postponement of the big event. I could not wait to shop for groceries when the first clear day came along. Good weather would mean a take-off at 5 A.M. Not only did we have to get up at 4 A.M. for fourteen straight days, but I was also frantic over the daily mounds of fresh salad which would not keep. I put the steaks and bread into the freezer, and the rice and canned baked beans were no problem, but our neighborhood was kept well supplied with lettuce and carrots.

I grew so tired of looking out our windows for signs of McKinley, of listening to hourly weather reports, and especially of those early rising hours, that I was ready to pull out of the whole venture. Just at that point, the clouds finally got the message, the weather cleared, and we were on our way. While I had built up a towering hatred of Mount McKinley, fervently wishing that it and Don's cabin would vanish from sight, the flight up the Ruth Glacier through the Great Gorge was enough to win me over completely. On many trips past the mountain, en route to Fairbanks, I had always been deeply awed by its great size and majestic beauty. Now, as we flew low over the deeply crevassed Ruth Glacier, gigantic white mountain slopes rose everywhere ahead of us. In a few more moments we could see the gorge through which we would fly—a narrow passage over the glacier, enclosed by towering rock walls. I made a mental note to avoid that flight on anything but a perfect day. While I was debating just how many feet of clearance lay between our wing tips and the cliffs, the gorge suddenly opened onto a great amphitheater of dazzling snow fields encircled by high mountain walls. I doubt that I have ever seen a more dramatically beautiful sight in all of our travels anywhere, not even among the Karakorams and Himalayas of central Asia.

As Lowell began to descend for a landing on the hard-packed snow, we could see Don's little cabin up ahead. Perched on a rock outcropping, it was a tiny brown dot in the midst of a sparkling white world. In another few moments we spotted Don's plane, already on the ground, its tracks clearly indicating the "runway" we should use. Landing on snow is quite different from coming down on an asphalt or gravel strip, or even grass or sand. It is almost impossible to gauge one's distance and to know just when the skis will touch (a little sunshine makes a tremendous difference, and after having sweated through a few white-outs, Lowell never lands without it). The jolt of landing caught me by surprise, and the subsequent rough bouncing told me that snow fields aren't necessarily as smooth as they look from five thousand feet up.

Once we had left the plane, we also discovered that the snow was a lot softer than it had looked from the air. With every step we sank up to our hips, so that the walk up to the cabin several hundred yards away turned into far more than just a stroll. The next time I'll take snowshoes! We finally did reach the rocks, and while the children played on a nearby snowbank (after all, they had not seen snow in three months) and some of the men enjoyed a tremendous ski run, I started to cook for thirty-two people. My stove was the small charcoal variety, cans made good pots for the beans and rice, and my admiring audience was Brandy, who never took his eyes off the sizzling steaks.

Just when I was ready to relax and enjoy the view, wispy white fingers of clouds appeared out of nowhere, and everyone suddenly began to think of a valid reason why he or she should be on that first flight out. What a shame, because I really would have enjoyed a few hours of quiet in the midst of such a soundless world. But to be stranded there, in the midst of a howling blizzard, with thirty-one other people and Brandy, was another situation altogether. We were all flown out in plenty of time, however, and Lowell and I plan to return with the children next summer—just the four of us for a change.

IV

We Take
to the Camping
Trails

According to ever-present statistics and polls, camping is one of
the most popular leisure pastimes for Alaskans, and our family is
no exception. There are few places left in the United States where
one can, within a short drive from home, set up a tent or park a
trailer, either in a relatively empty campground or almost anywhere just off a main road. We have often found ourselves the
sole occupants of a state or federal campground, and we have
spent many delightful hours camped in a solitary mountain
meadow or on the gravel bank of a swift-flowing stream.

When we do use a campground, it is easier to find a place to
park a trailer and we are guaranteed ample water supply, clean
"outdoor rest rooms," with a big pile of firewood beside an outdoor grille, and tables with benches. We have yet to find a lit-
tered or unattractive campground, but when using them, it's best
to avoid holidays or big weekends, and one does have to be prepared to share the beauties of the wilderness with at least one or
two other families.

When we feel especially independent and anxious for solitude,
it is relatively easy to find a stop where we can set up the tent or

park a trailer and be totally alone. To us this is a cherished opportunity, one which has been lost to most American families. The children and dog can roam at will, we can swim if we wish, even though we may have forgotten to bring bathing suits, and we can drink all the water we want from the clear, cold streams. We keep reminding Anne and David that this simple act is a rare privilege these days, that most of the waters of the world today are spoiled by man's pollution.

Of course, Lowell considers camping by car totally civilized, regardless of where we end up, and would much prefer taking off in "Charlie," heading for some remote field or beach to set up the tent there. I have a number of answers ready for this suggestion: the most potent one being, "That's fine, dear, and if the weather turns bad, no one will mind staying there a week." That's especially powerful on a Saturday when he has three important Monday meetings, plus some film editing which simply has to be done Sunday night.

My other answers are far less emotional but much more practical: It has become almost impossible to squeeze our two well-built, practically full-grown kids into the back of the plane along with tent, four sleeping bags, stove and utensils, food, clothing, and fishing gear. Besides, my favorite bear repellent and Lowell's great companion, faithful dog Bozie, would have to be left behind.

The collecting of camping gear for any kind of overnight family outing can be a monumental chore unless one does it regularly and follows some kind of system. Our first few sorties were disasters because I inevitably forgot something vital or brought the wrong item. And regardless of what I packed or forgot, I was totally exhausted from the hectic preparations before we even started. Now I keep a box of camping utensils: compact gas stove, extra pots and pans (including a large one for water and dishwashing), silverware, scrub brush, and pot holders; also a box of soap, tin foil, paper towels, and nonperishables, such as salt, sugar, powdered milk, and instant coffee, in plastic containers. These are stored together with our sleeping bags and tent, so that I am ready to go on a few hours' notice.

If we plan to take off for more than a night or two, we often rent a small trailer. While this simplifies much of the outdoor housekeeping, there are ways and then there are ways of packing a trailer! Bottles and other breakables simply will not put up with our rough roads, and any improperly stowed equipment will always end up in a jumbled heap on the floor. I have learned to tightly pack all our clothing into the little closet; to make great use of plastic containers, wrapping any necessary glass bottles in towels; and to tightly wedge sleeping bags, books, and other paraphernalia on the back bunks.

Whether we travel with tent or trailer, there are always items I label indispensable—such as a good supply of "nibble" snacks and comic books. Both commodities are not a part of daily home life but are a great help on long drives or during enforced stays in tent or trailer. Books and games are also a boon on long trips, and in addition, we take along plenty of rain gear and spare shoes and socks. One would like to be able to enjoy the out-of-doors regardless of weather, and this enjoyment inevitably involves wading in streams or hiking through puddles. Warm sweaters and jackets are a must, too—nights can be cold, and when camping near a glacier, it is surprising how cool the air can be.

At the risk of incurring the wrath of the Chamber of Commerce, another indispensable camping item is mosquito repellent. While these pesky varmints aren't nearly as prevalent in this area as they are farther north, there can be evenings when they will drop in in droves. At least we do not have to contend with any other insects, and there are no snakes in all of Alaska!

We have camped in many different locations within a two-hundred-mile radius of Anchorage, but all excursions begin with the same ingredient—an "hours behind schedule" departure. Fortunately for me, after late afternoon or evening getaways we can drop in at any of a number of good restaurants just forty-five minutes to the north or south of town. Lowell knows that after treating me to this one spree away from pots and pans, I will cheerfully tackle the rest of the meal preparations along the road all by myself. For visitors who may not want to cook every meal themselves, there are a number of excellent eating places along Alaskan highways, and overnight lodgings as well.

The tourist also need not be concerned over a choice of routes out of town—there is only one. Alaska Highway Number One takes us south to Seward, connecting with the Sterling Highway down the Kenai Peninsula, or north, through the Matanuska Valley to Gulkana and Fairbanks. Alaska's highway system is pathetically small and inadequate. While the state encompasses 586,000 square miles, we have only twelve hundred miles of paved highways and thirty-two hundred miles of dirt or gravel secondary roads. However, it is not the camper or visitor who suffers the most from lack of roads, it is the economic development of the state. While we have in the past bucked road conditions in this area similar to the rutted camel tracks of the Middle East (partly because of the '64 earthquake), most of the existing main roads are now in good shape.

The drive southeast from Anchorage, along Turnagain Arm, is most familiar to us because it leads to Alyeska, where we ski almost every weekend during the winter months. But no matter how often we drive it, we always enjoy the scenic beauty of the route. The arm is a narrow finger of water, like a Norwegian fiord, surrounded by six thousand-foot mountains whose vertical walls drop to the water line. Building the road and railroad along this precipitous shore line was a feat in itself, but the 1964 earthquake made things a lot more difficult for the highway and railroad people—most of the land along the arm (in fact, all of the Chugach Mountains, the Kenai Peninsula, and Kodiak) subsided seven feet or more, inundating much of the tracks and roadbed. It took over three years to bring the highway back to passable driving condition.

While negotiating the curves along the water's edge we are always fascinated by the effects of the tide, which one can easily see moving—sometimes as fast as six knots. The arm has thirty-seven-foot tides, among the highest in the world, similar to those off the coast of Nova Scotia. When the tide is at highest flood, the calm waters reflect the snow-capped peaks on all sides. With lowest ebb, mud flats are visible everywhere. A number of hunters and fishermen have been trapped in the quicksand-like mud and drowned by the extraordinarily swift incoming waters.

As we drive along the arm, our children prefer to watch the waterfalls on the other side of the road—small streams cascading down the steep rock walls. During the wintertime, snow avalanches are frequent, some blocking the road. However, because this land is a part of the Chugach National Forest, Rangers exercise excellent avalanche control. Since National Forest regulations are strict, to keep natural surroundings unspoiled, wildlife is abundant, and the "game" of scanning the rock walls for mountain goats can keep anyone occupied for most of the drive. And there is always a good chance that a brown bear or moose will amble across the road.

Thirty-seven miles south of Anchorage, one can turn left onto a dirt road going into Glacier Valley and the village of Girdwood. The Alyeska ski facilities and the many cabins of Anchorage ski enthusiasts are also there, within a mile of the main highway. The one-lane dirt road continues on up the valley, through a thick forest of giant hemlock and spruce trees, until it dead-ends at the Chugach mountain walls, the site of one of the earliest gold mines in Alaska. The first recorded discovery of gold in this state was in 1886, on the south side of Turnagain Arm, at Resurrection Creek. During the stampede which followed, prospectors came by boat to the western shore of Prince William Sound, then climbed over a glacier, later called Portage, to the head of the arm. At the height of the stampede (which was in full force from 1895 to 1900) several thousand miners lived in camps established at Hope (still in existence as a tiny village today), Sunrise, and Glacier—later called Girdwood, in honor of Joe Girdwood, who was one of the first to stake a claim in the valley.

Another 360-acre claim at the head of Glacier Valley belongs to Arne Erickson, who has mined gold there for more years than he cares to disclose. The old-timer now spends most of his time showing visitors around rather than mining, but bits and pieces of gold can still be found along the creek bed. In the summertime tourists are able to visit the old buildings of the mine, still containing much of the furnishings and equipment of the past. And best of all, one can rent a shovel and gold pan and try his luck along the stream.

Anyone who has tried to pan for gold knows it's hard work! Our children thought the project would be a most exciting chance to splash in the water, dig in gravel, and, of course, find lots of large gold nuggets. So they always lose interest after the first few attempts. Basically, the technique is to scoop up gravel, and while continually shaking the pan, gradually let water carry off the lighter pebbles and dirt, leaving the heavier gold at the bottom. It sounds so simple, but the constant moving of the pan is extremely tiring, and the hands (and usually the feet, too) become icy cold from the water of the mountain stream. One can find occasional flakes of gold, but anything larger is rare. Therefore, perhaps because we just don't have the proper gambling spirit, our gold-panning excursions seldom last for long.

Eleven miles on down the highway beyond the Girdwood area, one reaches the head of Turnagain Arm and the Portage Glacier Recreational Area. The glacier itself, the one traversed by the early prospectors, is five miles off the main route but can be reached by a good road. Up until 1913, the ice extended all the way to this road and the parking lot, but in less than sixty years it has receded two and a half miles, leaving a small lake, over six hundred feet deep, behind. While the deeply cleft walls of this river of ice are not within touching distance except to determined hikers, Portage Lake adds to the interest of the scene in that during the summer it is usually filled with icebergs of all shapes and sizes. It is great fun for children (and grownups) to try to hit or sink the floating ice, using some of the many stones along the gravel bank. And someone always tries to take away a cake of ice as a souvenir, inevitably leaving a puddle of water on the floor of the car or on the mattress in the back.

A glacier is an awesome and spectacular sight, and Alaska has some of the largest and most accessible in the world. While we who live here are familiar with the phenomenon, I suspect that some "outsiders" don't even know what a glacier is. Actually, this region hasn't yet recovered from the effects of the Great Ice Age —the Pleistocene period thirty or forty thousand years ago, when almost half of North America was covered by masses of snow and ice.

The experts say that there are four types of glaciers: The continental is the largest of all, the kind that covers Greenland and Antarctica. Ice caps are the type which accumulate on the top of a single mountain, such as Rainier, or on a range of mountains (the Juneau Ice Cap or the Harding Ice Field on the Kenai Peninsula are good examples in Alaska). Valley glaciers, the third variety, eminate from ice caps, flowing down mountain valleys. The Seward Valley Glacier is over forty miles long, while others may measure only nine hundred feet. The thickness of ice varies greatly, too—anywhere from two to eight hundred feet. A piedmont glacier, the fourth variety, is composed of two or more valley glaciers that flow together onto a plain. The Malaspina, near Yakutat, is a perfect example—a mass of ice as large as the state of Rhode Island!

The growth of a glacier depends upon ample snowfall (over the years the very weight of the snow compacts it into ice), cold temperatures, and the minimum amount of melting in the summertime. Even summer rain trickling into the frozen depths of the ice contributes to its mass. These days, however, most glaciers in arctic regions are retreating, a sign, I would think, that the warming trend which ended the last great ice age continues. On the other hand, a scientist friend of ours, Dr. Maynard Miller, who has been studying glaciers for many years and who spends each summer on the Juneau Ice Cap, states just the opposite. The theory involved is a highly complicated one made even more complex by the fact that a few glaciers in Alaska, rather than retreating, are moving rapidly forward. I had better leave further explanations to glaciologists, but I fervently hope that our beautiful rivers of ice won't vanish too soon in the future.

Portage Glacier is not the only attraction of the Portage recreational area. There are also three large camping and picnic grounds, plus a number of places where one can park off the road and camp along the gravel banks of the swift stream which flows from the glacier to the inlet. We have found that this is an ideal spot to put up a tent—Lowell has many climbing or hiking paths, and the kids love to wade in the shallow stream. The water is gray with glacial silt and icy cold, so it is not altogether conducive to swimming; but ten- and twelve-year-olds think it's great fun to don hip boots and just wade about.

We pitch our tent close to the water's edge, so that we are lulled to sleep at night by the musical gurgling and splashing of the stream. That, in addition to the cold air, warm cozy sleeping bag, and the companionship of the family together in our large and comfortable tent, makes sleeping outdoors perfect for us. The added sense of security for me is Bozie, who lies on a mat just outside the tent door. (While we were ensconced on one of these gravel beds last summer, a bear paid a midnight visit to an adjacent campground, tearing apart the garbage containers and thoroughly frightening some of the campers. If he had come near us, Bozie would undoubtedly have raised enough uproar to frighten him off.)

Housekeeping by that glacial stream is more fun than a chore. Water is plentiful for cooking, meals are strictly simple: grilled hot dogs or hamburgers, or "one-pot casseroles." Appetites are vigorous, and husband and children will eat anything, even foods ordinarily turned down at home. Afterward, while I first give dishes a quick washing in water heated on the stove, we rinse everything in the stream. And I have never had a problem urging the kids to wash and brush teeth while camping—nothing is more fun, and each vies with the other to see who can spit the farthest or just how far downstream they can spot the toothpaste or soap bubbles. Trees make dandy towel racks and laundry lines, or if worst comes to worst, we can drape shoes and socks around our roaring evening fire.

After these delightful visits to Portage, we either return home or head farther afield—due south seventy miles to Seward or southeast down the Kenai Peninsula. The road to Seward winds through the coastal mountains, past streams and lakes, thick spruce and hemlock forests, and alpine meadows. There are many more campgrounds here, and wildlife is abundant—in short, the whole area is a paradise for those who love the out-of-doors. The railroad parallels the road, and I have heard tourists claim that this train trip provides one of the most thrilling and scenic excursions they have ever experienced.

When describing travel in just about any part of Alaska, it is hard not to get carried away with superlatives, and this is also true when one talks about the town of Seward. Home to about three thousand people, the "little city" is nestled at the foot of the Chugach Mountains at the head of Resurrection Bay. The terminus of the railroad to Fairbanks and one of the main seaports of Alaska, the town is named for William H. Seward, secretary of state in Lincoln's cabinet, who arranged for Alaska's purchase from Russia. Resurrection Bay was named by Alexander Baranof, director of the Russian Fur Company in Alaska, when he discovered it on Easter morning of 1793. The Russians set up a shipbuilding operation in a cove near the present townsite.

Seward itself was established in 1903 as a supply center when a private group of northwestern businessmen began to build a railroad into Alaska's interior. The corporation went bankrupt after laying down about seventy-one miles of track. The many bridges and tunnels that had to be built proved too great an expense; after one tunnel had been dug out entirely with shovels, the rest were machine-driven—at twenty-four dollars per foot more money. In 1915, when the federal government decided to build a railroad to the interior, it purchased the already existing track, and Seward remained the terminal seaport.

While the drive to Seward is through beautiful countryside and we have taken this route many times over the years, we discovered two summers ago that the ideal way to approach this little seaport town is from the water. We were riding the Alaska State Ferry—it was a clear, calm day, and the snow crests of the Chugach Mountains rimming the shore line were actually reflected in the blue, mirror-calm waters of Prince William Sound. Wisps of fog drifted about the rocky promontories up ahead, and as we wove our way among great stone cliffs, Resurrection Bay suddenly opened before us. Now I can imagine how the Russians must have felt on that Easter Sunday. The harbor is large, with obviously deep, dark blue waters, but well sheltered—being completely surrounded by the snow-capped mountains.

The town itself is on the northwest shore line, and as we slowly made our way toward it, we noticed a number of avalanches at the foot of the rocky mountain sides. We had been aware that this area was especially hard-hit by the 1964 earthquake: A gigantic tidal wave wiped out the Seward docks and railroad yards. We had not known, however, that the quake had triggered so many large avalanches. In some places it looked as if half the mountainside had slid down into the water. What a horrifying spectacle if one had been offshore on a boat at that moment.

While Seward, with its single main street and odd assortment of wood and cement-block buildings, is a favorite hangout all summer long for fishing and boating enthusiasts, two special occasions there are well worth planning a visit around—the July 4th Mount Marathon Race and the late August Salmon Derby. The Independence Day combination running-climbing race is considered to be one of the most rugged of its kind held anywhere in the world. It all began back in 1915 when two seamen and two old-timers bet each other that 3022-foot Mount Marathon, rising just behind the town, could be climbed in less than an hour. Five men lined up for the first try, and the winner's time was sixty-two minutes. While the bet was lost, merchants supplied the leader of the race with a new suit of clothes and the loser had to furnish drinks for the crowd.

The race has been held, although under different circumstances, every year since. The start and finish line is down the middle of Main Street, so that observers line the sidewalks to watch the eager young men (and a few women) start off. While one needs field glasses to watch the progress of the runners up and down the mountainside, it seems a matter of minutes before most of the group is roaring back down Main Street. The record time, set in 1964 by Swedish champion runner William Spencer, is forty-six minutes and fifty-five seconds.

Anyone can be a contestant, but it's wise not to decide to enter on the spur of the moment after a quick glance at a deceptively low and rounded mountain. (Many of the runners practice for weeks ahead of time.) Much of the slope is steep, some at a 45-degree angle, and covered with treacherous shale. Lowell climbed up most of the route one year in order to film the racers at close range. He reported that flying rocks were a great hazard, especially when racers were on their way back down, slipping and sliding most of the way.

Lucrative cash prizes offered by the annual Salmon Derby help lure thousands of anglers to Seward during the last week in August. The bay becomes dotted with boats of every size and shape, and most Southcentral Alaskans listen attentively to radio broadcasts of just who has caught the biggest fish. As I tune in on these reports, I dream of the chance to hitch a boat ride and fish for myself. One year we did go, dropping at the little Seward airport via "Charlie" just long enough to cast a few times off the nearest dock —again that basic conflict over how to fish.

Thirty-nine miles north of Seward, one comes upon that rare occurrence in Alaska—a highway junction. While the main road continues north, over Moose Pass to Anchorage, the Sterling Highway heads 135 miles southwest, down the Kenai Peninsula to Homer. Another of the more scenic Alaskan routes, it is also a sportsman's paradise because almost two million acres on this peninsula have been set aside for the Kenai National Moose Range. Countless numbers of clear lakes (over twelve hundred), streams, and coastal inlets can keep a fisherman busy for the rest of his life. Game Department people estimate over seventy-five hundred moose live in the area, plus an abundance of Dall sheep, mountain goats, brown and black bears, beavers, lynxes, minks, wolverines, and other smaller fur animals. There is just as great an abundance and variety of bird life, especially among waterfowl, and the rare trumpeter swan is still an important nester here.

Many of the lakes have boat ramps and docks, and a number of well-marked trails run between them. Maps of this canoe-portage system are available to anyone interested in the more rugged camping trips. For those of us more tied to the car and highway, there are excellent campgrounds all along the route. However, had I been writing this story previous to the past summer, all superlatives would have been thrown away when describing the highway itself. I could have summed up the conditions along most of the road as "horrible." In fact, the ruts, the stones, and mud were so bad that the road to Homer became a joke throughout the state. The following letter, appearing in a 1962 Homer newspaper, was a typical reaction to the situation:

Dear Ed:

. . . I know it is important that you make the trip to Homer. As I have explained in past letters, the map does show a road running from Anchorage to Homer. However, and let me emphasize this point, maps can be wrong. But I see you are determined and will make the trip regardless of my warning, so my only recourse is to give you some good advice. First, I would not advise you to make the trip alone. When you reach Anchorage, hire yourself a good guide. I would suggest that you retain *Lowell Thomas, Jr.* He made the trip from India to Tibet to gain basic training for the Soldotna to Homer run and is well qualified. Heed Mr. Thomas' advice in purchasing the necessary equipment and emergency supplies; you can be detained enroute for several months. This trip *has* been made on wheels; I would suggest a tracked vehicle, something like a D8 cat. You cut down the odds about 50% this way. Timbers are necessary for re-enforcing bridges; be sure you include an adequate supply. Beware of wet spots on the road. These are locally called frost boils; in other parts of the U.S. they would be called bottomless bogs. Recent excavations by public-spirited citizens unearthed a truck and trailer in one of them. By the condition of the bones of the two skeletons found in the wreckage, it was estimated that it had been there about five years.

Another thing I must warn you about. You will see figures along the road that resemble statuary. Leave them strictly alone. They are members of the State Department of Highways. Due to the many and frequent shake-ups and reorganizations of this department, these people are afraid to move in any direction.

I should think it would take about six or seven days to drive from New York to Anchorage. About another week in Anchorage to collect the necessary equipment and guide. So if you leave there on the first of May I will expect you in Homer about the last of July. If you have not arrived by that time, I will organize a rescue expedition. We have a well-qualified man living in Homer who normally takes charge of this type of expedition. His name is Mr. Stanley. Good bye for now and may the good Lord hold your hand.

> Your friend,
> D. E. Plorable
> Eugene D. Smith, Cohoe, Alaska[1]

While we never disappeared into a bottomless bog, we did have our share of miserable experiences along this road. We are all relieved now that conditions have improved, because the Kenai Peninsula is without a doubt one of the finest outdoor recreation areas in all of the United States. It is also rapidly becoming one

[1] *Inlet Courier Weekly,* Homer, Alaska, May 4, 1962.

of the largest oil-producing regions in the world, and the subsequent growth of the towns of Kenai and Soldotna has been spectacular. When geologists first bulldozed trails in parts of the peninsula to facilitate oil exploration, local conservationists were alarmed and predicted the demise of the Kenai moose. Now statistics reveal just the opposite—thanks to man-made trails, the moose can find winter food more easily, and their numbers have actually increased. While the wildlife officials keep a careful watch on restrictions in the area, the state has become acutely aware of water pollution problems. As a result, hopefully we can build some industry on the peninsula while also keeping much of the area open to recreational pursuits. Many have their doubts, and only time will tell. At least we, in such a new state, have a unique chance to learn from all the errors and pitfalls previously encountered by our sister states.

The big oil boom began with the discovery by Richfield Oil Corporation of a large petroleum field in the Swanson River area near Soldotna in July of 1957. In 1960, Standard Oil opened a ten-million-dollar refinery with dock facilities at nearby Nikiski (north Kenai). About twenty thousand barrels of crude oil are processed daily, and while the largest market at the moment is the U.S. West Coast (where an ever-increasing number of automobiles use more gasoline than anywhere else in the world), products for the Alaskan market include jet fuel, stove oil, diesel, and furnace fuels. Another large potential market is Japan, which has already contracted for shipments of liquid natural gas.

Since the 1957 inland discovery, a number of oil companies have concentrated on exploration in Cook Inlet, which the industry now nicknames "Oil Alley." At the moment, six major oil fields have been discovered in the inlet, and oilmen feel there could be over four billion barrels of crude oil beneath these waters. So exploration continues at a feverish pace.

In 1968, 30 per cent of Alaska's revenue came from oil and gas, but, according to oil-industry spokesmen, the future is even brighter, especially as so many oil-producing areas of the world are in the midst of political turmoil. While Alaskan production costs are unusually high, the quality of the crude oil is also high, the wells are faster producers, and the success ratio in new wells is at an almost unheard of high of 50 per cent. Also, the oil activity will inevitably attract allied industries, such as a fifty-million-dollar petrochemical complex now under construction by the Collier Carbon and Chemical Corporation. It will manufacture, among other products, the liquid natural gas for Japan.

(In late July of 1968, Alaska's oil industry made a dramatic announcement that drastically affects the future of the state: Atlantic Richfield struck oil in the Prudhoe Bay site on the arctic slope. Two wells showed flow rates of 2400 barrels a day and the company stated that they believe this north slope field may contain five to ten billion barrels of oil. This ten-billion figure increases known reserves in North America by a full 25 per cent and means a field twice the size of any ever discovered on our continent. This new oil bonanza is located on one small corner of state land—the big question now is about what might lie beneath the rest of the vast north slope region. Some experts feel that arctic Alaska may contain more oil than anywhere else in the world, including the Middle East.)

The town of Soldotna, one hundred miles down the Sterling Highway from Seward, owes its development to the oil discovery at Swanson River in 1957. When we first visited it in 1962, streets were being bulldozed before our eyes, houses were sprouting among the trees, and some brand new shops and a filling station lined the highway. Today the few homes have become large residential areas, and new apartment houses, businesses, schools, and an airport have been added. The population has mushroomed to around one thousand residents, who optimistically plan and build toward a bright economic future.

Eleven miles away from Soldotna and the Sterling Highway, high on the bluffs of Cook Inlet, is Kenai, an oil town which has grown even faster—from 778 people in 1960, to 2500 in 1967, and another 5000 in the surrounding area. "People are moving into this town faster than we can build," complained one contractor recently. Hammers and bulldozers are put to work from early in the morning until late each night—restaurants and cafés remain open twenty-four hours a day. Entire subdivisions of homes have sprung up within the last year, including many in the two-story, forty-thousand-dollar category, and one of the largest shopping centers in Alaska opened just recently. Kenai City Manager Bill Harrison says that he has signed over a million dollars in building permits for single-family dwelling units in one day alone.

Kenai, however, unlike its neighbor Soldotna, did not just grow out of the woods a few short years ago but can boast of a long history going way back to the days of the earliest settlements. As far as is known, the Kenaiohkotana (thank goodness the name was shortened!) Indians first lived on this bluff, where the Kenai River flows into Cook Inlet. In 1791 a trading post, Fort St. Nicholas, was established by the Russian American Fur Company, making Kenai the second oldest settlement in Alaska. Bloody uprisings of the Indian tribes and fighting between rival Russian fur companies marked many of the years until the United States purchase in 1867. While the Russians were mainly interested in furs, eventually greatly depleting the whole area, when the Americans took over, the major activity switched to fishing, and canneries were built along the river. No wonder, after the big oil discoveries and the completion of the refinery, the Kenai residents celebrated with the slogan, "From Whale Oil to Standard Oil!"

Although the Kenai Russian history is a blood-stained one, the Russians also chose it as the center of their missionary activity in the Cook Inlet area. An ancient Russian church and chapel, containing a wealth of historical religious relics, are still in use there today. Tourists can also see the hand-hewn timber remains of other Russian buildings, and the Kenai residents recently restored the old "Fort Kenay," built by the U. S. Army after the take-over from Russia.

A little farther down the highway one finds more traces of early Russian days. The tiny fishing hamlets of Kasilof and Ninilchik were first founded by the Russians. Ninilchik is one of my favorite Alaskan villages, with a quaint Russian Orthodox church sitting on a hilltop above the inlet, the shore line of the cove below lined with small boats, the tiny cluster of houses behind them made of logs or wood. Some of the people who live there are descendants of the original settlers and still speak Russian. The old log schoolhouse (which has now been turned into a museum) and a few other structures were built of hand-hewn logs during the middle 1800s.

Just north of Ninilchik is one of our favorite stops while traveling down the peninsula—the home of Mary Hawkins, a highly capable woman of great talent and a warm friend. In many ways, she and her home typify true Alaskan homesteading to us. The house is made of logs and is most attractive and comfortable. In the summertime, Mary and her sons plant a giant vegetable garden, one that makes me green with envy. They also make the most of the fish in the waters below the house and the berries in the woods around them.

Our children are more interested in the origin of the Hawkins' milk, however—they have goats, which are kept in a large pen out back. They join in the fun of milking with great enthusiasm, but I wish I could say the same for the subsequent drinking of warm goat's milk. I am most interested in another of Mary's many activities—weaving. A large loom occupies one corner of the living room, and during her "spare time," Mary has made everything from curtains to shirts for the boys. And as though she does not have enough to keep herself occupied, Mary also teaches home economics at a nearby school. Homesteading in Alaska is not a lucrative business, so many of those who tackle such a venture also take on jobs to help with the high living costs. (While farming is a big activity on the Kenai Peninsula, I will wait until we reach the larger agricultural area of the Matanuska Valley before going into the pros and cons of homesteading in Alaska.)

Just south of Ninilchik is another favorite stopping place for all of us. There are a number of beaches in this area, and it is possible to drive right onto some of them—we have even parked in a trailer on the hard gravel that must pass for sand. Not only is it fun to beachcomb along the water's edge (once the children even tried swimming), but these beaches are a happy hunting ground for clam diggers. In the early summer, people flock here from as far away as Anchorage, pails and shovels in hand to dig up the large razor clams.

My favorite occupation at this stopping point is to sit on a log and stare at the view—it is breathtaking! Directly across the waters of Cook Inlet rise the two snow-covered ten-thousand-foot volcanoes of Mount Illiamna and Mount Redoubt. They are both still active and are the beginnings of the mountains which stretch over seventeen hundred miles along the Aleutian Island chain.

Just south of our favorite beaches is another small Sterling Highway community with a rather unique distinction: Anchor Point is the point farthest west that one can drive on the North American continent. It was also a stopping-off place for Captain Cook during his search for the Northwest Passage. The explorer anchored his boat overnight in the sheltered cove there to wait out a storm.

From Anchor Point, the highway turns south and dead-ends at the western tip of the Kenai Peninsula, the site of another of the most scenic towns in Alaska. Homer was founded in 1896 by a group of gold prospectors, including a Homer Pennock. The gold mining petered out rapidly, the men departing for more lucrative areas, but at least Mr. Pennock left behind the contribution of his first name. In those days there was a brief flurry of coal mining, too, but this was also given up because transportation to markets proved an overwhelming obstacle. In fact, the original town burned down when a nearby coal seam caught fire.

Present-day Homer sits on one hundred square miles of flat, fertile land bordering the deep blue waters of Kachemak Bay and Cook Inlet, and I will never forget our first view of the area. Those last few miles of the Sterling Highway are built along high ground, so that one rounds a corner and suddenly comes upon the truly breathtaking panorama of Homer's low, green fields, the blue water beyond dissected by a long, thin sand spit and rimmed everywhere by jagged, snow-covered mountains and glistening blue glaciers.

The residents of Homer rightfully feel they live in one of the world's most beautiful locations, and they make the most of what nature provides around them: a number of homesteaders either raise cattle or vegetable crops, and fishermen, using a small-boat harbor along the spit, find plenty of sea food in the Kachemak waters for local processing plants. Diana Tillion, the artist-wife of fisherman-legislator Clem Tillion even makes black paint from a large local population of squid!

One of the most unique and profitable of the smaller Alaskan industries is also located in Homer—the Alaska Wild Berry Products. Begun in 1946 when it was discovered that the wild cranberries, blueberries, strawberries, gooseberries, watermelon berries, and other varieties were extra plentiful and luscious in the Homer area, Harry and Betty Brundage operate their business from a downtown log cabin. Natives, local homesteaders, and children do the picking for the jams, jellies, and sauces, and canned crab, salmon, and clams are included in over five thousand yearly mail orders going out to all states and many foreign countries.

Our favorite hangout in Homer is the long sand spit—a perfect place for camping or beachcombing. The fishing is great, and while it's best to go out in a boat, one can also dangle a line from the docks. Our most memorable catch was a Dungeness crab, caught by David when he was five. (Memorable because of all the fingers pinched while getting him off the hook.) This particular visit was before the 1964 earthquake, which greatly damaged all the waterfront facilities there—in fact, the entire spit sank from three to six feet, becoming completely exposed to high tides. We were greatly saddened, on our return in the summer of 1964, to find the attractive motel and most of the food-processing buildings propped up on logs in an attempt to escape high water. The road was largely eroded away, and many of the docks were gone. There was grave doubt that the spit would survive at all, but the Army Corps of Engineers has since rebuilt the boat basin, using the rock and gravel excavation to heighten the surrounding area, and other facilities have also been restored.

The little community of Seldovia, just across the Bay from Homer, on the southern of the two prongs of the peninsula, and only accessible by small plane or boat, also suffered extensive damage from the earthquake. While it shares the same spectacular natural setting, the village itself was more picturesque in that its entire business section was built on pilings overhanging the harbor. When we flew there in "Charlie" in 1962, it was great fun to walk down a main street which was really one long dock, stopping at restaurants, offices, salmon canneries, and crab-packing plants, all on stilts above the water. Our children were fascinated, insisting on peering below at every few steps to watch the dripping water or myriad barnacles, starfish, and jellyfish which made their homes at the lower levels. I clung desperately to shirttails, wondering how Seldovia mothers managed to keep from losing little ones off such an unusual main street. Another hazard was the little cars which zipped about the narrow boardwalk, forcing pedestrians to the very edge, but bicycles were the greatest menace because they were more quiet and numerous and bore down at great speeds.

When this land sank after the earthquake, the subsequent flooding and erosion threatened the entire waterfront. The whole area has now been razed, through an urban-renewal project, and most of the businesses, including the most modern crab-processing plant in Alaska, have been rebuilt on safe land nearby. I'm glad for the economy of Seldovia but sad that the old boardwalk street is gone.

Southwest of the tips of the Kenai Peninsula, 136 air miles from Homer, lies Kodiak Island, site of the oldest settlement in Alaska and the main base of the giant king-crab industry. Kodiak also suffered extensively from land subsidence after the earthquake. Massive tidal waves wiped out 75 per cent of the business section of the town of Kodiak, and the fishing fleet lay in ruins. But thanks to another extensive urban-renewal program, the coming of the state ferry system, and the rapid growth of the crab, shrimp, and fish industries (there are over thirty fish-processing plants on the island now), Kodiak has suddenly become a bustling town of over seventy-five hundred people. In fact, in spite of the relatively small size of the harbor and community, Kodiak ranks as the nation's third most important fishery port, with catches worth thirteen million dollars to fishermen in 1966.

I greatly regret that I have not yet visited Kodiak, not because I want to see its booming economic growth, but because it is scenically a beautiful island, about one hundred miles long and fifty miles wide, its shore lines marked by picturesque harbors and bays, its interior covered by precipitous mountains and a wilderness of dense green, almost junglelike growth. (The climate is mild and rainy, with little snow or cold during the winters.) While the island is oriented toward sea life, it is also the home of the gigantic Kodiak brown bear. He used to reign supreme in the early days when the Aleut natives (Aleuts live in the Aleutian Islands-Kodiak area and are a race related to the Eskimos) and Russians didn't dare venture beyond the shore line. But now that hunters have taken to light airplanes and ranchers have taken over the foothills for their cattle, the Kodiak bear is in grave danger of extinction.

I would also like to see Kodiak because it played such a big part in early Alaskan history. The first natives, the Koniaga, lived there from two to four thousand years ago, and the Russians arrived in 1763 after sweeping along the Aleutian Island chain, decimating the sea-otter herds everywhere they went.

In 1784 Gregory Shelikof, a shrewd Siberian merchant and fur trader, established the first Russian colony in North America at Three Saints Bay, on the south side of Kodiak Island (not far from the present village of Old Harbor). According to historians, he could not have chosen a better moment to land there—just at the time of a full eclipse of the sun! The hostile natives thought Shelikof must be possessed of supernatural powers, and subsequent relations were far more harmonious than otherwise might have been the case.

Those early Russian colonists built sturdy log houses, and they maintained large vegetable gardens. However, with the great growth of the Russian-American Fur Company under the leadership of Alexander Baranof, the colony was moved in 1792 to the present site of Kodiak town. It became the capital of Russian America until Baranof transferred headquarters to Sitka in 1804. While most of the Russian economic activities centered on furs and some on lumber and boatbuilding, they also developed a most unusual and profitable ice company—shipping tons of ice to western American and even central American seaports.

While so many of those early Russian buildings did not stand the test of time, the Baranof mansion, Alaska's oldest structure, does remain, restored by Kodiak residents for the state's 1967 centennial year. Two old Russian wells, a cemetery, and an old brick kiln can still be seen, and although the original church building burned down in 1943, the one built soon afterward also adds to the Russian atmosphere. On nearby Spruce Island stands a small shrine and chapel, built in the early 1890s to the memory of Father Herman. This saintly Russian Orthodox priest was the only one of the original missionary group which came to the colony to remain, living alone among the Aleut natives of Spruce Island for over forty years.

There are many stories about his work, his deeds, and his great love for the native people. It is said that when Father Herman first came to Spruce Island, he lived in a cave until he built a little hut which was to be his home for the next forty years. He wore the same clothing both summer and winter—mainly a simple jumper made of reindeer skin. A small bench covered with reindeer skins served as a bed, and for a pillow he used two bricks. He ate very little, his food consisting of fish he caught and vegetables he grew in his garden. His thin body, exhausted from labor and fasting, was constantly weighted down with a fifteen pound "chain-fetters," which he wore next to his skin.

At one time a local evil authority suspected the saintly father of agitating the Aleuts, and an inspection team was sent to his hut. In their zeal to find evidence, one man began to tear up the floor with an ax. "My friend," said Father Herman, "I am sorry you took up the ax; this instrument will end your life." One night a few years later, savage Kenai natives attacked this man while he slept and chopped off his head.

The Aleuts of Spruce Island were convinced that Father Herman could talk with all the animals. They told of seeing him feed the bears and other wild creatures. Beneath his hut a family of weasels made their home. These little animals are unapproachable when raising their young, but Father Herman fed them out of his hand. The island inhabitants also say that when he died, all the birds and animals suddenly vanished.

Another favorite story among the Aleuts concerns a tidal wave which approached the island one year. The terrified inhabitants rushed to the father for help. He calmly carried his statue of the Virgin Mary down to the beach, placed it above the high-water mark, and then knelt down to pray. After a short prayer, he told the people to return home unafraid. "The waters will not rise beyond the spot where the holy image stands."[2] And the words of the old man came true.

As I mentioned earlier, the island of Kodiak lies southwest of the Kenai Peninsula off the mouth of Cook Inlet, the twenty-mile-wide Shelikof Strait separating it from that part of the Alaskan mainland which extends on into the thousand-mile-long Aleutian Island chain. This large western Alaskan peninsula contains over thirty-six active volcanoes (including some of those

[2] Tay Thomas, *Cry in the Wilderness,* Anchorage, Alaska, Color Art Printing Co., 1967.

snow-covered mountains we see to the west of Anchorage), and the area is considered one of the world's greatest hotbeds of volcanic activity. Some of these volcanoes have been semidormant for many years, showing no signs of further life. A few are perennial smokers, while others, such as Redoubt, Trident, Illiamna, and Spurr, cause a flurry of excitement from time to time by spewing out great columns of smoke or erupting briefly with lava and ash. In July of 1953, Mount Spurr suddenly exploded, with a mushroom cloud of ash and steam rising more than thirteen miles into the sky. It was noontime, and in Anchorage, over eighty miles away, day turned into night as volcanic ash began to fall. Our friends who were here at that time say they had to turn on the headlights of cars and lights indoors. Over one fourth inch of ash covered everything like snow.

None of this volcanic activity comes close to matching the performance put on by Mount Katmai in 1912. Directly across the Shelikof Strait from Kodiak lies the 4215-square-mile Katmai National Monument, among the largest of all U.S. national parks and monuments. Forty-four years ago the area was a lush green wilderness covered with forests and grass. Caribou roamed the meadows, while several native villages trapped for fox and otter. Suddenly violent earthquakes and eruptions hit the whole area, frightening away all the people. Hot, glowing sand and gas spouted high in the air as fissures opened everywhere, and smoke rose from thousands of fumaroles. Then Mount Katmai literally blew her top—catastrophic eruptions blasted off more than one thousand feet of the mountaintop and spread ash and pumice stone a foot deep for over a hundred miles in all directions. On Kodiak, people thought the world was coming to an end and rushed for the boats in the harbor. There they waited for two days in total darkness while ash continued to fall. In fact, so much ash came down that the islanders had to shovel off roofs to prevent cave-ins and sailors had to clean out the ships to keep them from sinking.

The eruption was so large that dust and ash formed a haze halfway round the world, dimming the sun as far away as North Africa and Europe, and causing spectacular sunsets everywhere. While scientists knew that some great volcanic activity had taken place, no one was quite sure where or just what had happened.

A year later a National Geographic Society expedition entered the Katmai area and discovered a scene of total devastation: a wide smoking area (the Valley of Ten Thousand Smokes) of rock dust and lava that closely resembles our idea of lunar landscape. They also found a beautiful emerald-green crater lake where Mount Katmai had once been, and since the lake water never freezes, volcanic fire must still smolder below.

Although President Woodrow Wilson first proclaimed Katmai a national monument in 1918, few people have yet visited it because of its extreme isolation. The only way to get there is by air (eventually the state ferry plans a stop as part of its Kodiak run), and Wien Consolidated Airlines, which serves northern and western Alaska, takes an increasing number of tourists to Katmai each year. The airline has built several fishing camps on lakes within the monument, so that one can not only visit the Valley of Ten Thousand Smokes but also enjoy superlative fishing on the same outing.

I mention a Katmai visit in this chapter because while one can't drive there with trailer or land with a plane on wheels to camp out, a trip to one of these fishing camps is our idea of the ultimate in camping luxury. For the Alaskan visitors and tourists who want to enjoy Alaska's great out-of-doors but would rather not tackle a tent or sleeping bags on the ground, these camps of WCA's are ideal. And the fishing is the best one can find anywhere. In September of 1963 we took my mother and father there on a four-day outing we will all long remember.

The flight from Anchorage is short and easy, bringing one right to Camp Kulik, a cluster of attractive log cabins along the shore of a small lake. We were amazed to discover running water and electricity in all the units, comfortable beds, and a central dining area where we were served delicious meals—Lowell was obviously concerned that I might be spoiled!

Fishing occupied the first two days of our visit, and so of course our conversation centered on what could be caught (mainly rainbow trout and arctic char), the methods to be used (hip boots and casting rods—I had no choice), and who were our fellow fishermen (bears, of course). Of the latter, I, for one, wanted to learn as much as possible. It can be disquieting to know that one must share the lake and stream shores with the largest carnivore on earth, that his height, when standing on hind legs, is seven to nine feet, and that he can carry a two-hundred-pound deer under one arm. The biologist divides the brown bear up into many species and subspecies—the Kodiak brown bear, for instance, is slightly different from the Alaskan Peninsula brown bear, but to the layman, all the brownies are alike and closely related to the grizzly, who lives in the Alaskan interior (and parts of other western states).

These bears live mainly on fish but have a variety of other foods to fall back on (berries, vegetation, marmots, etc.) in case fishing isn't good. And according to the experts, in areas where the bear knows he may have to share the stream with man, he will fish only early in the morning or late in the evening. This is a comforting thought, and so is the fact that a brown bear usually will not attack a man unless frightened, and this is invariably when it's a mama with cubs. A bear has terrible eyesight but a keen sense of smell and hearing. So chances are that while he might not spot you from far away, he will smell or hear you and immediately give you a wide berth. Walking while singing as loudly as possible is considered a safe way to travel in this area, but if one is self-conscious about one's voice, he can copy what many veterans of the bush do—carry a bell or a couple of rattly, clinky metal items.

Thus forewarned and also relieved by this information about our fishing neighbors, we were then delighted to hear about a fellow camp guest, Charlie Brown. Charlie, a large brown bear between two and four years old, had appeared uninvited the previous summer and now was a regular visitor at meal-preparation times. In order to be sure we'd make Charlie's acquaintance, we got up at 5:30 the following morning. There he was waiting by the kitchen steps, and he didn't seem to mind that we all crowded onto the porch to take his picture. For some reason he loved chocolate bars—especially Peter Paul Almond Joys—and he begged for them by rising on his hind legs and waving his front paws in a ponderous sort of dance. He made a remarkably good catcher, too.

Needless to say, we did not push our luck, or Charlie, by mov-

ing any closer than eight or ten feet. John Walatka, veteran bush
pilot and camp manager, always cautions guests that no matter
how tame these brown bears become, they are still wild animals,
and every bear will act differently under different circumstances.
Over the years John has entertained a number of similar four-
footed visitors at the camps, with many interesting and delightful
results (and no human guests, or parts thereof, lost in the process). One year a whole family descended on Kulik Camp: mama
"Charlene," "Charlie Junior," and "Charlette." Apparently Junior had a highly developed sense of humor and delighted in
stealthily following guests at their heels as they went from building to building around camp. He simply wanted to play "follow
the leader," but some of the newer guests found such goings on
difficult to enjoy. Both youngsters would stand and wave and beg
for food by the hour, and when they tired of this, they would run
down to the lake and romp in the water like children. During the
salmon runs in August, the three of them spent hours fishing in
the river and often let the current carry them out into the lake
where they would dive and fish by the hour.

Our fishing methods were far less aquatic but just as much fun.
We spent two days along the shores of the lake or wading in the
streams, with no spectacular luck, but not really caring because
the weather was perfect (probably the reason the fish weren't
biting) and the autumn colors brilliant. While wading about in
the clear water we could see large schools of fish.

On our third day in the Katmai area, we flew with John
Walatka in an old twin-engine Cessna on floats to another camp
on Brooks Lake. Here we were closer to the Valley of Ten Thousand Smokes and, to our great surprise, discovered the lake shore
covered with pumice stones. The children were delighted to find
stones that could float and spent the rest of the day showering the
lake waters with pumice. I must say I found it a very intriguing
material myself—for stone it is extraordinarily light, and we had
great fun taking pictures of Lowell holding a large pumice boulder
in one hand high above his shoulder.

From Brooks Camp we took a day's excursion into the Valley
of Ten Thousand Smokes, piling into an old bus of pre-world-war
(it's debatable which one!) vintage, and driving along a road just

recently hacked out of the forest by the parks people. Needless to say, it was not a four-lane paved highway or even a two-lane dirt road, but anything other than the narrow, rutted, winding tracks would have detracted from the fun of our expedition. There were no bridges, of course, so the fording of streams was especially exciting, and we finally did reach our goal, a hilltop from which we could look out upon a vast expanse of desolation—miles and miles of nothing but barren sand and rock, the snow-topped volcano culprits on the distant horizon. An occasional stream, in its meanderings, had already carved a deep gorge out of the soft rock. The whole area was so eerie, so desolate and silent, totally denuded of living things, that I can understand why our astronauts have been brought there to train for their lunar trip.

The Park Service had built a small warming hut on the hilltop, so we ate some sandwiches there, signed the relatively new guest book (as far as we could tell, Anne and Dave were the first two visitors under twelve), and then began our hike down into the valley itself. We planned to cover about five or six miles, and I kept my fingers crossed that we would get our six-year-old back up the hilltop under his own power. I should have saved my energy—he literally ran back up, while wondering why Mother was so slow.

We found the valley floor a fascinating place, an area we would like to return to for a much longer time. While the thousands of smoke holes are dormant now, they are by no means dead. By touching a match to a fumarole the gasses trapped underground would ignite, and through close observation in some places we could see wisps of smoke coming from the ground. The soft stone was also covered with fossils or fossil marks, and we would like to have had more time to look for different kinds. We were most enthusiastic over the idea of returning with a tent the following summer and spending at least a week on the valley floor, until John Walatka told us that our perfect weather that day—the blue sky, warm sun, and lack of wind—was extremely rare. Almost 90 per cent of the time this area is wracked by cold hurricane-force winds and driving rain—not very conducive to camping.

While our ride back to camp and our last night there should have been something of an anticlimax, it turned into a rather morbid experience. During the return trip, our driver, a grizzled veteran of the bush, stopped the bus every few minutes, muttering to himself and rushing out to look for something along the roadside. At first we were puzzled but then were told that this man was a mushroom "expert" and was looking for different varieties along the road. By the time we reached camp he had collected several bagfuls and had also acquired a number of eager helpers. Since there is nothing we would rather eat, we were delighted when he gave them to the camp cook for dinner.

We were all thoroughly enjoying the tenderness of these wild little plants when Lowell opened a book on mushrooms and started to read a bit to us. When he got to the part about the deadly variety being virtually identical to the harmless one, the room became strangely silent. He finished reading on the sentence about the poisonous ones reacting within a few moments, and we just sat and looked at one another—at least we wouldn't have long to wait. While nothing gruesome did happen, naturally we did not clean up our plates, and the little bags of leftover mushrooms, so thoughtfully given to us to take home, were carefully left behind the next morning as we climbed aboard the plane. What we did eat was delicious, but why push our luck?

V

The Vast
Interior

Our camping trips also take us northeast of Anchorage, into the fringes of the great Alaskan interior—for us this geographical division refers to almost the entire state, excluding the seven thousand miles of coast line, the southeast panhandle, and the Aleutian Island chain. It is a land of few people, a gigantic wilderness of spruce forests, treeless tundra, lofty mountains, and broad river valleys. It is the home of the giant Alaskan mosquito and the land of permanently frozen ground; of endless summer days and equally long winter nights, with tremendous extremes in temperatures; the home of many small Athabascan Indian villages, of vast herds of caribou, of winter dog teams and summer fish wheels; and it is an area liberally sprinkled with early goldrush boom towns, now mostly existing in name only. In fact, this interior region most closely resembles the Alaska most "outsiders" believe is their forty-ninth state.

While the giant Alaska mountain range is generally considered the southern boundary of the interior, as soon as one leaves the coast, driving into the flat Matanuska and Susitna valleys, he becomes aware of subtle changes in climate, of less human habitation and more untouched wilderness.

Just north of Anchorage, the one main highway follows Knik Arm (unlike Turnagain Arm, it is surrounded by open, flat land) and then crosses Knik River into the fertile farmland of the Matanuska Valley. Way back before the days of Russian colonization there were at least four small Indian villages in this Knik River area. However, by the time the Russians came that far up Cook Inlet, the native population had been greatly reduced by a severe smallpox epidemic. The Russians built a trading post at the Knik Indian settlement about 1880, on a flat area along the north shore of the arm. It was accessible by water (in the days when there were no roads), the larger ships anchoring at what is now the Anchorage harbor, while smaller ferries and barges busily traveled back and forth to the flats of Knik. The Knik site was also a gateway to the Matanuska and Susitna valleys—the latter a large flat plain crisscrossed by the navigable Susitna River, an ideal access route to northern and western interior areas.

The Russians were only interested in furs, however, and it wasn't until after the arrival of Americans that gold exploration began. The first gold discoveries in the Yukon Territory posed a problem for American prospectors: They had the choice of a difficult inland journey through Canada from Skagway in southeastern Alaska, or a long boat journey to the mouth of the Yukon River and then another interminable water trip all the way upriver to the Yukon Territory. Therefore, as early as 1895, a U. S. Army group (one of several exploring parties) landed at Knik with orders to find a passable route inland. At about this same time the Alaska Commercial Company built a trading post at Knik, and within the next few years gold was discovered in nearby streams and hills. From then on, the town grew rapidly—to four stores, four hotels, just as many saloons, and five hundred people in 1914.

The settlement became the distributing point for the quartz and placer mines in the vicinity, but many travelers also came through, en route to or from the interior regions. One dog-team trail, coming from Seward to the south, led on north, through what we now call "Windy Pass" in the Alaska Range, to the mines of the Kantishna and Fairbanks area. Another route, the famous Iditarod Trail, led to the west, through Rainy Pass in the Alaska Range, to the McGrath mining area and eventually on to Nome. After the fabulous Nome gold strikes, the Iditarod became a well-traveled winter route for men, mails, and supplies. Roadhouses were built twenty-five miles apart all along the way— just the right hiking distance for the traveler of that day. It was easy for the northern prospectors to take their gold finds back to the States via boat during the three summer months, but during the many more winter days this dog-team trail was the only answer. Apparently the residents of Knik became quite accustomed to sleds piled high with gold worth thousands of dollars lining their streets, usually unattended!

Knik residents seemed to be unaware of the impending doom of their prosperous town when the first railroad survey crews set up tents at what is now Anchorage in 1914. The route decided upon ran a number of miles to the east of Knik, closer to the coal mines and potential farm land of the Matanuska Valley, and within two years the village had become a ghost town, leaving only a colorful bit of history which is recalled briefly each year with the running of the Iditarod Trail dog-team races.

These days, as we drive along the modern highway from the new city of Anchorage toward the equally new settlement of Palmer in the Matanuska Valley, we do not come near the old townsite and trails of Knik. However, we do pass one most interesting bit of the past, at the tiny Indian village of Eklutna. Russian missionary priests arrived there as early as 1794, and the original log church still stands. It is unusable now, and since the villagers still belong to the Russian Orthodox Church, a new structure, with the traditional onion-type dome, has been built nearby. We found the church's little graveyard especially intriguing because it so clearly represents a combination of Indian and Russian traditions. Each grave is covered with a miniature wooden house painted in a bright color—an Indian custom from earliest times. Orthodox three-barred wooden crosses stand beside the houses of those converted to the faith.

Just beyond Eklutna the road crosses Knik River, a favorite stopping place for our children because the many large gravel bars are an ideal spot for running and playing after they have been sitting in the car. On a sunny day the gravel is warm, and while the kids collect rocks (I never know what to do with the baskets full of "rare finds"—stones which gleam with shiny streaks of minerals underwater but look like piles of dull junk when placed on the bureau at home), I study the many endless varieties of wild flowers and Lowell hikes along the swift-flowing, heavily silted water.

Unfortunately, the most unusual and exciting feature of the Knik River and its glacier cannot be seen except from an airplane. Each year this glacier, a seven-mile-wide river of ice, advances until it plugs up the outlet of nearby Lake George. The waters of the sixteen-mile-long lake build up such pressure that by August an escape-channel tunnel has formed under the ice. As the tunnel widens, sections of the glacier begin caving in, and then for a few days we can witness one of nature's greatest spectacles: Huge sections of the ice, some hundreds of feet wide, fall with a tremendous roar and splash into the river. Raging torrents of water carry these gigantic ice cubes downstream at fantastic speeds. Within a week the entire glacial barrier has been swept away, and the glacier begins to advance toward the mountain again.

Once across the Knik River, the highway takes us to Palmer, the trading center for the Matanuska Valley, and we come to another of those rare highway junctions: One road heads east through the valley, while the other (a new one, with much of it still under construction) heads west and north, up the broad Susitna Plain. Matanuska is undoubtedly known to most Americans as the farming area colonized by a New Deal project in 1935. Actually, over 130 homesteaders were already there by 1914, mainly raising vegetables for local miners and residents of Knik. However, the arrival of the 230 families taking part in the colonization did do a great deal to boost the agricultural development of the valley, despite the fact that only one third remained after ten years' time.

I suppose it has been the dream of most Americans at one time or another to be given homestead property, to build one's own home, and to become self-sufficient with what can be raised off the land. A great dream, but most of the time it doesn't work out that way. In fact, I'll bet that this Alaskan homestead pot at the end of the American rainbow has caused more headaches for our state and local government and welfare groups than anything else. The necessary ingredients of great determination and hard work are too often lacking.

The federal government was thinking in such idealistic terms when it set up the colonization project in 1935, knowing little about the physical conditions of the valley. Some guidelines were drawn: The colonists came from an area with a similar climate (Wisconsin, Michigan, and Minnesota), they were supposed to be physically and mentally fit, and to have done some farming. Unfortunately, the actual selecting was not carried out properly, and consequently most of the colonists had little or no farming knowledge. Many of these families, not having the remotest idea of what they were getting into, faced much hardship and grief, but a few positive things did happen—the town of Palmer was established, with stores, a Farmers' Cooperative Association, a school, and hospital. Many more acres of land were cleared, and some of those 1935 colonist families are now the backbone of the Matanuska Valley farming community.

If someone is really intent on homesteading in Alaska, the hard cold fact he must first face is that to develop a homestead into a full-time commercial farm requires a cash investment of from forty to sixty thousand dollars! If one just wants to raise food for oneself, the costs are far less, but the great majority of all homesteaders are forced to hold other jobs in order to make ends meet. Frequently the men will go to the cities for wintertime work, leaving the wives and children alone on the homestead. Are you still willing, ladies? Some of the problems they face are the small size (160 acres) of the homestead in terms of modern mechanical farming, the terribly high cost of initially clearing the land, and the cool climate (with only about 110 frost-free days). Many crops cannot be grown here (soybeans, corn, alfalfa), and those that do all mature at the same time and cannot be stored easily. (Potatoes and cabbages are the exception.) And this local produce must meet intensive competition in the markets with fresh products trucked in swiftly from the "lower 48."

One of our friends in the Matanuska Valley is a "lady farmer," Louise Kellogg, the owner of one of the more successful dairy herds. We love to visit her "Spring Creek Farm" because, in typical womanly fashion, everything from the fields and fences to the barns and milking sheds is kept in spanking-clean, neat, tip-top condition. Her 860 acres are four miles north of Palmer—open, gently rolling fields surrounding a New England-style frame white house, barns, and other neat, freshly painted buildings. In fact, the only thing that doesn't look like New England is the ever-present backdrop of the rugged Chugach Mountains and glaciers.

We spent one Thanksgiving day with Louise on her farm which we will long remember. Inside the cozy farmhouse we shared the feast with other farm families and valley residents. All ages were represented, and while the children played and the men chatted, the women set the long table with many platters of traditional Thanksgiving fare, contributed by everyone present. I had the feeling that I might never again come so close to that celebration of the first Thanksgiving. When the meal was finally over, the farmer who takes charge of the dairy herd for Louise invited us out to watch the milking. The moment we stepped outside we were in another world. It was totally dark, although only 3:30, there was deep snow on the ground, and it was bitterly cold (a strong Knik wind didn't help). With this sharp reminder that we were near the arctic, we hurried to the well-lit, warm barns.

While Louise has always had help, usually a farmer and his wife, her story is still a most remarkable and unusual one. She grew up on a farm, just outside Chicago, but it was a "gentleman's farm." Nonetheless, her one desire in life was to be a farmer. World War II sidetracked her for a while, and she served in the WAC's. In 1948 she came North to homestead, going first to Homer. Louise is quick to admit that her two main prerequisites were electricity and a good main road. Since Homer had neither at that time, she moved on to the Matanuska Valley, buying a 240-acre place that had already been farmed for seventeen years.

Before you think, "that's the easy way to homestead," let me quickly add that Louise lived in a tent the first summer while a basement was being built, then lived in that for three years until her house was finished. The barn, already on the farm, housed about thirty cows (she now has eighty and gets a ton of milk a day), the fields were planted with brome grass, oats, and peas (grain was ordered from "outside" by the sack—expensive!), and she grew her own vegetables, went berrying and fishing—keeping as self-sufficient as possible.

Today Louise's farming operation has become more modern and mechanical. Now she buys her fish and produce at market, she grows the same crops for silage but buys grain for the cows in bulk locally (a highly nutritious mixture which includes soybeans). Her barns and milking shed have become thoroughly modernized, and she uses the new concept of the unheated "loafing barn." The cows are not tied in the stalls but come and go at will, growing heavier coats, needing less bedding, and generally staying a lot healthier.

When asked if Alaskan farming is here to stay, Louise says staunchly, "Well, I am!" She adds that while little Matanuska Valley land is available these days, there is still room for more farmers. But she quickly states that both husband and wife must like the life and must be prepared to face the great challenge for at least twenty years. When I wrote to her recently for more information on her farm, her reply was typically Louise:

I will be honored to be mentioned by you as part of the Valley agricultural scene, but please don't describe me as a person who has made good on her own, because (1) I have not made good —ask the mortgage holders, and (2) I have accomplished nothing by myself—friends and family are continually called upon to rescue me from the puddles of blood, sweat and tears I fall into.

The new road, heading north from Palmer through the Susitna Valley, is completed now as far as the small settlement of Talkeetna and gives us better access to another of the finest hunting and fishing areas in the state. Also, the lakes along the route are becoming increasingly popular for water sports and weekend cabins, and the number of farms and homesites is growing. As one drives farther into the interior, the summer weather becomes dryer and warmer (conversely, the winters are colder), and our family has spent many a delightful camp out enjoying the water of streams or lakes beneath a hot sun.

This valley covers hundreds of square miles, with few inhabitants and has what now seems like limitless opportunities for recreation. Many feel the same holds true for agriculture, and some homesteading families have already made good, beginning the hard way before the coming of the road. A particularly well-publicized group who settled in the Talkeetna area nine years ago were called the "59er's." These twelve families decided to pull up stakes in Michigan and start a new life in Alaska in the spring of 1959. Their record of success in homesteading has been better than that of the New Deal Matanuska Valley colonists—of the original twelve, six have proved up or are awaiting final patent on homesteads in the Susitna area, and another two have done the same on the Kenai Peninsula.

Carol and Marino Sik were among those to reach Talkeetna in the late spring of 1959. They pulled a house trailer across the rotting ice of the Susitna River and down a dirt track five miles farther westward. This was unsurveyed land, and they had been told it was probably the best available for farming. With meager capital, a baby less than a year old (later two more were born on the homestead), and only a background of city living, the young couple cleared, leveled, and planted the required one hundred acres, got their food from a large vegetable garden, a nearby stream full of fish, and ample game in the woods (during the first two years they bought no meat at all). Firewood for fuel was readily available—but civilization was not. Once the ice broke up in the river, the homesteaders' only connection with the outside world was bush pilot Don Sheldon of Talkeetna, who kept a regular check on the group.

In the past few years the Siks have had to spend the winters in Talkeetna, to be close to schools and a job for the father. The original homestead trailer has been expanded into a five-room log house, however, and the family hopes to live there full time before too long. The new Anchorage-Fairbanks highway goes right through part of their property, thereby solving school and job transportation problems. After eight years of homesteading, the Siks had some comments which I found most interesting: they felt that while they had worked much harder than they would have on a nine-to-five job, it had been a pleasure rather than a chore—their time had been their own, and they had been working for themselves. They also felt the privations they had had to face were worth it because of the great privacy and independence they could enjoy and the freedom from pressure which had bothered them so in city life. Above all, they felt there is no pat formula for homesteading success other than strong determination on the part of both husband and wife.[1]

The town of Talkeetna, the focal center for the Susitna Valley homesteaders and long the supply depot for the mining activity in the area, has also become the headquarters for big-game hunters and mountain-climbing expeditions. However, this impressive list of activities has done little to change the physical appearance of the sleepy frontier village. It is hard to tell just how many people live there—the only statistic I can find is that there were ninety-five voters in the last election. I never have seen more than a few homes in town, mostly log houses or trailers. The main street looks like a scene from an early western film. There is a saloon at the center of activity, two all-inclusive stores, a post office, and a variety of miner-trapper characters who wander down or lounge about the dirt street which is rarely used by cars.

Away from the "center" of town one does see a sign of the arrival of twentieth-century hunters and fishermen—two new motels which we found clean and comfortable, with a spectacular view of Mount McKinley. (In fact, the mountain views from anywhere in Talkeetna are far superior to those of many of the fancier tourist stops.) Most of the mountain-climbing expeditions, however, cannot afford to stay in these motels, and they bed down with sleeping bags in Don Sheldon's hangar. At one time, during a period of prolonged bad weather, Don counted seventy men bunking there. Don's own little airport, hangar, and home are right beside the main street, and landing there is quite a hair-raising operation. Since the single dirt runway is short (twelve hundred feet), ending at the Susitna River bank, one must come in low and set down as soon as possible to avoid a dunking at the other end. This easy-sounding maneuver actually involves coming within what seems to me inches of the roof of the saloon, the chimney of Don's home, and the electric wires thoughtfully strung along the end of the runway. And I don't think Lowell will accuse me of exaggerating! Much of the year large ruts and potholes make a landing even more treacherous, but such conditions don't bother Don—he doesn't want just anyone dropping in on him.

[1] *Alaska Sportsman,* Juneau, Alaska, September 1967.

One of our most delightful visits to Talkeetna was in July of 1963. The earth was to experience a total eclipse of the sun at that time, and the path of totality lay right across Talkeetna (the only other part of the United States in a similar position was a small section of northern Maine). The tiny village, basking in such unusual glory, was inundated with visitors for that one day. People danced to the ragtime tunes of a piano right on the main street, the saloon moved outdoors to do a rip-roaring business, and occasionally someone glanced at the sky to check the progress of the eclipse.

Our visit was more scientifically oriented, and we combined a family outing with picture taking for Lowell. He wanted to record the actual eclipse over Mount McKinley, and he set up his movie cameras on a high treeless hill to the east of town. We stayed overnight with friends who owned a cabin on a small lake nearby, and while Lowell saw nothing of the eclipse other than through the lens of his camera, the children and I went out in a rowboat and found the disappearance of the sun a most unusual experience. As we drifted over the mirror-calm water, we watched the reflections of the crescent-shaped sun until the moment of totality. It was a decidedly eerie feeling to have darkness slowly descending at ten in the morning, but it was actually frightening to have the day suddenly turn to night. (Now I can readily understand the terror which struck primitive peoples.) Although the period of total eclipse was very brief, while drifting on such an isolated, utterly still lake, we did notice two things—we quickly became very cold, and there was a sudden mass movement of birds, flying to the trees to roost!

Of course, we had warned the children not to look directly at the sun during the eclipse because of the danger to eyes, and we had given them sheets of unexposed film to peek through during the earlier stages. But best-laid plans, of mothers particularly, can certainly go awry—the moment the period of totality was over, Anne announced that she had seen the most beautiful halo all around the sun! I won't dispute the scientific findings on eclipses and eyes, but at least we survived that incident without injury.

While most of our trips to Talkeetna have been made by airplane, we have also stopped there a number of times while on the train. The Alaska Railroad runs 470 miles from Seward to Fairbanks and is a most unusual operation for a number of reasons. First of all, it is owned by the federal government and run by the Department of Transportation. It is also extremely comfortable and highly efficient, yet at the same time is undoubtedly run more informally than any other train system anywhere. About fifty thousand people ride this railroad annually, mostly summer tourists, and it acts as the road, or one outside link, for many homesteaders along the route. The twelve-hour run is made daily all summer long and twice weekly during the winter.

These days few residents of Anchorage ever take this trip—several airlines can zip one to Fairbanks in forty-five minutes, and thinking is no longer oriented toward train rides. However, the children and I (and definitely not Lowell) love this particular trip and have taken it a number of times—summer and winter. I especially enjoy the chance to relax in a comfortable chair in an air-conditioned car, with no telephone to answer, no meals to cook (the food is delicious), and no place to have to hurry to. In fact, there is nothing to do but relax, read, sleep, or look out the overlarge, tinted windows.

Actually, window-watching on this train is an exhilarating experience for anyone. The scenery is breathtaking, and there are frequent views of the mighty Alaska Range, myriad jewel-like lakes, streams (some of which are raging torrents, while others are quiet trickles), birch forests, and alpine meadows. To keep photographers happy, the engineer obligingly stops the train at a few of the most outstanding panoramic spots. Of course, such a wilderness is teeming with wildlife, and if one watches sharply, many animals can be seen from the train windows. The beavers and their dam homes are everywhere, and we have also spotted grizzly bears, porcupines, and scores of moose. On a wintertime trip, moose are such a common sight that one quickly loses count of the numbers. When the snow is deep, Mr. Moose finds it far easier to walk down the cleared railroad track than wallow through drifts up to his tummy. Obviously this situation creates problems for the engineer, who is often forced to stop the train while the critters amble down the tracks ahead. The government has spent thousands of dollars trying to solve this problem, but so far nothing has worked. Whistles, flare guns, and firecrackers seem to attract the moose in even greater numbers—they are curious enough to want to see what is up. And once, when a type of horn was tried out, it must have sounded like the mating call because all the bulls appeared, ready to charge and do battle.

A moose on the tracks is not the only unscheduled stop for the train; it will also pick up any person along the route who waves it to a halt. In fact, once it was known to stop when the engineer spotted a hunter by the tracks, sitting on his dead moose, apparently too worn out to give any signal at all. (When hunters come aboard, their game is stored in the baggage car.) Actually, this personal pick-up service goes even further—a hunter or fisherman can get on the train, inform the conductor he wants to disembark at such and so creek or meadow, be left there, and be picked up by the train returning from Fairbanks. In late summer or early fall, when the salmon are running and hunting season has begun, I have been on trains which seem to stop almost constantly, and yet we usually arrive in Fairbanks right on schedule. One of these days I'm going to ask the engineer just how he does it!

To many a Susitna Valley homesteader this kind of personal service is all-important—it is his one contact with the outside world, his way of receiving supplies and mail or of going back and forth to the big city. I always enjoy watching the homestead life as we pass by; many of the houses are built right next to the tracks, and in the wintertime paths are shoveled between the front door and the train. In the warm weather small children, riding tricycles on the paths, wave frantically. Fathers, with packs on their backs, a flag in their hand, and often pulling wagons, wait for supplies to be unloaded. Mothers are usually standing in the doorway, holding babies, wondering whether Father will remember to mail their letters.

Of course, there are also many scheduled stops along the route, where a "window-watcher" can observe a whole gathering of homesteaders, along with a sprinkling of miners, trappers, and road-construction workers. The names of some of these settlements are just as fascinating as the people waiting for the train, and while some succinctly explain the reason for their existence (Gold Creek, Fish Lake, Broad Pass), others are far more obscure (Sunshine, Curry, Sherman, Lagoon, Montana, Colorado, and Honolulu). Montana is at the center of a number of homesteads, so I suspect at least one of the settlers must have originally come from Montana. The same goes for Colorado, except in this case it must have been a miner instead of a farmer. Honolulu has long had me stumped, especially when one has seen both the big Hawaiian city and this pathetic cluster of wooden buildings in the midst of a treeless wilderness. I have heard rumors that the original settlers were from our fiftieth state and the name helped to stave off homesickness.

Another place of great interest along the route is Hurricane Gulch, a deep river gorge where winds undoubtedly roar with hurricane-like force. The crossing of the gorge itself is a hair-raising experience because the railroad bridge is 918 feet long and dangles nearly 300 feet above the river. While most travelers who have cameras record this sight on film, an Anchorage resident recently put down his reactions in a poem:

> Hurricane Chasm's a heart-thumpin' sight
> when you're buckin' the wind on the ridge,
> but it looks its deepest, bloodcurdlingest best
> from the middle of Hurricane bridge.
> Cheechakos can see it from inside a train,
> but up on the Railbelt it's said
> that a few men have walked it—with knots in the middle,
> or maybe with rocks in the head . . .[2]

McKinley Park is the next stop for the train, and the getting off-getting on point for a majority of the passengers. McKinley is the second largest U.S. national park, 3030 square miles in size (Yellowstone is the largest). Of all the scenic and wildlife wilderness areas in Alaska, this park is an absolute must for tourists and residents alike. Sadly, though, in keeping with the hectic pace of modern living, most visitors allow a day and a half at the most to "do" the park—on a mad dash down the road they are not likely to see any of the limitless wildlife inhabitants, and the mighty mountain itself may remain totally hidden behind clouds.

The park hotel, an unimaginative barracks-type building (with no view of the mountain) is usually crowded in the summertime but comfortable and a good base for those visitors who do not

[2] "The Phantom of Hurricane Gulch," Lew Turner, *Anchorage Daily News,* Alaska Living, February 11, 1968.

1. The author, leaving "Charlie," which Lowell has just landed at the 5500-foot level on the Eagle Ice Field among the Chugach Mountains. The family plans an afternoon of skiing under the hot July sun.

2. "Charlie," Lowell, and Swen Johanson, Olympic skier and U.S. Biathalon coach, spend another warm summer's day in the Chugach Mountains, enjoying every moment of a ski run.

3. During a weekend camp-out into the Chugach Mountains in the fall of 1962, Anne and David take refuge from a rain shower. Their stuffed rabbit companion traveled all over Alaska with Anne in 1958, and now spends his declining years, minus ears and a considerable amount of stuffing, on Anne's bed.

4. The family tent, pitched on a carpet of wild flowers, with a gurgling brook and a few lingering patches of snow in the background. While Lowell climbs the mountain slope behind, Tay and the children set up housekeeping, ably assisted by their bear guard, Bozie.

5. Lowell and the children could be spending the day on any beach in the "lower 48," from the looks of the bathing suits, sand, and water. However, on the beach at Ninilchik the background cannot be matched anywhere—the white snow cone of Mt. Redoubt, one of the many active volcanoes on the Alaska Peninsula.

6. Mother lands a big one—a twelve-pound silver salmon, during a day's outing to Johnson River. Just an hour's flight in "Charlie" from home, and Lowell lands the plane right on the beach.

7. Don Sheldon's Mt. McKinley cabin, an hexagonal hut perched on a rock outcropping in the vast Ruth Amphitheater, about 5500 feet high beneath North America's highest mountain.

photo courtesy of Joseph S. Rychetnik

8. Anne and Dave carry their skis from "Charlie" to Don's mountain cabin. The summit of McKinley is on the left. Summer skiing is excellent at these altitudes but can only be reached by climbing or with an airplane.

9. Lowell, Anne, and Dave visit the Point Hope Eskimo village grave-yard during the anniversary celebration in 1965. Over a thousand whale jawbones form the fence, and others mark some of the graves.

10. A good catch of Beluga whales lines the Kotzebue beach, while the children appear to be watching for more hunters to return. Most Eskimos use the modern boats with outboard motors these days, but the people of the North still prefer whale meat to the best cuts of beef flown in from "outside."

photo courtesy of Rev. Bob Jones

12: Lowell takes an afternoon stroll on Arlis II, a floating ice island in the Arctic Ocean near the North Pole. The wooden buildings of this most remote scientific station are in the background.

photo courtesy of William Bacon

11. Anchorage's annual Fur Rendezvous is an exciting holiday for the young and old alike. Although many native people come to the big city just for the sled dog races, Anchorage now also has the largest native community in the state. The Eskimo ladies, from left to right, are: Mrs. Anokazuk, of King Island, Mrs. Adaline Hendricksen (Pa nia gon), of Mary's Igloo, and Mrs. Ku vi suk, of King Island.

13. The Eskimo town of Kotzebue sits on the tip of a long, sandy peninsula, virtually surrounded by the frigid waters of Kotzebue Sound. The tents and boats in the foreground belong to Eskimo summer visitors.

photo courtesy of Rev. Bob Jones

14. Fairbanks, the "Golden Heart of the North," a city of 17,000 people now—a pleasant mixture of tall, modern buildings and early-day wooden and log homes. The Chena River, responsible for the terrible flood of 1967, meanders through the background. The author took this picture from a helicopter just two months before the disaster.

15. The author explains the action of the earth slide which, when triggered by the earthquake, destroyed their home and almost killed her and the two children.

16. The bedroom section is the only part of the Thomas home that remained intact. Lowell, in the right foreground, is beginning to salvage belongings two days after the earthquake.

17. Tay, Anne, and David look for possessions just after the earthquake, which was the strongest ever recorded on the North American continent. It was a gruesome treasure hunt which lasted for many weeks—many items totally vanished, perhaps down a crevasse, but others, like a favorite crystal vase, were found undamaged, lying on the ground.

18. A large section of the main street of Anchorage sank many feet, leaving the buildings twisted wrecks. It is amazing, considering the damage, that no one was killed in this area. It has been said that some of the customers caught in the D&D Bar during the quake have never touched another drop!

19. During the earth slide the remains of the Thomas house were scattered over a fifty-yard area. The antique cupboard in the foreground was salvaged and repaired, but many other Early American pieces of furniture were totally destroyed.

have camping outfits. Park Rangers conduct eight- and twelve-hour tours by car, but the ninety-four miles of road opens only a fraction of the two million acres; some of the area remains virtually unnamed and seldom seen. To truly enjoy the tremendous advantages of the park, one should be prepared to camp (there are excellent campgrounds) and hike (much of the land is treeless, tundra meadows) or even use a foldboat or canoe. Such a visit is on our "has-to-be-done" list, right at the top. Since we have already enjoyed many unexcelled views of Mount McKinley from the air, our main reason for a visit on the ground would be to enjoy the wildlife—there are over thirty-five different species of animals, many more kinds of birds, including the bald eagle, the rare surf bird, and the wandering tattler, and the lakes and streams are filled with grayling and trout. (Fishing is permitted, hunting is not.)

Probably the animal most unique to this area is the *Ursus Horribilis,* the most ferocious and feared of North American carnivores—the much-maligned grizzly bear. Once he ruled supreme over the entire American West, but now he is threatened with extinction, and some naturalists feel Mr. Grizzly doesn't like being "crowded"—perhaps the reason behind increased bear attacks on people in some of the parks. In McKinley Park these animals have far more room and freedom from human intervention. It takes a lot of food to keep a grizzly going, especially when the snacks are small, such as berries, grass, roots, squirrels, birds, and fish. Fully grown, a male weighs from eight hundred to one thousand pounds, and like his brownie cousin, he can measure up to eight feet when he stands on his hind legs. Unlike the brown bear, the grizzly has a slight hump on his back, and his coat, which may vary in color from brown to gray and black, is silver-tipped. Despite his horrifying-sounding scientific name, I suspect the grizzly is more shy than ferocious, wanting to be left alone, and when I visit McKinley Park, that's just what I intend to do!

Beyond the McKinley Park station, the train winds its way through the Alaska Range, the tracks perched precariously on the steep mountain slopes and above deep river gorges. The stops are fewer now, it is usually dark, or in the summertime the sun turns the white mountaintops a rosy pink. This is mining country, but these days coal rather than gold is being sought. The coal mines at Healy are the major supply source in Alaska.

Once through the mountains and on the north side of the Alaska Range, at long last the traveler reaches the true interior and the city of Fairbanks: "the Golden Heart of the North," the gateway to the towns of the arctic coast. Fairbanks itself is a mixture of the earlier-day mining town, with log cabins, saloons, and dirt roads; and the new Alaska, with the latest-style homes, paved suburban-style streets, stores, apartment buildings, and the modern, ever-expanding University of Alaska.

In July of 1902, Italian prospector Felix Pedro found gold in a valley near the Tanana and Chena rivers, after three long and fruitless years of searching. Word spread quickly, and within a year a busy settlement had sprung up on the banks of the Chena. The usual trading post, hotel, and saloons were among the first structures erected, and by 1904, a courthouse, log jail, two churches, and over two hundred cabins had been added. One early writer claims that over ten thousand people were living in the area at that time. The name of the community, unlike many of the other early settlements, was not that of a local miner, but of a U.S. senator who had never even been to Alaska, and from Indiana of all places—Charles W. Fairbanks. The senator was one of the few members of Congress at that time who showed an interest in Alaska and a willingness to help.

The new town of Fairbanks received its supplies from steamers plying the Tanana and Chena rivers and via an overland route to Circle City on the Yukon River. A winter trail followed the rivers from Fairbanks to Nome, and as the hoards of miners headed for the latter community along this inland route, its snow cover became so hard-packed that a few intrepid gold-seekers rode bicycles the whole way! A third trail, the Richardson, connecting Fairbanks with the southern port of Valdez, was gradually widened into a wagon road and became the key link with the outside world until the opening of the railroad in 1925.

Gold mining was the major activity in the Fairbanks area for many years. This was done not so much by individual prospectors with their shovels and pans, but by companies that used sluicing and dredging methods in large-scale operations. (Only one still exists today.) When the gold-mining industry finally collapsed in the '20s, Fairbanks did not become a ghost town like its many sister communities (Circle City dropped from a population of three thousand to thirty in two years) because the town had also established itself as the trading center for the interior. Today, since the coming of two military bases, the University of Alaska, and a large network of airline routes, Fairbanks has become the state's second largest community, with a population of nineteen thousand and an area population of close to forty-five thousand.

One thing we in Anchorage never discuss with our Fairbanks neighbors is the weather—any mention of the subject is certain to bring on a violent argument. We wonder how anyone can endure their long, dark, extremely cold (minus 40 degrees is not uncommon) winters with the added misery of ice fog which settles in for days at a time. Visibility is reduced to zero, air traffic comes to a halt, driving is virtually impossible, and most people remain indoors. But Fairbanksians are fiercely loyal and staunchly defend their climate. Their winters, they claim, are dry and therefore much more livable than our "dampness," and they are justifiably proud of their hot (80-degree temperatures), dry summers. Also, because of a climatic oddity called "temperature inversion," a warmer layer of air often exists above the intense cold lying close to the ground. So for many years Fairbanks residents have skied on nearby hills where temperatures are twenty and thirty degrees warmer than downtown. Now more and more people are building their homes high on these slopes, escaping the extreme cold and the ice fogs which cling to the valley basin.

Most of our visits to Fairbanks have been during the summer months when I will readily agree that the dry, hot air feels wonderful. And there is always an unending round of exciting summer activities, geared partly for tourists but more, I suspect, for the townspeople, who have been cooped up for so long and are determined to enjoy every moment of their all-too-brief warm weather. The first big events are held on June 21, the longest day of the year, when the sun barely sets at all, and the same goes for the residents of Fairbanks. They celebrate with a "Midnight Sun Baseball Game," beginning at 10:30 P.M. (played without artificial lights), and also a "Midnight Sun Golf Game," which tees off at the stroke of midnight.

The Golden Days Week, in mid-July, commemorates the first

discovery of gold in the area, and in the process of celebrating, the town recovers much of its early gold-rush atmosphere. Everyone wears pioneer costumes, men sprout beards, there are street dances, parades, a bean feed, an old-timers' baseball game, gold-panning contests, and a re-enactment of the landing of the first riverboat and the founding of the town. While this holiday commemorates the coming of the prospectors, the Eskimo Olympics, held in early August, is a celebration for the native peoples who lived in the northland long before the arrival of the "outsiders." Fairbanks itself has a large native population and has close ties with the Athabascan Indian villages of the interior and the Eskimo villages along the arctic coast. Age-old Eskimo and Indian contests, such as the blanket toss, seal skinning, seal-hook throwing, teeterboard jumping, and dancing are the activities of the day.

My favorite outing, on a summer visit to Fairbanks, is an excursion on the old stern-wheeler *Discovery*. Our good friend Jim Binkley, who shared in Lowell's forced landing near Fairbanks, pilots the ship. In fact, the Binkley family has owned and operated Alaskan riverboats since 1898. Captain Jim provides one of the most interesting tourist trips in the whole interior—taking people on a four-hour cruise down the Chena and Tanana rivers. Besides the fun of the boat ride itself, there are many interesting sights which Jim tells about along the way; at first one sees old homesteads and modern homes lining the Chena banks, with boats and seaplanes moored to docks, and then comes Cripple Creek, a small stream which in gold-rush days yielded over one hundred million dollars in gold. The scenery quickly changes when the Chena merges with the Tanana; in fact, there is even an abrupt difference in the water—until the junction, the ripples are gentle, green-blue in color, and suddenly the boat enters the ruffled, swift, and gray (silt-laden) Tanana. Civilization has been left behind now, and the Tanana Valley is a green wilderness. The many islands, channels, and sand bars obviously indicate the need for a good river pilot.

The riverbanks have been badly eroded by the strong current (a great problem facing many interior river villages), and one occasionally sees an abandoned cabin sitting precariously at the water's edge—probably once built well back from the bank by an early prospector. Fish wheels are frequent and a unique feature of these Alaskan rivers. The Indians must depend upon a large supply of fish to feed their sled dogs, so they let these unique contraptions, built of bits and pieces of wood and wire, do some of their work for them. The wheels are built on the principle of the windmill, only in this case, it is the water current rather than the wind which does the turning. Fish are caught in the wire scoops and then slide into a wooden box, built safely above the water line. The stern-wheeler *Discovery* also stops at an Indian fish camp, and passengers can disembark to watch the salmon that have been caught in the wheels being smoked in cook sheds and dried on racks nearby.

Most of our trips to Fairbanks also include a visit to the University of Alaska campus, a sprawling complex of modern buildings perched on a hilltop a few miles north of town. Alaska has probably one of the smallest of the state universities but undoubtedly one of the fastest growing. Outstanding work is being done in specialized and graduate fields, such as the School of Mines, the Arctic Research Lab, and the Geophysical Institute. More down to earth and understandable to me is the experiment involving the musk ox herd. This arctic animal, whose home was originally Greenland, looks like a Tibetan yak, with long, shaggy hair, large body, and short, stubby legs. While he might not win a beauty contest, the musk ox does produce from three to six pounds of fleece each year which is as soft as silk and finer than cashmere—a potential industry for herdsmen of the Far North.

For the residents of Fairbanks, the summer of 1967 in particular will be long remembered—for a triumph of personal achievement and for a catastrophic natural disaster. Fairbanks was selected as the center of Alaska's Centennial Celebration, marking the one hundredth anniversary of the purchase of Alaska by the United States. Over five million dollars was spent in constructing a forty-acre Centennial site between the city and the airport, and most of the residents were caught up in a feverish rush of preparations for the grand opening. We had heard a bit about the many projects: moving a number of original log buildings to the site, docking the 238-foot stern-wheeler *Nenana* there to be a restaurant and entertainment center, and other ambitious-sounding ventures. But we were totally unprepared for what we found when we flew up for the opening day. The huge crowds were delighted with what was truly a highly professional Alaskan Disneyland; the gold-rush town was a perfectly done copy of the real thing, the Eskimo and Indian village buildings had been carefully reproduced and were most interesting, as was Mining Valley, Wilderness Park, and a cultural center containing many exquisitely done exhibits on Alaskan history and life.

Naturally, our children thought the amusement park (something Alaska has never had) was "the greatest," and we all loved the ride on the Crooked Creek & Whiskey Island Railroad, which ran through or near all the attractions on the site. The cars were made in turn-of-the-century style, and the engine had a true potbellied smokestack. At a certain time each day, the passengers were even treated to a full-fledged train robbery. We were traveling through a short but dark tunnel when the first shots rang out, and we all nearly jumped out of our skins. The masked outlaws willingly settled for a box of fake gold, however (with an occasional pretty girl thrown in to boot), and we were soon chugging on our way.

August was to be the peak month for visiting the Centennial Park, and since July had been unusually rainy, officials were hoping for more normal dry weather. That was not to be the case, however; by August 12, Fairbanks had already received 3.42 inches of rainfall, when the usual average for the entire month is 2.20. Then in the six days before August 15, the entire Chena-Tanana river plain became saturated under a constant drizzle amounting to another six inches. For the semiarid interior, a summer flood is highly unusual (the last serious one to hit Fairbanks was in 1937), while spring flooding, as a result of melting snow and ice, is more common, especially for small villages perched on the edges of river banks. At this time of year the Chena has occasionally crested to twelve feet in the Fairbanks area—causing slight flooding along the river bed itself.

By August 13, Fairbanks residents were becoming annoyed at so much rainy weather and at the dampening effect it had on crowds at their Centennial Park. Fishermen were also losing patience over the swollen streams; tourists and residents were going downtown just to gape at the angry, swollen Chena. First reports were coming in of the total flooding of the town of Nenana, about thirty miles to the southwest, but still no one in

Fairbanks was overly concerned about a possible flood. River advisories were predicting that the Chena might crest at fifteen feet by midnight Monday, more rain was forecast, and people in outlying lower areas began evacuating their homes. On Monday, August 14, Civil Defense officials became alarmed and, with the help of the Red Cross, started preparations for evacuation centers. The river was rapidly rising at a rate of six inches an hour, and parts of the city and the Centennial site (on a bend of the river) were already several feet underwater.

Even then, most residents remained unconcerned—those who could see water creeping up their streets or into their basements felt this was happening to them because they were in low-lying areas. Besides, the river would be cresting at the predicted fifteen feet soon and then would retreat in the normal pattern. The Chena did reach fifteen feet as predicted but at 4:30 Monday afternoon, and then the water continued to rise. By 9:00 that night, the level reached sixteen feet, and Governor Hickel declared Fairbanks a disaster area. By 1 A.M., the water had risen to 17.8 feet and was pouring down most of the streets in the city. By 10 A.M. on Tuesday, the level hit 18.8, an unheard-of high for the Chena, and 95 per cent of the homes and businesses were inundated: in many areas the water reached the tops of first-floor windows. While residents had first casually watched the water creep up their streets, many now were trapped in their homes by raging torrents rising around the houses at first-floor level. The force of the water eroded away streets and caved in basements. Cars were now useless (at the height of the flood, most were totally covered); wading, in many areas, became impossible. So there was no escape, except by boat or helicopter. Also, because the water had come so quickly, few people had had time to rescue belongings from the lower levels of homes or to collect any food or clothing to take away with them.

Fortunately for the trapped Fairbanks residents, over fifty boats began rescue operations, along with nine helicopters from nearby Eielson Air Force Base and several more belonging to a local private company. While the boat owners and private 'copter pilots worked around the clock for the next thirty-six hours, not taking the time to count the people they rescued or the number of trips they made, official Air Force records show their nine helicopters alone flew 593 sorties, picking up 1436 people. Boat travel down the deeply flooded streets was hazardous, with some capsizing in the swift currents and others running aground on flooded cars or other obstacles. One young boat operator, ferrying three children and four adults, hit a submerged parking meter and tore a gaping hole in the bottom of his craft. Expecting to sink on the spot, he gave the engine full power and crashed into the side of the police station. The boat sank, but the passengers were thrown onto the roof of a nearby car and were quickly rescued.

Seven thousand of the evacués were taken to the high ground of the University of Alaska, three thousand found temporary refuge at relatively dry Lathrop High School, four thousand were taken directly to the airport (which miraculously stayed dry) to be flown out to Anchorage and Seattle, and another four thousand found their way to the houses of the fortunate few living on hills outside of town. Friends of ours, Kathy and Merrill Wien, had just built a home high on a ridge, a twenty-minute drive from the center of town. We had stayed with them when we attended the Centennial opening in May, using a downstairs playroom for a guest room. Upstairs they have three small bedrooms for themselves and two young children. I am sure that we crowded them slightly over that weekend, but it didn't matter because we are all close friends and the visit was most informal. With the evacuation of Fairbanks two months later, Kathy and Merrill took forty people into their home, and their stay was not just for a weekend but in most cases close to two weeks! We tried to figure out just where everyone slept, but then decided it was simply a question of using every available inch of floor space.

To compound the situation, there was no electricity or running water at the Wien home, and the women were forced to cook all meals over two small camp stoves. To make matters even tougher, Kathy had to take complete charge because Merrill, who is a senior pilot for Wien Consolidated Airlines, was away flying a helicopter during all of the emergency. Merrill's brother Richard and his wife Sally, living next door on the hillside, took in an equal number of refugees, and the situation was virtually the same for those other families fortunate enough to live on high ground out of the city. Other friends of ours, Bishop and Mrs.

William Gordon, took twelve people into their small home, one of the few in the downtown area which remained dry on the first-floor level. Of those twelve refugees, four were teen-age boy friends of their attractive young daughter—they just happened to be in the vicinity when the waters surged down the streets.

By Tuesday night the space problem at Lathrop High School had become acute. Fortunately, many of the evacués had brought some form of bedding, even if just a thin blanket. But others who had been plucked from roof tops by helicopter arrived with just the clothes on their backs, and these were wet. In the beginning, family groups took over corners of the rooms, but they were soon full, and the overflow began to bed down in the corridors. The floors became wet and muddy—such a mess that one woman was heard to say, "I'll never ask for anything in my life again but clear skies and sunny weather!"[3]

Adding to the crowded, chaotic conditions at the school were a large number of pets: dogs and cats which families simply could not bear to leave behind. Although no one ever complained and not a harsh word was spoken, it was obvious from some of the stories that the animals felt differently, that dog and cat fights were common, complete with plenty of loud barking. While the pets argued, the people all pitched in to make the most of a tough situation. Two tourists on vacation were among the evacués—neither had laid eyes on the other before, but both happened to be former army cooks—just what was needed to start up a kitchen! And the Red Cross and Salvation Army (both organizations did a wonderful job throughout the emergency), with the aid of army trucks and helicopters, supplied helpers, food, and clothing for the refugees.

Because of extremely difficult conditions, the high school itself was evacuated after forty-eight hours; all of the people there were either transferred to the university or flown out to Anchorage or Seattle. When the flood waters first started to rise, university officials counted the number of available beds in their facilities—there were three hundred. By Tuesday night the high-and-dry campus was home to seven thousand refugees. Beds were not important; blankets brought by the military were handed out,

[3] *Daily News Miner,* Fairbanks, Alaska, September 14, 1967.

and people were assigned to classrooms, laboratories, recreation rooms, and faculty homes. Feeding so many was a mammoth undertaking—all the emergency relief agencies helped supply the food, and the quantities were staggering: for one day, 1000 loaves of bread, 900 dozen eggs, 1200 cooked hams, 2500 pounds of flour, and 5000 cans of milk! Refugee volunteers helped to fix and serve the meals, as many as 15,000 a day, beginning at 6 A.M. and continuing to midnight without a break. More volunteers organized other services: an infirmary was established by nurses and doctors (many people had upper-respiratory infections after wading through the cold water and standing about in wet clothing), a recreation program for children was organized in the gym, and a kennel, staffed by a refugee veterinarian, was set up for the one hundred some odd evacué dogs. Someone even began publishing a mimeographed daily newspaper. At first it was called the *High Water News,* later changed to the (*Lower*) *High Water News,* and finally the (*Even Lower*) *High Water News.*

While the university was able to take in one third of the population of Fairbanks, because of the widespread flooding there was no other place to handle large groups of refugees, and so many thousands had to be flown out by National Guard planes and the regular airlines. Stranded tourists were taken directly to Seattle, as well as mothers and children who wished to join relatives "outside." But most of the women and children, over seven thousand altogether, were flown to Anchorage, to stay in homes here until flood waters receded. With only a few hours' notice, our local churches, the Red Cross, and the city government set up a system of meeting planes, cataloguing refugees, finding homes, and providing transportation and clothing. The efficiency of these volunteers was astonishing, and the wholehearted response of the Anchorage population was also tremendous. Most of the residents offered to take people—in fact more homes were available than were needed.

We had just returned from a vacation trip to the East coast and were debating how best to get word (the phone system had broken down when underground lines had become flooded) to Fairbanks friends that we had plenty of room available when three families of twelve people were brought to our door by a local Methodist minister. It was one o'clock in the morning and they were total strangers, but it was obvious that they had been through a frightening ordeal and were coming with nothing but the clothes on their backs (most of the children were barefoot). As we took them in and found blankets and sleeping bags for everyone, I couldn't help but think back on the night after our earthquake, just three years before, when the children and I were given shelter in the same way.

The following ten days were a bit hectic in our household, and yet in many ways the experience was the most rewarding and enriching we have ever known. When we took stock of the situation the next morning, it was obvious that we would first have to send out appeals for clothing for the three mothers and all nine children. Before that day was over, our front hall was jammed with boxes of clothes—far more than our three families could use. The next step was a trip to the grocery store: Shopping for sixteen was a new experience for me. Then we tried to create some order out of chaos within the house—while we have only three bedrooms, three couches in our study and Lowell's office can become beds. So we located Shirley DeVries and two children in the study, her sister Ida Burud and her three in the office, and Mary Lou Hollett and her four on sleeping bags in the downstairs playroom. Games, comic books, and a TV set were judiciously placed in the living room, and the six boys (all between eight and ten) virtually lived there, while the four girls closeted themselves in our Anne's room to giggle and chatter as though this were just another social visit. Ida Burud's youngest was not yet a year old and spent most of her time in a crib which we were able to borrow from a friend. Unfortunately, it rained for most of the ten days, so the children were unable to play out-of-doors. Considering this inability to let off steam, everyone was remarkably well behaved—there were no broken heirlooms or crayoned walls, but all the cats did retreat to shelves high above the reach of eager little hands!

The crowd at mealtimes certainly couldn't compare to that at the Wiens, but we did eat in two shifts; the eleven children first, and then Lowell and his four women. Housework was never so easy—all three mothers wanted to pitch in and help: They were not used to being idle, and the busier they were, the less time there was to worry. One can become inured to stories of tragedy in newspapers, but if the events are recounted to you by an individual, that is an entirely different matter. Our three families had lived in the most flooded area of all; water was pouring down their streets when they realized they should flee, but by then it was too late. When Shirley last checked her basement, it was totally flooded, and they heard a loud roar, probably a wall caving in. They then all joined forces in one home, and as the water rose to window level, they climbed out onto a flat roof. The only moment of real panic came when two helicopters passed them by. One person crawled back down to a bedroom and found several bright yellow raincoats to wave. This must have helped, because they were all soon being hauled aboard the large army helicopters via baskets and slings. They were among the group taken to the high school, and at that point it was decided that the women and children should go to Anchorage while the husbands remained behind in order to enter the houses the moment the water retreated.

For several days all attention was focused on the drama of the rescue, but then thoughts began to turn to what would be found once the flood waters receded. Two of our three families knew that the water had reached ceiling level in the first floors of their homes. This meant the end of all appliances, pianos, and books, and most furniture, drapes, and rugs. And as the days went by while the waters receded with agonizing slowness, the women began to think more about the huge cleaning task ahead. When dirty, oily water fills your home for five days, everything is going to be in a pretty messy state. All of Fairbanks faced a gigantic clean-up operation of almost insurmountable proportions. The city officials were concerned primarily with restoring electricity, water, sewers, and telephones, carting off debris, and repairing roads and the damaged schools, which were scheduled to open in less than three weeks. All downtown stores had been badly flooded, destroying or damaging merchandise. Large sales and auctions were the immediate order of business, and buyers flocked down streets closed to cars, while soggy merchandise lined the sidewalks. Buying was brisk; at least some of the items weren't as waterlogged as belongings back home.

Once the flood waters had receded and our refugee families

had returned to face mop-up operations, Lowell decided to see for himself how everyone was doing and also attend a briefing session set up by our governor. (The legislature was later called into special session to tackle some of the financial problems caused by the flood.) While other legislators were planning to stay with friends or in some of the few hotel rooms emerging unscathed, Lowell decided to fly up in "Charlie," take a tent, and camp out. He felt that he simply could not impose on families like the Wiens after what they had just been through. At first he thought he would camp in the hills south of Fairbanks, then fly in before the morning meeting. He ran out of time, however, and landed instead just before sunset at the small light-plane field west of town. He parked "Charlie" in the most distant corner of the strip and set up the tent beneath one wing, feeling most thankful that because it was late in the day, no one was around. Camping may be a popular pastime in Alaska but not usually at an airport right next to a city!

After hastily cooking a light meal and enjoying a good night's sleep (not worrying about bears or a noisy party in the next room), Lowell then decided that it simply would not do for a state senator to appear at a briefing looking the way he did. While he was thinking about shaving and getting out of his oldest camp clothes and boots, an official-looking car roared down the airstrip, stopped, and two uniformed Fish and Game men came toward him, with highly puzzled expressions. Lowell hastened to assure them that he was not about to do any poaching (duck season was just over), that he was Senator Thomas, in Fairbanks to attend the governor's briefing. Now the men were more puzzled than ever—state senators just didn't dress like that or sleep in tents beside runways. They don't know my husband. They reluctantly accepted the story, and after he'd cleaned up a bit, even drove him to the meeting. (Maybe this was to make doubly sure he was telling the truth!) Lowell faced one more embarrassing moment at the briefing—before the proceedings began, the governor asked him where he was staying. My honest husband mumbled, "at the airport," hoping the governor would forget that there was no such thing as a hotel in that vicinity. Fortunately, Mr. Hickel had far more on his mind than Lowell's accommodations, or lack thereof.

Once the briefing was over, Lowell spent a few hours wandering about town, checking up on friends and seeing for himself just how things were progressing. He came home in a much subdued mood that night, truly appalled at the frightful mess left by the flood. The actual damage to basements, streets, and utilities was bad enough, but he was especially shocked by the scenes he saw in front of almost every home in Fairbanks—soggy, stained couches, chairs, and cushions spread all over the lawns to dry out; chairs, tables, bureaus, and other wood furniture piled high on the driveways, hopelessly warped beyond repair; piles of dirty, wet clothing laid or hung out wherever there was space; tragically large trash piles of books, photo albums, and family records; and on every roof wall-to-wall carpeting and rugs spread to dry. (Jim Binkley had hung a pair of pants from his chimney—a touch of defiant humor in the midst of a pathetic situation.)

Floods have hit and will continue to plague areas in all parts of the United States, but seldom has an entire city of nineteen thousand people been so totally affected. And aside from the staggering personal and financial losses, the people were faced with a gigantic recovery effort which had to be completed within a few weeks' time—the Fairbanks winter was about to descend. The interior is usually hit with hard frosts by Labor Day, and snow covers the ground before mid-September. (Fortunately, the fall of 1967 was exceptionally mild, dry, and long, co-operating with a hard-working, determined people, so that most major repairs were completed before the onset of cold weather.)

In other, happier summers, we have flown to Fairbanks and then have followed the usually more quiescent Chena and Tanana rivers westward or the Steese Highway northeastward to the largest river in Alaska, the Yukon. The juncture of the Chena and the Tanana is just a short hop in "Charlie," compared to the leisurely travel of Jim Binkley's riverboat, and the broad Tanana, with its numerous "ready-made landing-strip" sand bars is a delight to follow. In the summertime, after flying over miles of jagged mountains, rough tundra, and timber-covered hills in a single-engine plane, a big river is always a welcome sight. It is fun, also, to watch for the small settlements all along the route, but one must look carefully because these Athabaskan Indian villages consist of a small cluster of log buildings and that's all. They all have airstrips (aside from the river, the one means of reaching the outside world), but most are simply short, bumpy runways of dirt and grass. A few of the larger villages have paved strips and a semblance of a main street.

Nenana, the first river village west of Fairbanks, is different in that it is also on the railroad route from Fairbanks to Seward, and so is a good-sized town, an important transshipment point for goods from the rails to the water. In Alaska, Nenana is best known for its annual ice classic—each spring people all over the state make guesses as to when the river ice will break up. Tickets are bought, and the pool usually contains many thousands of dollars. The contest was started forty years ago and is big business for the town of Nenana. Excitement runs high each April and May as thousands of Alaskans begin debating over the thickness of the river ice. An elaborate timing device, attached by wires to a tripod in mid-river and carefully watched by a round-the-clock guard, tells the exact second that the ice lets go.

From Nenana, the Tanana River meanders north and then west to where it joins the mighty Yukon. In the early days, when river navigation was vital to interior communities, this juncture was an important link in the system—sometimes called the "Hub of Alaska" during the gold-rush period. An Indian settlement has existed there for longer than anyone really knows. Later, the U. S. Army built Fort Gibbon, a military post and telegraph office at the junction, because of the strategic importance of the area, and with the coming of mining and trading, the "outsider's" village of Tanana began to grow alongside the fort.

However, unlike most nonnative settlements in the interior, Tanana did not depend upon an adjacent mining camp but rather owed its existence to Fort Gibbon. The two settlements sat side by side with only a fence in between, the postal authorities of the little town refusing to be called Fort Gibbon, while the fort was just as stubborn about taking on the name Fort Tanana. As a result, letters addressed to Fort Gibbon were usually lost, and telegrams sent to Tanana were refused. But regardless of the animosity between them, the town was necessary to the post for two reasons: whisky and wood! Most of the buildings of Tanana were saloons, and civilian employees of the post chopped approximately three thousand cords of wood a year.

Since those rowdy earlier days, Tanana has reverted to a quiet village (115 voters in 1966), the families, mostly Indians, largely dependent on fur trapping and catching fish in the river. While I have been there for only a brief visit, I was most impressed with the beauty of the natural surroundings—the wide river and the spruce forests on all sides. We walked down the dirt road running from the airstrip along the river, past the log homes, a Public Health Service hospital, the Episcopal church, the store, and the post office. It was a hot and dusty July day, and the water looked most inviting. A few villagers were racing about in outboard motor boats, but this was the only sign of life other than a couple of women working in healthy-looking vegetable gardens. Everyone else was either staying indoors to escape the heat or off at nearby fish camps, working on the all-important summer catch.

We have often flown "Charlie" on west from Tanana, along the Yukon toward the arctic coast, but the story of our arctic travels belongs in the next chapter, and instead I will turn eastward, toward other interior villages we have visited from time to time. While one can only reach most such places with little planes like "Charlie," the Steese Highway, running northeast from Fairbanks, does take the road-bound tourist a bit more into the interior, ending at the famous old mining town of Circle, on the Yukon River. This small settlement of about one hundred people now has the distinction of being the most northerly point reached by highway on the North American continent. Gold was first discovered in many of the streams of this area in 1893, and a camp was established on the banks of the Yukon where steamers could most easily land supplies. The miners named the village, soon to be the largest log-cabin town in the world, Circle, thinking that it sat squarely on the Arctic Circle. Actually, the town is a few miles to the south of the circle.

Another settlement farther down the Steese Highway is called Circle Hot Springs, and it, too, is south of the Arctic Circle. It is neither a mining town nor a native village but a "hot springs resort," and before anyone conjures up a picture of Warm Springs, Georgia, or White Sulphur Springs, West Virginia, and their elegant facilities, let me hastily add that the word "resort" has a little different meaning in this case. There is an airstrip of sorts and a motel of similar caliber. At the time we stopped in for the night, we were longing for some swimming, and we were intrigued by the idea of hot water springs so close to the Arctic Circle. The water was warm (about 140 degrees), and there was lots of it (over three hundred gallons a minute gushing from the ground), piped into two big pools, one indoors and one outside. But swimming in an oversized, steaming bathtub lost its novelty in a very short time, especially when the water was a murky green. For us, the most interesting part of Circle Hot Springs was the large, luxuriant gardens. To counteract the short growing season, pipes carrying the warm water crisscross beneath the normally cold ground, and the vegetables being grown were the largest we have ever seen.

We have also admired vegetable gardens at Fort Yukon, a large Indian village right on the Arctic Circle and on a great bend in the Yukon River. This town—the first interior Alaskan settlement by English-speaking people—was established in 1847 by Alexander Murray, a trader for Hudson's Bay Company. Gold was discovered in the surrounding area in the 1850s, but the town's main interest has always been trapping. It is the trading and transport center for over sixty thousand square miles of northeastern Alaska. We were intrigued by the great number of pelts hanging in the Northern Commercial Company Trading Post—ermine, mink, fox, lynx, beaver, and wolf furs. (The value of furs harvested in Alaska is about four and a half million dollars a year.) We were also most impressed with the beautiful beadwork done by the Fort Yukon women, especially the exquisite pieces we saw in the St. Stephen's Mission building. The altar frontal was made by the ladies of the village in 1917, in honor of the World War I dead, and it remains in perfect condition today.

This settlement was also the first site of English-speaking church work in Alaska. Church of England missionaries reached the area from Canada just after the building of the trading post. In 1862, Archdeacon Robert McDonald, a Scotsman who spent fifty years working among Yukon Indians, went to live at Fort Yukon. He translated the Bible, *Hymnal,* and *Book of Common Prayer* into the Tukudh dialect of the Athabascan Indians. When

American Episcopal Bishop Peter Trimble Rowe came to the town in 1896, he found that Christianity was well entrenched, and since that time the Fort Yukon area has played a major role in the Episcopal Church's work in the Alaskan interior.

We have enjoyed our summer visits to this town, when the temperature is hot (it has been known to reach 100 degrees); the broad river looks like a lazy section of the Mississippi, the fish wheels turn continually, scooping up salmon which have already swum twelve hundred miles upriver, and the villagers sit out-of-doors basking in the warm sun. But seeing Fort Yukon in mid-winter was an experience I will never forget. In fact, flying "Charlie" over the Alaskan interior to get to Fort Yukon in mid-January was one of the most memorable of all our journeys.

After our "practice survival camp out" on the lake near Tal-keetna, we were ready (at least Lowell was) to tackle a long winter flight, but despite all our careful planning, we almost never made it off the ground. We had set our take-off for eleven in the morning, allowing ample time for the winter flight preparations, which are such a nuisance that a lot of pilots put their planes to bed between fall and spring. First the engine has to be warmed up with a special heater, and frequently one has to join a waiting line for this service. Then all wing and tail surfaces must be carefully brushed off to get rid of any ice or snow—a tedious chore when there is a wind and the temperature is below zero. Finally, the plane must be carefully loaded with all the gear, including ample emergency equipment, hopefully leaving enough room for the children; and just before take-off, Lowell makes one last check with the weather office and files a flight plan.

Lowell was finally ready for his passengers at noon, and by then our beautiful clear sky was suddenly being filled with omi-nous black clouds moving in from the sea. As we sped to the airport, the visibility was decreasing rapidly and it looked like it would snow at any moment. We squeezed into the plane, man-aged to close the doors just as the first snowflakes were falling, and then to climax an already frantic situation, the engine refused to start. Lowell exploded out of the airplane, rushing off to bor-row the heater again, while I almost collapsed, keeping one eye on those black clouds. The children went right to sleep. At 1 P.M. the engine finally roared to life, and we were moving, our skis

clattering on the smooth snow and ice. After taking off and crossing Cook Inlet, heading due north, I looked back, and Anchorage
was already disappearing behind the snowstorm.

While we were now in the clear weatherwise, it was going to
take us two hours to reach Fairbanks, our immediate destination,
and the sun would undoubtedly set first. The timing was close
and reminded me exactly of that day over six years ago when
we were so late in taking off from Tehran but determined to go
anyway. At that time darkness caught us, the airfield at our
destination of Meshed had no lights, and we had to land over the
headlights of the American consul's jeep. But we were a few years
wiser now—we knew Fairbanks had a large, well-lighted airport,
if we could just get through the mountain pass before darkness came. As usual, the flight past Mount McKinley was spectacular, but this time the dazzling snow of the many peaks was
a deep pink color. The sun was setting directly behind "Mighty
Mack," and it threw a shadow into the sky to our right. We knew
then that we were ahead of nightfall, so we relaxed and enjoyed
the beauty of the scene.

From Fairbanks we had originally planned to fly on to Kotzebue,
but at this time of the year if one wants to go anywhere, flexi-
bility is the rule, and when the weather bureau reported snow-
storms all along the arctic coast, we decided instead to fly on
north to Bettles. This Indian village lies at the foothills of the
beautiful Brooks mountain range, and we had especially enjoyed
visiting it during our Alaskan travels in the summer of 1958.
During the usual lengthy take-off preparations, the children and
I waited in the airport terminal, growing hotter every minute in
our mukluks and fur parkas. At one point a Pan American jet
from Seattle landed, the passengers streaming into the waiting
room in far more conventional travel clothing. From the way they
stared at us, I gathered we were providing most with their first
look at Alaska. Fortunately, Lowell rescued us before we had to
prove whether or not we could speak English, and we were off
the ground that day by 11:30.

As we flew on north, over the low mountains behind Fairbanks, I started one of my favorite pastimes when flying in a
single-engine plane—looking for places where we could land if
necessary. This is a comforting game which almost continuously

supplies me with at least one emergency landing site. That day, over those brown, rocky mountains (there was almost unusual lack of snow) and narrow, forested valleys, I couldn't find a single small clearing; no lakes or rivers—only tiny, threadlike meandering streams—, and the one road going north eighty-one miles to Livingood seemed just as narrow and winding. To make matters worse, the engine was running rougher than normal, a condition which was giving me gray hairs, but Lowell had calmly attributed it to the cold winter air. I was still searching desperately for places to land when I suddenly noted what looked like a great white ocean just up ahead. Little tentacles of that dreaded ice fog were already covering the ground beneath us when Lowell switched on his radio and called Bettles. "What is your latest weather?" he asked. "Light snow and fog banks at all quadrants," was the reply. We immediately turned back, but the thought of having to return to Fairbanks after all those hours spent getting ready to take off was most disheartening. "We might just as well head straight for home," Lowell said, disgusted. He tuned into a weather broadcast, took a look at his map, then brightened considerably. "Why not head northeast for Fort Yukon?" was his highly welcome suggestion.

So "Charlie" headed north again, over the Beaver Creek river valley—the terrain around us quickly changing appearance now to a wild, rugged winter landscape. The valley beneath us, bisected by the river and dotted with small lakes, was completely covered with snow. The now-scarce trees and bushes were hidden beneath their coating of white. The mountains on either side were higher: treeless, precipitous, rock- and snow-covered slopes. The wilderness of the Yukon again—the same general region we had flown over in 1958 and which we thought Robert Service so aptly described as the cussedest land he knew:

> From the big, dizzy mountains that screen it
> to the deep, deathlike valleys below . . .

I was now feeling the same awe and admiration that I had felt before, but something new was added—I had never felt so alone in my entire life. "Charlie" was a tiny dot over all that snowy emptiness. Loneliness was never shattered so dramatically—at just that moment in my reverie I nearly jumped to the ceiling, seat belt not withstanding: A red and silver jet swooshed across our path a bare mile away. "A fighter," I yelled, but Lowell, who had been looking at the map, merely said, "Impossible," and went back to his navigating. He had just changed our flight plan and was computing the distance to Fort Yukon. I was beginning to relax again when the jet came back, this time close enough to see his markings, and Lowell saw him, too: a delta-wing F102 supersonic fighter. We decided he was patrolling the border— Canada was less than fifty miles away. We learned later, when we checked in with the FAA man at Fort Yukon, that due to our sudden change of flight plan, radar in that area considered us an "unknown."

The broad, flat Yukon valley was a welcome sight that day, the three-mile-wide river now a frozen sheet of ice, which bush pilots had used for a landing area in earlier days. We chose the large airfield to the north of town. I use the word "town" loosely because all we could see was a group of log houses seemingly huddled together, half-hidden by the snow. The temperature was minus 30 degrees when we got out of the plane (we were lucky —it can and frequently does dip to minus 60 degrees), our breath turned to white clouds in the frigid air, and our boots crunched and squeaked on the hard-packed snow. The air was absolutely still, the sky was blue, the sun just peeking over the horizon, totally devoid of any warmth.

As we walked down into the village, the log homes were half-buried in snowdrifts, thick curls of white smoke coming from the chimneys. There were no other signs of life, except for a few sled dogs curled into furry balls behind some of the houses and an occasional large and noisy blackbird—"bull-bulls" we heard them called. How such a bird can survive the arctic winter is beyond me. A further sign that winter there was indeed long and cold were the woodpiles beside each home—the highest and longest I had ever seen. A resident told us later that wood was stacked by the 100-cord. Central heating in all homes at Fort Yukon consisted of one potbellied central stove. The large oil-drum heater in the center of the living room of the small hotel where we stayed put out an amazing amount of heat—enough to keep us perfectly warm, even in the bedrooms on the floor above.

Any story on interior Alaska should logically conclude there at Fort Yukon, on the mighty river, but this particular journey ended with a family experience which I must recount, even though Lowell is likely to censor it before it leaves the house! From Fort Yukon, we followed the river on toward the southeast, over country which was the center of much feverish prospecting during the early gold-rush days. South of Circle, we flew over Woodchopper, Sam Creek, Millers Camp, and then Eagle, which is where the Yukon River crosses into Canadian Yukon territory. From the village of Eagle we followed the Taylor Highway south over Bonanza Bar and the Fortymile River, one of the most famous of all names in gold-rush stories. We would liked to have spent more time in this eastern interior region because it played such a big part in the early prospecting days, but we had to think of heading home. We were still a full day's flight from Anchorage, and so we decided to spend the night at Northway, a small settlement which is the first stop for planes and cars en route from Canada to Alaska.

It was then that Lowell decided it would be fun to camp out again, on a lake just south of the airport. I could agree only halfheartedly because after our four-day winter odyssey I had begun to run out of bravado. It didn't take me long to run out completely. We made a smooth landing on a small lake but quickly discovered it was covered with deep snow. It was a little difficult for us to maneuver about, but after an initial bit of floundering-for-fun, the kids (still under six at that time) were reduced to tears. Amidst the wails (and my complaining), we heard the sound of an engine, and much to our amazement an army helicopter, coming out of nowhere, settled down beside "Charlie!" A young lieutenant hopped out and came running over to tell us that a bad snowstorm was just about to move in on the area. We didn't bother to ask how they knew we were there or to get any further details. (I should say "I," for Lowell was highly disgruntled by the military invasion of our privacy and by being told what to do.) I did not give him a chance to object, however; while the 'copter was still hovering nearby, I shoved the kids into the plane, threw in some of the items we had already unloaded, and then hopped in myself. Poor Lowell had no choice, especially with our "military escort" standing by.

As soon as we had taken off, dark clouds crept in over the lake, and the snow squall was right on our heels all the way back to Northway. This obvious fact did not help Lowell's disposition at all, however, and he was furious when a young major greeted us with, "I'm sure glad we were able to rescue you." In fact, my husband was so mad that instead of sleeping at the warm and comfortable motel that night, he walked off into the woods beyond the runway and, in a grand gesture of defiance, pitched his tent in the midst of the snowstorm. I never dared ask him if he had a good night's sleep!

VI

Eskimos Don't Live in Igloos Either

We took off on our first family flight to the arctic coast in late July of 1962. The four of us were most excited: While David, at five, was simply happy to be going on a trip, seven-year-old Anne had already heard stories about Eskimos, igloos, and walrus hunting. We just hoped that she would not be too disappointed. We also knew little about these natives of the Far North, and we were aware that great misconceptions (even among Alaskan residents) existed.

The twenty-seven thousand Alaskan Eskimos are in many ways a most unique people—only by becoming ingenious masters of their environment have they been able to survive for centuries in one of the harshest climatic regions of the world. Now, facing the impact of twentieth-century technology, Eskimo ways are changing rapidly. While most of the people still live in their small arctic settlements, many, especially the new generation, have left home for the bigger towns and cities. And while most of those remaining in the villages continue to live on a hunting and fishing economy, an ever-larger number are also taking on jobs to obtain the cash needed for the modern conveniences of today.

The early-day sod homes, the fur clothing, the dog teams are now being abandoned during the change to modern ways. Even the art of igloo making is threatened with extinction! While Eskimos don't live in these often-depicted round houses made of blocks of ice and snow, over the centuries Eskimo hunters have built igloos for protection when out on overnight winter hunting trips. Now the young people are more interested in schooling and job trades than in igloo building. Juke boxes and the latest records have crowded out traditional dances, and candy and soda pop are more popular with the youngster than muktuk and oogruk meat.

There is an equally great misconception about the land of the Eskimos—the Alaskan arctic region of two hundred thousand square miles is not all flat, frozen wasteland. On the contrary, the Brooks mountain range, from fifty to one hundred miles in width, stretches east and west over six hundred miles from the coastline to the border. (It is the only major mountain system in all of North America which runs east and west.) The summits are only from four to six thousand feet high, with a few reaching nine thousand feet, but this is certainly far from flat land. The slopes in wintertime are gentle and deeply laden with snow, but as we flew over them during the short summer period, they looked like giant rock piles, bare of vegetation. And during all our flying in the region just south of the Brooks Range (no roads or railroads there), we were constantly aware of the many large, meandering rivers, their banks lined with trees, and countless lakes of all shapes and sizes. To the north of the mountains, the coastal plain is crisscrossed by a myriad of small streams, and during the summer months the tundra is covered with pools of melted snow—the water trapped by the permanent ice beneath the muskeg.

Our first flight to the Far North, to visit the large Eskimo villages of Unalakleet and Kotzebue and the historic town of Nome, began under most unarctic conditions. The temperature in Fairbanks and Tanana, where we stopped for gas, was 85 degrees. We found a beehive of activity at the Tanana field: Thirty-four forest fires in the Hughes area just to the north were keeping army helicopters and Bureau of Land Management personnel on the run. A perennial headache to the state but a source of lucrative employment for the native people, these fires are started by lightning from gigantic thunderstorms which we in Southcentral Alaska almost never experience. Along with snakes, moths, and gnats, thunder is something I don't miss!

After we had left the Yukon River behind and were flying over a short stretch of wooded hills between Kaltag and Unalakleet on the coast, we spotted our own forest fire, much to the great excitement of the children. Lowell immediately reported it to Unalakleet, and they asked us to take a closer look. We circled back and descended to one thousand feet. (If Lowell had been alone, he undoubtedly would have gone to two hundred!) The flames formed a perfect circle about one fourth of a mile wide, apparently just started by a nearby storm. The blaze was still confined to the tundra but was obviously heading for a grove of trees. Later we heard that a number of men from Unalakleet were flown out to fight this particular fire.

As we turned and headed back again for the coast, our first glimpse of the Bering Sea and Norton Sound was most exciting and a breathtakingly beautiful sight. The water was calm and a deep blue, the land beneath us was heavily forested, and along the sandy shore, on a sand bar by a river mouth, was Unalakleet. The Eskimo village looked very much like the larger Indian river communities from the air. A handful of little wooden houses lined the beach, and a number of boats were drawn up on the sand. The gravel airstrip paralleled the shore to the north of the village, and on a high hilltop behind sat a most incongruous, futuristic Air Force radar site and also a White Alice long-distance communications facility. The latter belongs to the Air Force, too, but is maintained and operated by the Radio Corporation of America. While I do not know too much about this elaborate communications setup, I am aware that all public and military long-distance phone calls in Alaska are handled by White Alice. We were most intrigued by the name and later learned that the letters in Alice stand for *A*laska *I*nterior *C*ommunications *E*lectronics. The White simply refers to the color of the scenery in the Far North during most of the year. (All the buildings are painted white for camouflage purposes.) Air Force personnel sign up for duty at the radar sites on the basis of a one-year "hardship post."

Despite the military "hardship" category, Unalakleet has long been considered a garden spot in the arctic. When the first missionaries arrived there in 1887 (of the Swedish Evangelical Covenant Church), they were most impressed with the fertile soil and started large vegetable and flower gardens which gained great renown in the Far North. Unalakleet was off the beaten track during the coastal gold stampede, however, and so has remained a quiet, sleepy little Eskimo village, one of the few in Alaska to decide to take on reservation status.

We enjoyed every moment of our two-day visit there, partly because we were blessed with hot, sunny weather, a rarity along the northwest coast. We stayed at the home of a Federal Aviation Agency family because the little local hotel was jammed with construction men working on state and federal projects (the usual occurrence in most of the larger villages during the few short summer months, when all such activity must take place). Our hosts, Mr. and Mrs. Don Baker, lived in the typical FAA neat white frame house seen all over Alaska, but theirs was perched right on the beach. All the while we were there, we found it very hard to remember that this was the Bering Sea coast and not a New England or even a Florida beach. Children were swarming all over the sand, barefoot and in shorts, so our two joined right in playing, beachcombing, even wading. The thermometer read 70 degrees, and the sun was hot.

I took time out to make use of the Bakers' washing machine, hanging the laundry out on their clothesline along the beach. As I walked on the warm brown sand in my bare feet, I kept pinching myself—it was almost impossible to believe we were on the arctic coast, with Siberia just over the horizon. When we wandered on down into the village itself, we found many sights similar to the Indian settlements of the interior. The plain, wood houses (not made of logs, however, but of weather-beaten gray siding) were all more or less the same size and shape. The usual teams of dogs were tied in back, curled up in holes in the sand, obviously suffering from the heat. The sleds were parked up on the roof tops (a very sensible place!), and racks laden with drying salmon were everywhere (so was the aroma). A large old tublike ship was tied up among the many smaller ones in the lagoon, and we were told that it served as a summer fish cannery: a common sight in many of these coastal villages during that season, bringing added income to the inhabitants. The fishing in this area is excellent—we tried our luck one morning, going upriver a short way, and bringing home some Dolly Varden trout for the Baker dinner table.

We knew that the weather there could be miserable, with chilly, driving rain in the summers and frigid, howling winds during the rest of the year, so we made a point of finding out as much as we could from the Bakers about how they coped with such an adverse climate. Father and mother and all four children didn't seem to feel the least bit handicapped—they thoroughly enjoyed every moment when they could be out-of-doors, and if housebound, their home was bursting with books, games, paint sets, victrola, radios, a Hammond organ, parakeets, and a big black cat. We first found out about Mrs. Baker's rather unusual hobby the day we arrived at their doorstep. As we entered the house, she called from upstairs: "Be down in a minute—I'm talking to Australia." Mr. Baker quickly explained that she was an ardent ham radio operator.

We left Unalakleet with some reluctance, yet at the same time most excited over what lay ahead. Our flight that day was due north along the coast and then directly west, following the southern shore of the Seward Peninsula, to Nome, one of the most historic of all Alaskan towns. Many of the geographical names along this northwest coast are of English origin, thanks to explorers Captain James Cook and Captain F. W. Beechey, and a few are strictly Eskimo, such as Unalakleet and Kivalina. The name of Nome, the most famous gold-rush town in Alaska, is a mixture of the two. The story goes that when the first whalers landed at that part of the Seward Peninsula and attempted to speak with the natives, they invariably heard the words "No-me" or "Ki-no-me." In Eskimo, they mean "No" or "I don't know." The visitors assumed "No-me" was the name of the area. Many of the gold miners used this word for their camp near Anvil Creek (it was also called Anvil City for a while), and it was quickly shortened to Nome.

Another story is told about the derivation of the name Nome, and the residents of that city apparently accept both, without choosing between them. An old English chart of this northwest coast placed opposite the present-day Cape Nome the word "Name": meaning that the cape was still unnamed. When this chart was later copied, the copyist misunderstood the meaning and wrote "Nome." The gold-mining town then took its name from Cape Nome.

Late in the fall of 1898, three prospectors found gold along Anvil Creek, and a short while later quantities of the magic mineral were found among the sands of the shore line there. Not only was this Seward Peninsula area much more accessible to American gold seekers than the Klondike, but also the gold was readily available on the beach and along the streams. So Nome became the goal of all prospectors at the turn of the century, and, in one way, this was a big "break" for Alaska. The gold fever kindled a tremendous revival of interest in all of Alaska's resources, eventually bringing new harbors, docks, roads, and railroads to help get the riches out. For the first time, also, Alaska was brought to the attention of millions of Americans—through gold-rush stories in newspapers, magazines, and books written by Jack London, Rex Beach, and others. And Nome and the Seward Peninsula brought new wealth to the nation. In 1899 alone almost three million dollars in gold was found there, and the total for all the years since comes to roughly 136 million dollars. Unfortunately, little of this bonanza ever remained in Alaska, par for the course in the state's long history of exploitation by "outside" interests.

Because the first news of gold found at Nome came in midwinter, boat travelers had to wait until spring, and the stampede began in the Alaskan interior. Discouraged and disillusioned miners from the Klondike and other northern mining areas made haste to reach Nome by the overland Yukon River route before the hordes from the lower states could descend in the spring. The first prospectors to arrive by boat were greeted by a most desolate sight. Nothing other than gold could have caused the building of a city on that spot. There was no harbor or roadstead, no shelter or protection of any kind. Yet Nome became the perfect example of how men of the North could conquer local conditions and bring comfort amid the bleakness and desolation of nature.

These early sea arrivals in 1899 also saw a few cabins made

from driftwood and several hundred tents. A snug little log house was the deputy recorder's office (the most important service there), and an adjoining tent of blue and white stripes housed the inevitable bar, of second-most importance. A restaurant, barber shop, and Alaska Commercial Company store made up the rest of the town, and within a few years, more stores, several churches, and a hospital were added.

By 1903 Nome was a bustling tent and log-cabin city of twenty thousand people—the buildings lining the beach for twenty miles. While the creeks were staked out first, gold was soon found on the sand along the ocean, and thousands of prospectors rushed out with buckets, shovels, and wheelbarrows. In two months they found over one million dollars in gold right at their doorsteps. Amidst such incredibly available wealth, racketeers had a field day, and Rex Beach's famous novel *The Spoilers* was one of the many stories written about those rip-roaring early days.

One such tale had a "good-guys-can-win" ending: When a party of newcomers asked about the best place to find gold, a couple of old-timers suggested they head for the top of a distant hill and sink a deep shaft. Every resident knew that the creeks and beaches were the only gold-bearing areas, and all were thoroughly enjoying this particular prank. The "Cheechako" party, the laughingstock of Nome, did head for the hills, sank shafts, hit pay dirt, and in one year took out 750 thousand dollars' worth of gold.[1]

Once the surface supply of gold had been exhausted, a number of larger mining companies moved in with heavy equipment to dig underground. However, even these large-scale operations declined, along with the others elsewhere in Alaska, and virtually came to an end in 1934, when the gold value of the dollar was lowered considerably and the United States officially went off the gold standard. Fortunately for tourists, there are still a few dredges operating in Nome and one can find an occasional nugget in the streams nearby.

The Nome of today, with its population now of just a few thousand, still retains much of this early gold-rush atmosphere, and so is quite different from the Eskimo towns of Unalakleet, Kotzebue, and Barrow (although 70 per cent of the present resi-

[1] *The Alaska Travel Guide,* 1967 edition, published by Lake Advertising Agency, Salt Lake City, Utah, p. 285.

dents of Nome are Eskimo). As we circled the large airfield
(which was used to deliver airplanes to the Russians during
World War II) in "Charlie" that sunny July day, we found the
town much larger than we had expected, and we were most excited by our first glimpses of that famous beach. Once on the
ground we again found a place to stay right on the seashore—a
rather rickety run-down hotel (which later burned down). We
could have gone to a much more modern one farther down the
street, where the summer tourists were put up, but this was just
what we wanted to avoid!

Mr. and Mrs. Paul Mandeville, owners of the place we chose,
were a most cordial young couple, and we were invited into their
family quarters—sunny rooms with large windows overlooking the
sea. Their two young boys took our kids in tow, and once again
they all headed for the beach. The weather continued warm and
sunny (I gather Bering Sea coast residents are still talking about
that summer), with not a cloud in the sky. Some of the Eskimo
children were actually in swimming (to be more accurate, playing
in the water, because no Eskimo knows how to swim—where and
when could they learn?). Of course, ours wanted to go in, too, but
after feeling the frigid water, we decided wading would be
enough.

We had to spend a little time on that beach ourselves—who
could help but want to look for signs of gold there. And we scrambled over the giant granite boulders which form a three-thousand-
foot sea wall along the front of the town. We were told that during
storms the angry Bering Sea sends huge waves crashing into them,
the spray splattering the windows of the nearest buildings. What
a feat it must have been to land thousands of men and tons of
supplies right on that beach: The large ships anchored farther
out, while small boats braved the surf, some unsuccessfully. Early
Nome stories are full of accounts of men arriving soaking wet,
having lost everything they owned beneath a big wave. (Today
the summer supply ships use a big dock, but the operation is
almost as hazardous as before.)

When we could finally tear ourselves away from the waterfront,
we wandered down the main street of town, dropping in on a few
of the storekeepers who had been there since the very early days.
A brand new school was quite a contrast to the older, weather-

beaten buildings. Construction in this arctic region is fraught with problems, and the school is an example of the newer attempts to thwart Mother Nature. Permafrost is the big headache—the permanently frozen ground will melt unevenly when warmly heated buildings are placed on top of it. Of course, this results in cracked foundations and crooked houses. When constructing the school, the builders decided to try a "refrigerated" basement. It solved the problem but at a terrible expense. Now northwest builders are experimenting with refrigerated concrete pilings—houses on cooled stilts!

Our final visit was to the newspaper office, run at that time by a pioneer woman, the late Emily Boucher. (*The Nome Nugget* is the oldest Alaskan newspaper still being published.) She asked us to dinner (delicious reindeer steaks) at her home that night, an invitation we were delighted to accept, partly because it would give us a good chance to learn more about Nome and its colorful past. I learned, too, not to wear high heels while walking down the city sidewalks—those walkways are made of wood slats, the better to shift with the heaving permafrost, and heels inevitably catch in every gap. By the time we reached Emily's home, I was carrying my shoes, much to the delight of children playing nearby, and to the mortification of our own.

The Boucher family home was one of the oldest in town, built as a saloon in 1902, complete with a three-story Victorian façade. Emily's father bought it and converted it to a home in 1904. While these dates are not old for New England or other states with early histories, a building of 1902 vintage is a rarity in Alaska. The antique woodwork, the Victorian furniture, and stained-glass windows all blended together to enfold us in a most mellow, homey atmosphere.

We would have liked to stay longer in Nome and to get out into the surrounding countryside by riding the Wild Goose Railroad, which used to run eighty-five miles to gold mines near Anvil Mountain, passing Rex Beach's cabin on the way. But we had to move on in typical hurried tourist fashion (only most of Nome's summer visitors spend a half day there as part of a guided tour to the northern towns). However, we had long been looking forward to this next leg of our flight to Kotzebue, because it would take us along the westernmost tip of Alaska. If the day was clear, we would see the Russian island of Diomede barely thirty-three miles off our coastline. In the early days, Siberian and Alaskan natives frequently traveled back and forth over this short stretch of water. But now all that easy exchange is over, and instead, our Air Defense Command worries constantly over our light planes (usually out polar-bear hunting) straying into Russian territory. It can be the other way around, too—there have been numerous incidents of Russian planes along our coastline, and in fact, while in Nome we heard that four different local small planes had been buzzed by Russian jets during that past month alone. This was an experience I could do without—it had been frightening enough to be buzzed by our own fighters near Fort Yukon.

So it was with mixed feelings on my part that we were forced to change our flight plan at the last minute that day, due to bad weather along the coast. Our route now lay directly north across the Seward Peninsula, over wild mountainous terrain which many experts believe has one of the richest concentrations of minerals in Alaska. There may be vast quantities of tungsten, tin, iron ore, and copper there, but the area is so inaccessible that little has been done in the way of any large-scale mining yet. This inaccessibility factor is certainly understandable when one flies low over the peninsula—we have seen much rough terrain from "Charlie" but seldom any that can match this land. Some of the area was such a jumbled mass of mountainous rock and scree that I'm sure we could just as easily have been skimming over lunar landscape. The children became most excited over what looked like an old lava flow and then a large area of pure sand dunes, which seemed most out of place in an arctic region. And all the while never a sign of any human life.

Our maps did indicate a few settlements but along the coast and many miles to the west of our course. One was the small town of Teller, which played a most unusual role in Alaska's early history: It was there that Presbyterian missionary Sheldon Jackson brought the first herds of reindeer in 1892. Dr. Jackson, while on several trips to Siberia, had been most impressed with the native reindeer economy there. He decided that this might be the answer for the Alaskan Eskimos, who were facing starvation at that time, thanks to increased activities by large whaling ships.

Congress, however, was most unreceptive to pleas from Jackson for funds (one of his few strong supporters was Senator Henry M. Teller of Colorado—another "outsider" lawmaker whose name is now found on the Alaskan map), so the missionary was forced to finance the project himself. During those first years he made a number of trips to Siberia, bringing back a few animals each time, and he even traveled all the way to Lapland to bring back some herdsmen to train the Eskimos. Their Siberian counterparts had proved most unco-operative and unhappy.

This Teller experiment was a complete success—the herds grew rapidly (by 1930 they were estimated at six hundred thousand), and many of the animals were turned over to other northern villages. The Eskimos now had a dependable food supply to fall back on when hunting and fishing efforts failed and a good source of cash income besides. These herds have since fallen into a great decline, partly because of government bungling after the Bureau of Indian Affairs took over herd supervision and also because the Eskimos, unlike the Siberians or Laplanders, are a more sedentary people, their living based on hunting and fishing. The reindeer herds need special attention in the springtime, and yet for the native Alaskan this is the most important time of all to be out getting whales or shooting walrus and seal. Consequently, great numbers of reindeer have wandered off to mingle with the wild caribou or have been killed by wolves.

As we told our children a little about Teller that day, they immediately began searching beneath us for any signs of reindeer and, of course, Santa Claus, too. I was more interested in another most intriguing name on the map just to the east of Teller: a tiny settlement called Mary's Igloo. Apparently, as I learned later, a particularly hospitable Eskimo lady named Mary lived at this point long ago, and her home happened to be right on one of the main trails going to lucrative inland mines. So, of course, everyone stopped while en route, thereby making Mary's home such a well-known landmark that she ended up on the map! Actually, names on the Alaskan charts make navigating here especially fun and interesting. It is also a perfect way to entertain the children: they went into gales of laughter when I read them the name of the coastal mountains ahead of us. And who wouldn't, over Asses Ears Mountains! While we were debating over whether some prospector really had seen ear shapes or whether he was simply pleased with the performance of his favorite heavily laden mule that day, another unusual place appeared beneath our wing—the tiny settlement of Candle. It is hard to believe from appearances now, but Candle was a pretty important place back in early gold-rush days, when over fifty million dollars of gold was taken from Candle Creek.

We might have shown more interest in such a spot if we hadn't already been looking across the deep blue waters of the Chukchi Sea and Kotzebue Sound, toward the Eskimo town with one of the most unique locations in the arctic. Kotzebue, home to eighteen hundred people, mostly Eskimos, sits at the end of a long and narrow sandy peninsula. With such an obviously accessible location on a sheltered body of water, it is understandable why this second largest Eskimo community has for centuries been the summer trading center and hunting and fishing grounds for Eskimos from the Kobuk, Noatak, and Selawik rivers. (They all drain into Kotzebue Sound.) In the early days traders also came from Nome, St. Lawrence Island, Diomedes, and even Siberia. With the arrival of whaling ships and gold seekers the Eskimo name of the settlement, Kitkitagamute, was changed to the slightly more pronounceable Kotzebue, in honor of the Russian naval officer who first sailed into the sound while looking for that illusive Northwest Passage.

This great influx of peoples from the neighboring villages still takes place during the summer months. Although Kotzebue has many permanent residents now, who live in little frame houses lining the shore, we spotted a number of tents on the beaches as we flew in to land. Later, while on the ground, we watched the arrival of large Eskimo skin boats (oomiaks) loaded with all of the members of a family, plus dogs, kitchen equipment, blankets, tents, seal skins bulging with seal oil for cooking, and goods to sell or trade. Undoubtedly the only difference between this scene now and that of a hundred years ago is the outboard motor at the stern of the boat.

Naturally Kotzebue is totally oriented toward the water, and after finding ourselves a couple of rooms at the small hotel run by Wien Consolidated Airlines, we walked along the "Waterfront Boulevard." The broad gravel beach takes the place of a main street, and that day it was bustling with all kinds of fascinating activity. It was still warm and sunny, so many children were actually splashing about in water which less than a month before had been dotted with ice floes—brrr! Our two spotted several young Eskimo boys playing with a toy boat made out of half an oil drum, and they immediately joined in on the fun of trying to ride it. No need for formal introductions at that age.

All along the shoreline, drying racks were loaded with thick chunks of reddish-black whale meat and black squares of muktuk (whale skin with an inch-thick layer of blubber). Overhead, screaming gulls were circling endlessly, while underneath, curled into their usual balls, were the many dogs of the village teams. Out on the water, modern wooden rowboats and their ancient skin counterparts were busily scurrying about. Unfortunately, the waves were also dotted with a great amount of garbage, and for that same reason we had to watch our step as we walked along the beach. This ugliness could ruin the scene for a finicky tourist, and in recent years the town council, cognizant of the growing importance of the visitor trade, has conducted extensive spring clean-up campaigns. For a settlement unable to afford expensive garbage collection services, the easiest way to dispose of wastes during most of the year is to dump them out on the ice. This has been the custom throughout the North, and it works fine until spring breakup, when much of the winter's accumulation is suddenly left high and dry all along the shore.

Other sights in Kotzebue also point out most graphically the grave problems developing as a result of the impact of modern western ways on the old Eskimo culture. Most of the waterfront activities are a fascinating part of the past: The Eskimos must, to some extent, still live off the food from the sea. But they cannot, nor do they want to, continue to live in their ancient-style half-underground sod homes, effective as they were in insulation and structure. The houses along the waterfront now are, for the most part, one- or two-room 16 by 18 square shacks, frequently made of pieces of driftwood, with tar-paper roofs. There is no timber for construction in this region, not even any for fuel, and these frame houses are far more difficult to heat than those airtight, underground homes of earlier days. Housing is an acute problem in all of rural Alaska today, and the conditions are far worse than the poorest in Appalachia. Many factors further complicate the problem, beginning with a zooming birth rate, which is causing even more crowded living conditions. The size of families is increasing, despite the fact that Alaska's infant death rate is the highest in the nation. (Along this northwest coast, the rate is 69.3 infant deaths per 1000 live births, while for the nation it is 31.5 per 1000 live births. Fifteen to 55 per cent of the babies in these villages are born at home.)

In addition, the native Alaskan's annual income is so small that he cannot even qualify for any of the federal housing-assistance programs. To further eliminate his eligibility, the village lands have not been patented, a prerequisite for federal housing schemes in impoverished areas. (In fact, the entire native land-claims issue is yet to be settled in Alaska and is fraught with potential injustice to the native and problems for the state.) Those few units of housing which have been built in some areas are totally unsuited for the climate of the Far North—they are difficult to heat, and the walls become coated with ice from condensation. Yet no one seems to have a better substitute. In the meantime, thousands of American citizens continue to live in shacks, with no plumbing and no electricity (some villages are just now beginning to set up their own electrical co-operatives).

Even if the Alaskan native did have adequate housing, he faces the additional burden of the lack of income jobs in village areas. The Eskimo must now have cash to pay for fuel to heat his home, run his outboard engine (perhaps a snowmobile, too) and his wife's gasoline-powered washing machine. The children have been to school long enough now to appreciate clothing other than that made from seal skins; frilly white curtains line many of the windows of the homes; and a radio, phonograph, and even a tape recorder are becoming proud family possessions. So is the mail-order catalogue, which does a landslide business in the villages today. And when I visited the Kotzebue grocery store, Eskimo housewives were casually selecting canned and packaged goods of all kinds, even the latest in cereal fads.

An evening visit to the Kotzebue jukebox hangout gave us a graphic picture of the tastes of the younger generation: they were dressed in the latest teen-age styles, dancing the newest dances to the most popular tunes of that particular day; the thick cigarette smoke was mute evidence of the popularity of smoking, and while soda pop was the drink that night, it can all too frequently be liquor. This last importation of the "outsider" has caused the most trouble of all.

Just where is the cash to come from to pay for all these fringe benefits of twentieth-century life? It is a problem that is being tackled by concerned people from federal to state to local government levels, and while some significant progress has been made, a few well-informed sociologists and anthropologists predict the inevitable end of native village life, with the absorption of the people into larger communities closer to job opportunities. Some feel that this would be a better solution than the segregating of native peoples into isolated reservations (such as has occurred in the lower states) where they would continue to live in abject poverty as second-class citizens.

Whatever the ultimate solution to the problem, one of the brightest hopes to emerge at this moment is the sudden rapid growth of articulate and able native leaders. Even at the time of our first visit to the arctic in 1962, the Eskimos and northern Indians had no centralized organization or effective leadership. Each village was led individually by its town council, and spokesmen and advisers were the local BIA (Bureau of Indian Affairs, under the federal Department of Interior) schoolteachers (who usually rotate annually) or the clergy of several denominations, many of whom also don't stay long enough to really get to know the people and their problems. There have been some able native leaders, men who have served in the state legislature in the past, but they were members of the past generation, unable to cope with the problems of today. And they tended to drift away from their own people, losing the necessary ties to be effective spokesmen.

Within the last five years, however, a new group of dynamic young men has taken the lead: They have united the villages into a native federation and are speaking out for the rights and needs of their people. The very emergence of these few able and dedicated young people most graphically illustrates the single greatest handicap which should have number one priority: an improved and more complete education, so that more and more Eskimos and Indians will be better equipped to handle their own problems.

The new leaders of today are the fortunate few in that most are college graduates or at least have finished high school. Far too many children drop out at the end of the primary level because few villages are even close to high schools and many families don't want to send their children hundreds of miles away from home to BIA schools in southern Alaska or to the "lower 48." Therefore, an even smaller ratio of young people ever reach college level, and of those who do, many are not adequately prepared and must drop out.

So it is not only the availability of a higher education that is needed but also improved quality of primary instruction. The Eskimo people are especially handicapped with language difficulties, which must be handled at grade school level: Elementary class teachers have had to start with youngsters who do not for the most part speak English at home and then have been even further handicapped with a curriculum designed for children in the "lower 48." The lives of Dick and Jane, their dog, home, car, city, for that matter even a farm, are totally foreign to an Eskimo youngster. If any of you teachers is motivated by a great challenge, come North to teach!

Following three most interesting and thoroughly enjoyable days in Kotzebue, this particular arctic visit of ours had to come to a close. However, we did return as a family in July of 1965, when our primary goal was a little village on the northwest coast, between Kotzebue and Barrow. Point Hope may be just a tiny dot on the map, totally unknown to most Americans and seldom visited by outsiders, but some archaeologists believe it is the oldest steadily inhabited village in North America. And if this isn't enough fame for such a diminutive settlement, it is also called the "Polar Bear Capital and Whaling Center" of the United States. For a village of 350 Eskimos, this is quite a build-up! In addition, for a number of reasons Point Hope is considered the ideal Eskimo village of the North: ideal in terms of harmony among its people, with respect to strong community spirit, and beset with far fewer problems stemming from the conflict of old and new cultures. It is also a community without extremes of wealth or poverty.

This little dot on the map with such a big reputation was going to experience an extra-grand occasion that July 4 of 1965—the seventy-fifth anniversary of the arrival of the first Episcopal missionary to the arctic coast and also the beginnings of education in this same area. The celebration was considered so important that the villagers were preparing for the arrival of about 110 visitors, including the presiding bishop of the Episcopal Church of the United States and the governor of Alaska. Lowell and I felt that attending this event would be a wonderful experience and a perfect time to make another family trip to the northwest coast. And, of course, we had to go in "Charlie," which meant not just planning on a weekend visit but allowing two or three extra days in case of poor flying conditions. (Despite our delightful sunny weather in 1962, anyone traveling to that area in a light plane can easily be grounded for days because of rain and fog.)

We decided to leave Anchorage early on the morning of July 2, and our start was far from encouraging—we had to follow the Susitna River all the way to Talkeetna just two hundred feet above the trees. From there on, the clouds gradually lifted, and we went through Windy Pass without trouble. If we had postponed our departure by a few hours, the Point Hope trip would never have come to pass. Once in Fairbanks, the weather was sunny and mild, and with the forecast promising it would remain so, we decided to spend the night. We awoke at five the next morning to discover that the rain had followed us, and again we thought we would get no farther. Over the trees we went, hugging the Tanana River this time. When it was time to turn north, over rugged and desolate mountains to the Kobuk River, the ceiling lifted. Now, however, we had to thread our way through towering cumulus clouds, which became more threatening as the day advanced, and just when I was thinking we still wouldn't make it, there, right ahead of us was the arctic coast, and under a clear blue sky.

We landed at Kotzebue, three and one half hours from Fairbanks, but stayed there only long enough to refuel and munch sandwiches in the warm sun. We had an hour and fifteen-minute flight left, straight north along the coast, and clear skies stayed with us all the way. The Chukchi Sea was a deep blue and calm, with the pack ice plainly visible about ten miles offshore and chunks of it here and there beneath us. The ice on some of the inlets and coves was just breaking up. The beautiful sand beach looked so inviting under the warm sun until a big piece of ice floated into view. We flew very low—about two hundred feet, in order to "flight-see" but saw no human habitation other than an occasional trapper's cabin until we reached Kivalina, a small Eskimo village halfway to Point Hope. The next landmark was Cape Thompson, only a point of land on the map, but actually a spectacular series of rocky cliffs rising straight out of the water several hundred feet. As we flew past, birds—thousands of them—rose from their nests and circled about.

One just can't miss Point Hope (in good weather, that is)—a long, narrow sand spit, (the Eskimo name for this village is Tikeraq, or Tigera, meaning index finger) with a maximum elevation of eight feet, sticking way out into the Chukchi Sea. Point Hope is treeless and bushless, of course, but sections of the sand and gravel dunes are covered with green tundra growth. A glance at the map showed us that nothing lies due north but the North Pole, and Siberia is just to the west. From there, the bleak Alaskan coast line curves northeastward to Point Barrow. I suppose no inhabited place could better be considered one of the ends of the earth, but once we were on the ground, the friendliness and hospitality of the village people quickly made us forget the bleakness of the location.

After our warm welcome, we parked "Charlie" near a sign which told us that New York was 4200 miles away, Barrow 325 miles, and Siberia just 200 miles! Now that we knew where we were, we looked about us, and what we saw we loved. The village was neat and clean, with an attractiveness that one doesn't always see in the Far North. The ground around the some fifty well-kept frame buildings was not muddy but covered with a tundra growth of mosses, lichens, and grasses. And everywhere we walked on a carpet of masses of exquisite wild flowers.

While most of the homes looked like those in Kotzebue, a few of the old-style semisubterranean sod houses still remained at the west end of the village. And in the usual arctic style, all the sled dogs were staked out in back, with nearby racks hung with pieces of seal and whale meat. (These coastal people also store much of their meat in underground cellars—perfect natural refrigeration.) Five or six large frame buildings stood on the north side of the spit—the new four-room Bureau of Indian Affairs schoolhouse, quarters for the teachers and their families, and four dark green and white frame buildings of St. Thomas' Mission: the church itself, the parish hall, the old mission home (now used for offices), and the missionary's residence (at that time the Reverend Keith Lawton was priest-in-charge). We were told that less than thirty years ago, a schoolhouse, the one local store, and the mission buildings were the only frame structures at Point Hope.

While the sun was still so warm, we decided to walk about a mile to the east of the village buildings to visit a most unique graveyard—completely encircled by several hundred eight-foot-tall gigantic whale jaw bones. And while some of the graves were marked by white crosses, for others the tombstone was a single bone. Obviously the whale has long played a most important role in the lives of Point Hopers. In fact, men have lived at this bleak and isolated spot for centuries just because of the excellence of the sea-mammal hunting. The whales, seals, and walruses in turn attract the polar bears, which have also been a source of food for the Eskimo. In recent years polar-bear hunting has become increasingly popular with trophy-minded sportsmen. From Point Hope and Kotzebue they fly out over the ice, spot the giant bears, land nearby, and shoot them. Lowell and I are totally opposed to this type of operation—what can be more unsportsmanlike than hunting down these animals with a plane? We are also gravely concerned that these beautiful creatures will soon go the way of the giant blue whale. (Over four hundred are killed each year.) Little is yet known about them or just how many there are, and we can only hope that the countries of the North Pole region will join together and agree to give some protection to the polar bear before it is too late.

The tradition of whaling is still most important to the people of Point Hope; in fact, the whale-hunting season each spring is treated with a feeling of reverence—it is their key to survival in that a good catch of four or five whales means food for the village for a year. Whaling is also tremendously challenging and dangerous, so the annual preparations and actual hunting procedures are of utmost importance to the entire community. These people usually hunt the bowhead whale (more than the much smaller beluga), which can weigh sixty-five to seventy tons, with baleen (long, flexible strips in the whale's mouth) measuring up to fifteen feet and jaw bones up to twenty-one feet. This great size might not mean much to large, modern whaling ships with the latest in equipment, but the Eskimos use their oomiaks with paddles and harpoons (to which the modern mechanism of a small bomb has been added).

The preparations usually occupy most of March and April and involve the men as well as the women. The ladies begin their work by preparing seal skins to be used as floats (a whale when killed sinks to the bottom). They then go to work on walrus skins because the oomiaks must be re-covered every few years. The whaling oomiak is about twenty-four feet long, taking six skins over its wood framing. It might sound like a fragile craft, but it is really extremely sturdy and watertight because the skins are sewed together with sinew threading and are then pulled over the frame as tight as a drum. Also, the skin is too tough to be cut by ice, and yet the boat is light enough to be carried to open water.

It is the wife of the captain of the oomiak to be covered who calls together six or seven of her close friends, and during many gab or gossip fun sessions they tackle the sewing. The men usually put the skins on the oomiak, and at this time the villagers follow an ancient custom by supplying all the children with goodies in honor of the occasion. In the past this meant pieces of muktuk and Eskimo ice cream, but now the women hand out candy, cookies, and Kool-Aid!

While the ladies hold their sewing sessions, the men are busy with their own preparations, including long consultations with the older and experienced but retired captains of the community. Whale-hunting skills are of utmost importance, and these include paddling (because the Bowhead whale has a keen sense of hearing while submerged), positioning the boat when approaching the animal, and knowing just where to strike. It is also important to know much about the weather, the currents, the whys and wherefores of open leads, and the movements of the ice pack.

The actual hunting, involving four or five boats, takes place in early May, and it is a time of great excitement and tension for everyone in the village. Naturally, the end of a successful hunt calls for a great celebration; in fact, the butchering of the whales (done within twelve hours) is a festive occasion itself: The most successful ship leads the others back, the mission bell is rung to proclaim the good news, school is let out, and everyone goes to work. The victorious captain must act as host to the whole village, cooking fresh whale skin right then and there for everyone present. He must also hand out gifts to certain people within the village, and because this generosity can be quite expensive, whaling captains have to be continually successful and wealthy men. Every procedure, from the moment the dead whales are beached until the final three-day spring feast, is done strictly according to age-old custom—a most unusual and fascinating bit of the American past which hopefully will not be drowned out by our modern, mechanized ways.

These were our thoughts as we stood at the very tip of the spit where, just a few weeks earlier, the ancient celebration had taken place. Because the sun never sets in Point Hope at this time of year, it is easy to lose track of time, and when our kids interrupted our thoughts with complaints of hunger, we suddenly realized that it was dinnertime and our village wanderings had to come to a temporary halt. While we were unloading our gear from "Charlie," Father Keith Lawton told us that the villagers had spent over fourteen hundred man hours preparing for this great celebration. All the public buildings had been scrubbed clean and repainted, and mountains of food stuffs had been collected and prepared. Bishop William Gordon, head of the Episcopal Missionary District of Alaska and co-ordinator of the celebration, had already flown in nine hundred pounds of ham, potatoes, and oranges to supplement the Eskimo menu. This amount might not seem staggering in terms of air cargo these days, but the bishop flew it all in via his Cessna 180.

Aside from his position as head of the Episcopal Church in Alaska, Bishop Gordon is also a veteran bush pilot, logging hundreds of hours of flying every year as he visits each of his twenty-one isolated and widely scattered northern missions. When the bishop first came to Alaska twenty-five years ago as a newly ordained priest, he was assigned to Point Hope for five years. He knew nothing about flying at that point—in fact, he had to learn how to drive a dog team in order to get around. When he was elected bishop in 1948 (six months before his thirtieth birthday) and moved to Fairbanks to take charge of the immensely wide-flung district, Bishop Gordon realized that he would have to learn

to fly a small plane in order to keep in regular touch with many
of the missions. Today there are very few other bush pilots who
know the Far North as well as he.

While the task of feeding 110 visitors to a community of 350
people was an enormous undertaking in itself, housing such a
horde, with no Hilton hotel available, was something else again.
The undaunted village council decided to set up dormitories in
the school and mission office, and the guests were asked to come
equipped with sleeping bags. We elected to use our tent, mainly
because we had our children in tow, and there would be no other
youngsters among the visitors. This was a perfect arrangement
for the first day and night because the weather was so sunny and
mild. We were beginning to think that the arctic coast climate
was pretty nice after all, although Bishop Gordon (who had flown
in just behind "Charlie") warned us that in all his five years at
Point Hope he had never seen a day that compared with that one.
Sure enough, our luck changed, and on Saturday we were awakened by the racket of a madly flapping tent being buffeted by
strong, frigid winds, obviously blowing right from the North Pole.
We hastily abandoned our camp and found just enough space for
four sleeping bags in a small storeroom off the mission office. This
building was going to be the visiting women's dormitory, but our
particular cubbyhole had an outside entrance, so Lowell and David would cause no problems.

We were delighted to have had one day in Point Hope before
the arrival of the crowds, partly because we could see the village
as it really was and also because we had a most unique opportunity to spend the evening with three men who had served as
priests in the community. Along with Bishop Gordon and Father
Keith Lawton, the Reverend Rowland Cox, now Episcopal chap-
lain at Princeton University, had at one time spent five years at
Point Hope and had just flown all the way up from the East coast
to be on hand for the celebration. From them we were able to
learn much about the settlement and something of its early
history.

While Eskimo peoples had lived there for centuries and the
remains of earlier villages still lie hidden beneath grassy mounds
on the spit, it was not until 1826 that Point Hope was placed on
the maps for the explorers and navigators of the outside world.

English Captain F. W. Beechey, in command of a ship with the incongruous name of H.M.S. *Blossom,* was responsible for the first charting, but it was another twenty-five years before the whaling ships began to drop in at the spit. In fact, Point Hope became a way station for many of the whalers in the arctic in the early 1900s, an ideal location because of its proximity to the hunting grounds and also because of the eager co-operation of the natives: either to work on the ships or to trade their baleen—in great demand at that time for corset stays.

Unfortunately for these Eskimos, the impact of the whalers on the native inhabitants of the arctic coast is a sordid story of the trading of liquor for whale bone and the bringing of white man's diseases. While the outsiders brought little but misery and death, they only compounded already existing problems: The witch doctors of the Far North were wicked and powerful shamans, and the dean of all medicine men was Attungowruk, a chief of Point Hope. For many years he reigned supreme by declaring whatever laws and taboos he decided were needed. The most gruesome example of his ruthlessness was his highly successful technique for telling newcomers just who was boss. He simply gave them an escorted tour of the village graveyard, where bodies were kept above the frozen ground (in preparation for a mass burial in the summer when the earth thawed), carefully pointing out all the men he personally had done away with.

It is also said that Attungowruk was indirectly responsible for the secret of whisky making coming to Point Hope. A white visitor to this area had been badly treated by the witch doctor, and he took revenge by showing local Eskimos how to distill alcohol. Now liquor was readily available all year long, and it was very nearly the undoing of both Attungowruk and his people—when Eskimos drank, they were unable to hunt, and whole families frequently starved to death. Attungowruk's grab for power and other men's wives brought about his eventual downfall—he was shot to death in the winter of 1889, in his home, among his many wives.

The U.S. revenue cutter *Thetis* patrolled the waters of the Bering Sea during that period, trying to maintain a semblance of law and order. Its captain, Commander Charles Stockton, was shocked by the conditions he was continually finding, and appealed to both Presbyterian leader Sheldon Jackson and the Board of Missions of the Episcopal Church. Jackson had just become general agent for education and was making plans to extend schools to other parts of the territory. So he set up a historic meeting for a number of interested denominations, and it was agreed that the Congregationalists and Episcopalians would take on arctic coast schools, while the Presbyterians planned to start one up at Barrow.

In the summer of 1890, Dr. John Driggs, a medical man and Episcopal layman, was set ashore at Point Hope. Once settled in a two-room house which would serve as school and living quarters, the doctor had to persuade the children to come to classes. This was easier said than done because no one in the village really knew just what a school was all about. The story goes that John Driggs lured his first pupil with a molasses cake and almost immediately found himself faced with fifty students, all eager to learn to read and write.

A further complication for the teacher in starting classes was the problem of time. The Eskimos had no clocks, and the school had no bell. And in the arctic one just can't tell time by the sun, when sunrise varies from midnight to noon in six months' time. Also, the number of pupils varied greatly according to the season —when the whales were being hunted, the school was packed with newcomers to the village. When it was time to shoot caribou, there was a mass exodus for the interior and the school was virtually deserted. The school was also emptier on the rare good days, when everyone took off to hunt or fish, and crowded during the stormy weather.

Despite all this confusion, John Driggs's school was a great success, and he was also kept busy with the treating of the sick. For those too ill to come to him, he would make his calls after school hours, often traveling many miles to outlying hunting camps. And when he had finished caring for the Eskimos' needs, he still had to hunt for driftwood for fuel, cut ice for his water supply, and do a bare amount of cooking and housework.

Dr. Driggs faced many hardships with the people of Point Hope during his eighteen years there. When storms battered the land, waves frequently drove the people from their homes, often in frigid weather. In some years, when winter came early, the annual supply ship could not get through at all. Fuel for heat was a serious problem, and so was an adequate food supply. Tragedy was a part of everyday life in the arctic. During the doctor's first year there, he lost three students to drowning and bears. Another was killed by dogs, and over the years many succumbed to white man's diseases. One year a measles epidemic killed every baby in the village.

However, something better was also spreading: word about the many good changes taking place at Point Hope. The liquor problem had diminished, and the stills had disappeared; polygamy had gone, and women were being treated with much greater respect; the old witch doctors' taboos were being abandoned; the school had broadened the intellectual scope of the young people, and even some of their parents were learning to read and write enough to protect themselves against unscrupulous whalers and traders. But Dr. Driggs had been wise in the selection of these changes—his goal was to help the people of Point Hope become educated Christian Eskimos, not imitations of the incoming Caucasian Christians. It is obvious today that his labors and their results are a most important factor behind the harmony and spirit of that community.

By 1908, although the doctor was only fifty-four, his health had failed, and he was obliged to turn over his mission work to others. He found it impossible, however, to adjust to living in the southern states again, so he returned to the arctic coast, making his home at Cape Lisbourne, fifty miles north of Point Hope. He spent the last five years of his life there, trapping and hunting for his food and supplies. When he became ill in 1914, his Eskimo friends tried to take him by dog team to the mission at Point Hope. He died while en route and was buried near the storm-swept cliffs of Cape Lisbourne.

Seventy-five years after Dr. Driggs and his belongings were dropped off on that remote beach, airplanes were about to fly in visitors from as far away as New York City to help commemorate that event. True, the gravel airstrip was no paved runway and the planes would not be the latest jets, but on that Saturday morning of July 3 the village of Point Hope was all agog in anticipation of the arrival of three twin-engine beechcrafts, a DC-3, and on Sunday the governor's National Guard C-147. Now I can understand the feelings of a village over the arrival of the weekly mail plane! At the first sound of engines we all raced for the air-strip, wondering who was about to appear, eager to greet the newest arrivals. Bishop Gordon was acting like a mother hen, rushing from his plane, where he gave frequent weather reports over his radio, to greet the passengers of the next incoming plane. The villagers turned out en masse, and each arriving guest was engulfed by the warmest welcome one could find anywhere. The excitement was contagious, and in those brief moments of happy anticipation and then warm, heartfelt greetings, we felt a close kinship with our new Point Hope friends.

And how fortunate that we had brought "Charlie" in on Fri-day—all the planes were having weather problems. Fog was roll-ing in and out of Kotzebue, bringing zero visibility, and we were not at all sure the DC-3 from Anchorage would make it until we actually saw it coming in low under our three-hundred-foot clouds. Between dashes to welcome planes, everyone gathered in the lee of the church to watch games and foot races for the children. We were bundled up in all the warm clothing we had brought along, but I was distressed that I had not included mittens and fur parkas.

Of the many activities, the Eskimo blanket toss was the great favorite—partly, I suspect, because of the chance for grownups to warm up a bit, but also because it is one of the most colorful of native games. Anywhere from twenty to thirty Eskimos form a circle, grasping the edges of a walrus-hide "blanket" (seven or eight skins sewn together). Someone volunteers to jump, and this person must stay on his feet as he is tossed higher and higher by the undulating of that blanket. It sounds easy but is really very hard, and each year one or two know-it-all "outsiders" hit the ground instead, spraining or breaking ankles and legs.

Saturday night the villagers put on a great feast and dance for all Point Hopers and the 110 visitors, a tremendous undertaking which was greatly appreciated by those of us who came as guests. We gathered in the Parish Hall, and late-comers had a hard time finding even a few feet of floor space to sit on. We were amazed at how easily those in charge could feed so many, and the amount of food was astonishing. Villagers passed among us with platters of ham, great pots of caribou stew, dishes of muktuk, whale-meat steaks, slices of bread, Eskimo ice cream, mounds of doughnuts and oranges, and an endless variety of cakes. I suspect our two children made their meal of the latter and maybe a few handfuls of doughnuts, too. They sat with a group of Eskimo youngsters, doing their best to be part of the "gang" but never getting past the first nibble of the blubber and leatherlike black skin of the muktuk, which the village children consumed by the fistful. Anne and Dave perked up at the sound of Eskimo ice cream but quickly discovered that the resemblance ended with the name. The Eskimo version is made of pounded berries, snow, and rancid seal oil, and the latter ingredient provides by far the most dominant flavor.

The evening was a most memorable and exciting occasion in other ways, too. There was the chance to become better acquainted with our Point Hope hosts, to visit with the guests from all over Alaska, and especially to talk to Bishop John E. Hines. Because he is the leader of three million Episcopalians from every part of the United States, there are heavy demands upon his time. Consequently it is most difficult for anyone to have the opportunity to "just plain chat" with him. So we were most appreciative of the fact that we could share such an unusual experience with Bishop Hines and to get to know him as a friend. We had known that Alaska's Bishop Gordon is more at home in "the bush" than in a grand cathedral and that pretense and stuffy formality are foreign words to him, but we were surprised and pleased to discover that the presiding bishop was the same! He was so easy to talk to and he took such an active part in the festivities that it was all too easy to forget that he was our "P.B."

We awoke on Sunday to more promising weather—the wind had quieted and the sun was poking through the breaking clouds. But while the early morning fog was still quite thick, Governor William Egan's National Guard plane arrived, and we all held our breath as they circled overhead, wondering whether or not they would get down. They finally did, slipping in between fog patches, and from the airstrip the entire gathering trooped over to St. Thomas' Church, barely squeezing in despite many extra rows of chairs. While the exterior of the building is of plain wood siding with simple windows and steeple, all in keeping with the ruggedness of its surroundings, the interior is a great surprise—truly beautiful, with a magnificent mural behind the altar depicting the meeting between St. Thomas and Jesus after the crucifixion. The many gold candles lit before it gave the painting a soft, warm glow.

The service itself was just as beautiful and a most memorable one for everyone there: The joyous singing could never be duplicated by the grandest cathedral choir. The Eskimos have a great talent for harmony, and most of the hymns were sung in their own language. The stirring sermon was given by the presiding bishop, and Holy Communion was celebrated by the Reverend Milton Swan, a native from the tiny village of Kivalina and the first Eskimo to be ordained a priest. He was assisted by twelve other priests from Episcopal missions all over Alaska. But beyond all the words and pageantry of the service, no matter how meaningful and beautiful, I shall always remember the faces and expressions of our Point Hope friends as they came back from the Communion rail. In a bleak land with little of the comforts, luxuries, and conveniences on which we place so much emphasis, they share in the peace and joy of a tremendous faith which few Christians elsewhere could match.

A historical commemoration of the anniversary was held that afternoon in the church, with speeches by the governor, Mr. Robert Bennett of the Bureau of Indian Affairs, Mr. Tony Joule, one of the early school teachers and a native of Point Hope, the Reverend Rowland Cox, and Mr. Bernard Nash, president of the Point Hope village council. My thoughts at this point, and I know others felt the same, were of the weekend coming to a close and how sorry I was to have to leave. I knew it might be hard to explain to friends back home why we so loved our visit to "an end of the earth," but no matter—I would be forever grateful that we had been fortunate enough to be there!

There was a last-minute flurry of sight-seeing, packing, and good-bys. Then, one by one, the planes roared off, and we tagged to the rear, reluctant to leave, yet concerned that we beat the bad weather rapidly rolling into Kotzebue. The remainder of our trip, which should have been a routine flight back to Anchorage, turned into quite a hair-raising adventure. This time the beach did not look warm, sunny, and inviting but bleak and desolate, the shore line almost hidden by rain squalls and fog. When it was time to leave the coast and cross the sound to Kotzebue, I was most unhappy (so was Lowell, but he did not admit it until later). The clouds hung just a few hundred feet above the gray water, and the visibility through the driving rain was poor. We were greatly relieved to sight the airstrip, and there was no doubt that we would have to over-night in Kotzebue.

We were distressed to wake up to the same rain, cold, and fog on Monday morning, and under those conditions any lengthy stay in that community was less enticing. While checking with the forecasters at the airfield, Lowell met Bishop Gordon, who was headed back to Fairbanks in his Cessna. He suggested that we all fly out together, and this idea appealed to both of us because we knew the bishop was more familiar with that terrain than almost anyone else in Alaska. However, I was in a predicament—it must be obvious by now that I am a fair-weather flier, that there have been many times during tricky weather conditions when Lowell would just as soon have booted me out the Cessna door. We usually make an agreement before each flight that I will refrain from such comments as, "Isn't the ceiling too low," or, "But we can't see a thing," and he will make the decisions about when to turn back or go around. When we climbed into "Charlie" on Monday afternoon, Lowell was jubilant—obviously I would not be able to voice one fear—weren't we following our bishop, who has few peers among the fliers of the bush and who commands our total confidence and respect?

So off we flew, scooting under low scud clouds, the two little planes flying practically wing to wing, with occasional brief radio reports between the pilots. The rain showers grew denser, and the bishop suggested we follow him through a pass in the Hog River Hills. Our only navigation now was the bright taillight on his Cessna ahead, and as we literally skipped over the tops of the rain-shrouded mountains, I felt more anger than apprehension—he was deliberately testing my faith!

We finally broke out into clearer weather and found the nerve to ask where we were. "Just west of Hughes," was the reply, and then came the terse radio message, "Having oil troubles; think I'll land at Hughes." There was no alarm in the bishop's voice, but we were most concerned—we were still ten minutes from that village, over rugged hills, and there were no possible forced-landing sites. Lowell told the bishop we would follow him into Hughes, and we stuck close to his tail, holding our breath, our eyes glued to his plane. We could see no signs of oil leaking, and the fact that he did not change course to head for the sand bars along the Koyukuk River far to our right was most encouraging.

We were relieved to finally spot the tiny village just ahead, after one of the longest ten-minute periods I can remember, and both planes landed quickly and without incident. The bishop already had his engine door open and was peering inside when we ran up. What a sight! A thick coat of oil covered the whole engine, and after lifting the cowling off, he found that one of the magnetos had broken completely off its mounting. We were amazed that the engine had continued to run as far as it did. The bishop said that he had heard a slight pop and that the engine began to run "a little rough." His unruffled passengers, the Reverend Rowland Cox, the Reverend Dale Sarles, and Joyce, his bride of two weeks, had no inkling of any great trouble—only the one brief and unemotional radio message and then the unscheduled stop.

Both pilots agreed that nothing more could be done until a mechanic was rounded up. Since there was no such thing in the little village of Hughes, and the one Wien Consolidated Airline flight that week had just gone through, we flew "Charlie" immediately on to Fairbanks, where Lowell located a mechanic and ferried him back to the stranded bishop. It did not take long to make the repairs, and everyone returned to Fairbanks in the early afternoon. All in a day's work for fliers in the arctic, and a fitting climax to our visit to Point Hope.

As a family, we made one more visit to the arctic coast but, regrettably, not in "Charlie." In the early fall of 1964, when Lowell was campaigning for Alaska's lone seat in the U. S. House of Representatives, he decided to make a quick visit to Barrow, the northernmost village on the North American continent. Since he had only a few available days, using our single-engine Cessna was automatically out. (Although Lowell has flown the eight hundred miles between Anchorage and Barrow a number of times, it is easy to run into adverse weather conditions along the Alaska and Brooks mountain ranges, and the frequent fogs and storms along the northern coast in the fall can be a real problem.)

Because I had never been to Barrow and was most anxious to go, I talked Lowell into taking the kids and me along. The flight from Fairbanks takes less than two hours on a Wien Consolidated F-27 prop-jet, and with cloud cover beneath us almost all the way, we didn't have the same feeling of traveling vast empty distances to an isolated area that we had had when going to Kotzebue in "Charlie."

However, one look at Barrow from the air is enough to convince anyone that it isn't just another suburban community! It is the largest Eskimo village in Alaska, with a population of twenty-eight hundred, but the small frame buildings lining the shore are surrounded by the incredibly flat, treeless tundra on one side and the bleak and hostile Arctic Ocean on the other. The polar ice cap recedes slightly from the beach only briefly during the short summertime. On the land, the ground is permanently frozen just beneath the grass, wild flowers, and puddles ad infinitum. The temperature can rise into the fifties in July, but a good average is just above freezing, despite the fact that the sun never sets for eighty-two days. It is all too easy to remember that the North Pole itself is just twelve hundred miles away, especially on rainy, windy days, of which there are many. During the long winter months, the temperature ranges from minus 40 to plus 15 degrees, and the period of total night is three months long. However, the snow and ice cover the puddles and dirt and the muddy gravel in the village itself. In fact, Barrow residents say that their late winter days are beautiful, with the white ground cover everywhere, sparkling beneath frequent blue skies and almost perpetual sunlight.

When we arrived in early October, snow had already fallen and the ice was hard against the shore. The weather, however, was cloudy and gray, and the strong wind, blowing directly from the north, was frigid and penetrating. It seemed to have little effect on the people of Barrow, though: we saw more activity than we had seen in many of the other villages during the summer months. Many women were walking about (not hurriedly and hunched over against the wind as we were), dressed in long, colorful cotton parkas lined with fur and the native fur and hide mukluks for boots. Some carried babies on their backs, completely hidden beneath their parkas. Most of the men were dressed in western-style jackets and pants, while the large number of children wore an odd assortment of the old and the new.

And what fun the youngsters were having, oblivious to that icy wind. For once ours made no effort to join in! Some were playing with sleds, behaving just like youngsters in the "lower 48" when they have not seen snow in a long, long while. Others were heatedly involved in snowball fights, and a few of the older boys were roaring over the snow on small motorcycles. (I suppose this year it will be snowmobiles.) We saw a number of people standing about before the two-story frame grocery store, and a few were strolling in and out of the quonset-hut bank and post office. We were making a dash for the warmth of the two-story frame Wien Consolidated Airlines hotel! Other public buildings in the village included three churches, two schools, a hospital, a movie theater, and two restaurants. The homes were like those in Kotzebue—a random assortment of worn and weather-beaten box-like structures. Again no sidewalks, street lights, water or sewer systems. Drinking water had to be carried in from a pond almost four miles away, in the form of ice during the winter months.

The Arctic Ocean, despite its harsh, unfriendly characteristics, has always played a most important role in the lives of the people of Barrow. Like the Point Hopers, they have been and still are skillful whalers, in the past totally dependent on the meat for food and on the bones for sale to the outside world. Barrow, even more than Point Hope, was the center for hundreds of giant whaling ships coming from all over the world each summer. In the early days they roamed the arctic waters in search of the now-extinct gigantic blue whale, a valuable source of oil for lamps and other products in great demand at that time. It is difficult to understand today how much income could be derived from this activity—the bones of just one large bowhead whale were worth about eleven thousand dollars in the 1880s and 90s.

Although many ships visited the arctic during that period, the danger to men and boats was great. History and adventure books are full of accounts of ships caught and crushed by the constantly moving pack ice. So many seamen were cast ashore along that northern coast every summer and fall (some estimate that two thousand men were stranded in the years between 1880 and 1890 alone) that the U. S. Government decided to build a rescue station at Barrow in 1886, to be supplied annually by the U.S. revenue cutter, which also took the yearly group of beleaguered sailors back to the lower states.

Among the first outsiders to settle down in Barrow was Charles Brower, a native of New York City, who went to sea as a boy, was hired by a whaling company to find coal on the northern coast to refuel their ships, and later became known as the "King of the Arctic." He soon branched out on his own, starting a trading store, marrying a local Eskimo girl, and firmly establishing his empire with fifteen children. He left such an impact on Barrow that part of the village is still called Browerville, and one of his sons is now running a number of successful family enterprises, including, two general stores, a hotel, and a souvenir shop.

Another of the earliest outsiders to settle in Barrow came on the same ship which left Dr. John Driggs at Point Hope in 1890. Professor Leander Stevenson was a forty-five-year-old Presbyterian missionary teacher. After being deposited on the wind-swept beach, he was given a rear room at the Government Rescue Station for his school and living quarters, and he later took complete charge of this government rescue work. Over the years ahead, the missionaries of this farthest-north post faced the additional burden of feeding and caring for hundreds of shipwrecked sailors.

Professor Stevenson's primary task, however, was to start the school, and he was faced with the same problems that confronted Dr. Driggs. By the end of the summer, he had collected thirty-five pupils, and throughout the long, dark winter, he gained the confidence and friendship of all the people. The professor rapidly outgrew his single room, so when the Presbyterian Mission Board sent him some lumber four years later, he turned carpenter and built a schoolhouse and mission home. When seven years had gone by and his work was well established, he returned home to his wife and children. Stevenson originally promised the mission board (and his wife) that he would go for one year only!

In 1897 Dr. and Mrs. Horatio Marsh replaced Professor Stevenson at Barrow, the doctor having just married and graduated from a New York medical school. They were welcomed in a most dramatic way—no sooner had they settled into the mission when word came that a whaler had been crushed in the ice just off shore. The doctor went to help rescue the captain and crew and brought them to Barrow. These particular whalers were lucky —once fed and oufitted from the Marshes' meager supplies, they were able to take the revenue cutter south before winter set in. A few years later, the situation was a lot more crucial. The polar ice came early that fall and crushed eight large ships. More than three hundred seamen escaped with their lives and descended upon Barrow. Dr. Marsh filled the station and schoolhouse with bunks, built some native-type structures, and eventually he and Mrs. Marsh even had to turn their own home over to the unexpected guests. They moved in with an Eskimo family, and in the midst of all this crisis and chaos, Mrs. Marsh gave birth to a baby, the first white child born on the arctic coast.

It has been many years since the arrival of these first white men to Barrow, and while some aspects of village life there have changed drastically, others have remained the same. Although the large commercial whaling operations of the late nineteenth century came to an abrupt halt in the early 1900s, when ladies' corsets no longer required whalebones, the people of Barrow still go whaling. Their livelihood now does not depend on how many whales are caught, but coastal Eskimos love this meat more than anything else, including the caribou, which they also continue to hunt for food. Hunters now use the latest-model rifles, and while dog teams are still in great evidence, a newspaper report in 1967 told of a shipment of thirty snowmobiles on its way to Barrow. Another innovation has been the piping of natural gas from nearby newly discovered fields to the homes for heat.

However, modern technology has still not been able to completely conquer the severe climate and isolated location of this northernmost town. Although airplanes fly in daily now, the village residents must continue to depend on a once-a-year visit from a ship for most of their supplies. The freighter *North Star,* operated by the Bureau of Indian Affairs to service the remote coastal areas, is unable to reach Barrow before the end of August because of arctic ice conditions. This usually means that any building materials being brought in cannot be put to use until the following spring because of the rapid onset of winter weather. It also means that most commodities must be ordered for an entire year, and six months ahead of time. To further complicate the logistics and send prices skyrocketing, the *North*

Star must anchor at least a mile off the beach because of shallow water, and all supplies (usually five thousand tons of cargo) have to be lightered in by LCM's and crude barges. This operation usually takes a week, but bad weather can lengthen the time and compound the problems of an already difficult operation.

Outsiders and modern technology have also moved into Barrow in the form of federal aviation operations (with radio facilities to control all transpolar jet airline traffic), White Alice communications facilities, and an Air Force radar site. However, undoubtedly the most interesting and unique organization to set up headquarters there is the Arctic Research Laboratory of the University of Alaska, under contract to the Office of Naval Research. ARL has grown into a fair-sized community of its own, a few miles to the east of the village. A number of scientists and their families live there on a year-round basis in comfortable quonset huts, and the variety, importance, and caliber of the research work is, I gather, most impressive.

When Lowell produced a film on the programs of the University of Alaska in 1962, ARL was high on his list of priorities. The biggest lure for him, I suspect, was the research group's floating ice-island station, "Arlis II." Anyone bitten at all by the "exploring bug" seems to go wild at the idea of floating around on an ice cake in the Arctic Ocean. When Lowell announced his decision to go north, in February of 1962, taking cameraman Bill Bacon with him, I did not react like the brave wife of an explorer should—at least I knew that weeping and pleading would do no good, but I am sure he was aware of a total lack of enthusiasm on my part. I had visions of his hanging onto an ice floe which threatened to split apart at any minute, and looking back on the experience now, I really wasn't far from wrong, only fortunately I had no inkling of all the other problems that could arise as well.

"Arlis II" was really a floating ice island, deep in the Arctic Ocean, at that time only about three hundred miles from the North Pole. However, it was not just another bit of pack ice but rather a thicker fresh-water chunk, several miles in area, which probably broke off of a glacier on Ellesmere Island sometime within the last hundred years. Caught in the circular currents of the polar sea, it was gradually circling the pole. Lowell actually made three visits to the island, but just when I was beginning to worry that this trek north might become a yearly event, his vacation retreat drifted into the Greenland Sea and came to an ignominious end—melting in the north Atlantic Ocean.

At the time of Lowell's first visit, the island was a six-hour flight north of Barrow and ARL was supplying it with a twin-engined Navy R4-D. Lowell landed there just as the sun was returning after a five-month-long winter night, and immediately settled in with the ten scientists and support personnel there. His plan was to spend three days on the filming, catching the next plane out. In the meantime, the R4-D developed engine trouble, and there began a series of unbelievable events, including the misplacing of a new engine, which lengthened Lowell's stay to a month and added many gray hairs to my head.

His film venture was most successful, however, as he had ample time to cover the many activities going on about him. The scientists had drilled a hole through the thirty-foot ice and were catching and studying samples of all sorts of arctic marine life. Others were working on micrometeorology—using complicated equipment to measure and record weather phenomena. All in all, that floating ice cube sounded like a pretty busy place, with men constantly working or checking on equipment, seemingly unaware of their total isolation. One person worked solely as a radioman, keeping in continuous touch, not only with Barrow, but with ham operators all over the world. However, undoubtedly the most important man on the island was the cook, who saw to it that the men ate like kings. Their living quarters were most comfortable quonset huts, and they had an ample supply of books and games to while away the evening hours.

There were even several pairs of skis for daytime recreation. Lowell took many hikes out over the pack ice but always carrying a gun because polar bears were frequent visitors to "Arlis," smelling the good cooking, no doubt. One especially brave bear even stuck his head in the kitchen window one day, gobbling down a sack of flour before the surprised cook could shoo him off. Unlike their brownie cousins, these huge but shy beasts did not hang around long enough to become tame. However, the camp did acquire a mascot of sorts—a white fox named "Oscar." These arctic creatures frequently attach themselves to the bears, following them about and feeding off the remains of their larger friends' food catches. Unfortunately for "Oscar," he also developed a taste for rubber, and the scientists had to spend most of their evening hours repairing the electrical wires which were strung all over the camp and had been gnawed through by their persistent pet. Lowell never went into details, but someone on that island ended up with a magnificent white-fox pelt.

All this while, "Arlis II" was drifting farther and farther away from Barrow, closer to Siberia, and I was climbing the walls back home. As the days stretched into weeks, I became frantic: The children were sick, I got sick, and also tired of trying to carry Lowell's work load as well. I felt helpless because no one seemed to know just when the plane would be ready to return. I finally discovered that it had been flown to Seattle and that that was when the new engine was lost somewhere in the mails. Then to make matters worse, I learned that if the delay was much longer, the island might drift beyond the range of the R4-D. A front-page article in a New York newspaper about ten scientists and Lowell Thomas, Jr., drifting toward Russia and in danger of being "captured as spies" did not help at all, and when I called my parents to seek their support, my father's only comment was, "Well, a navy ship could always get them off next summer!" When I turned to a military friend for possible help, his reply was they could respond only in an emergency. I was stumped as to how there could be any more of a disaster at that point, although I did think about getting my cold to turn into pneumonia, going to the hospital, and thereby declaring an emergency at our end.

To make matters even more difficult, I received an occasional telephone call from a local ham operator who was in touch with the island. (He could never tell when or how often—it all depended on sun-spot activity!) This meant dashing to his house, talking via a microphone: a "How are you, dear—over," conversation with at least ten other people listening in; also disguising my "coldy" voice, and trying to sound most cheerful as I heard all about their nightly steak feasts (the kids and I were eating TV dinners), the many books he was reading (I was lucky to find time for the daily paper), and the long hours of sleep he was enjoying (the less said about my insomnia the better).

Of course the R-4D finally found its engine, it actually did reach "Arlis," with a few drops of fuel to spare, and Lowell was whisked home, as tanned and bearded as any intrepid arctic explorer should be, totally sold on ice-island living, and ready to return at a moment's notice. My feelings were mixed, like those of any wife whose husband returns much later than expected at night—relief that he is unharmed but anger at the tardiness. The only difference being that my experience involved polar ice, bears, broken-down planes, and communists as well!

VII

Rivers of Ice
and Highways of Water
in Southeast Alaska

Southeast Alaska is a long, narrow coastal strip of high mountains heavily laden with glaciers, their steep slopes descending almost perpendicularly to the fiords, inlets, and bays of the Pacific Ocean. The climate is mild and rainy, similar to that of the Pacific Northwest, so the mountainsides are heavily forested with lush stands of cedar, hemlock, and spruce.

The Southeast is home to Tlingit and Haida Indian peoples —famous for their totem poles and ceremonial dances. It is also home to many small fishing villages of Indians and Caucasians, dependent on the sea for their livelihood. Even the larger towns, which have pulp mills, a big tourist income, and other economic advantages, also have many citizens employed as either fishermen of salmon and halibut or as workers in the numerous canneries.

The sea and ships are an integral part of life in Southeast Alaska for another reason, too: because the mountains fall abruptly into the sea, the settlements must cling to the shorelines, some of the buildings perched precariously on the steep slopes behind. Roads, other than those in the towns themselves, are nonexistent—it would not only take an engineering miracle but millions of dollars as well to connect the communities with a road network. The only solution has been to develop a marine highway system, with state-owned and -operated ferries carrying people and cars to all main points along the Southeast coast.

Our family visits to the southeastern towns of Juneau, Petersburg, Sitka, and Ketchikan took place in 1962, before the inauguration of the state ferry, and we had to fly instead. However, we have ridden on a northern extension of the system—between the towns of Valdez, Cordova, and Seward on Prince William Sound. For this reason I will also include these travels in this chapter, although the Prince William Sound area is geographically a part of Southcentral rather than Southeast Alaska.

In July of 1967 my brother, Tap Pryor, his wife Karen, and their three children decided to come see for themselves why we love Alaska. Since they live in Hawaii, there was considerable doubt on our part as to how they would take to the much cooler climate. We should never have worried—aside from their kids not getting accustomed to wearing shoes (an impossibility, we all decided), there were no problems. In fact, thanks partly to a whole week of blue skies and warm sun, they fell totally in love with their sister state and talked of regular yearly trips in the future.

We wanted to take them on a short camping trip into a wilderness area and decided on a drive into the Copper River Valley, with a return on the ferry from Valdez to Seward. Ever since coming to Alaska we had heard people call that particular region the most beautiful part of the state. Our curiosity had been aroused because we had already seen so much unexcelled scenery elsewhere. Here now was our chance, and the ferry ride would be a delightful extra.

Planning a camping trip for nine people can be rather complicated, especially when it involves two families. However, daughter Anne made logistics slightly simpler when she flatly refused to leave town: her favorite singing group was coming to Anchorage on a rare visit, and she would go nowhere but to the arena to stand amongst a vast mad mob and shriek for five hours straight. Fortunately, she could stay with friends, and while Lowell would not have normally given in to such a request, he knew that we could squeeze eight people into our Travelall, whereas nine would have been impossible.

We decided to use both a small trailer and tents for sleeping accommodations, partly to give some of the Hawaiian members of our expedition a warmer place to sleep. A trailer would also be a good spot to store the camping gear while we were driving the already-crowded car. Planning food for four days was the biggest headache, especially when one's brother is a gourmet cook and our usual dehydrated and canned fare simply would not do. Tap stormed our supermarket in typical male fashion and presented me with numerous boxes containing everything from a whole chicken (somehow to be cooked over an open fire) to fragile bottles of wine, cheeses (in great need of refrigeration), and many exotic (and space-consuming) loaves of bread. We finally managed to squeeze it all in, and I must say, we did eat like kings!

The first leg of our journey was along the Glenn Highway, through the Matanuska Valley. Since we had gotten a late start (naturally), we didn't go far, and unfortunately, the beautiful scenery along this route was hidden by low clouds and drizzle. We stopped for the night at one of our attractive state campgrounds, and although I fretted over our Hawaiian guests being out in the cold rain, it was needless: No one noticed the conditions in the excitement of pitching tents on a riverbank, discovering fresh moose tracks in the mud, and catching a fish to be cooked for dinner. And anyone who enjoys camping knows what fun it is to go to sleep listening to the patter of rain on the canvas tent. (As long as it is waterproof!)

The next morning dawned clear and sunny, to our great joy, and as we drove toward Glennallen, at the junction of the Glenn and Richardson highways, and then south to Copper Center, the scenery became more and more spectacular. For Hawaiians, who live in a small, heavily populated area, it was almost unbelievable to look across a hundred or so miles of forests and meadows totally void of human occupants. And we rarely saw another car, no billboards, and only an occasional roadside gas station or eating place. Just south of Copper Center, as we followed the deep wide gorge of the Copper River itself, high clouds lifted to reveal the breathtaking panorama of the Wrangell Mountains to the eastward. As Alaskans we should have been used to mountain scenery, but we found this particular range, which covers over five thousand square miles, especially beautiful. Mount Sanford and Mount Blackburn rise as high as sixteen thousand feet, and Mount Drum, Mount Wrangell, and Mount Jarvis are just slightly lower—altogether eleven peaks surpass ten thousand feet in elevation. This towering mass of snow slopes and glistening glaciers feeds northward to the immense Tanana and Yukon river systems and southward via the Copper and Chitna rivers to Prince William Sound.

With our eyes constantly drawn to the peaks in the sky, it was a while before we became aware of the beauty of our more immediate surroundings: a wilderness of lakes, rivers, and forests. We stopped for a while beside Willow Lake, its calm water a perfect mirror for the Wrangell Mountains. Then we turned east onto a thirty-nine-mile dirt road leading to the ghost mining town of Chitna, and fortunately, we were still so absorbed in the scenery that the large ruts and bottomless potholes, reminiscent of Kenai days, went virtually unnoticed.

One small lake, with the unimaginative name of One Mile, squeezed into a gorge between two forested mountain slopes, looked so enticing under the warm sun, with a most attractive campground along its shore, that we decided to stay there overnight. The picnic table and outdoor fireplace were right by the water, and we parked the trailer and pitched two tents in a small grove of birch and aspen trees nearby. It was close to 80 degrees at that point in the early afternoon, so we all had one thought uppermost in our minds—swimming. Since we had brought no suits, Karen and I elected to wade, but everyone else splashed merrily in the crystal clear water. The temperature of the water, fed by the Wrangell glaciers, was a slight shock to the youngsters used to the balmy climes of Hawaii, but the hot sun more than made up for the chill.

After hanging the wet clothes on all the nearby branches to dry, we settled down on the still-warm rocks and gravel to watch the sun drop behind the mountain, eat a delicious meal (cooked by Tap) at the water's edge, and then turn in early, although the brightness of the midnight sun, even though shielded by the mountainside, defied early sleep. And of course, that same ever-present sun made it very easy to rise next morning at 5 A.M. to try our luck at fishing.

We were highly tempted to spend another whole day enjoying our hidden paradise, but a most intriguing man-made point of interest lured us onward. Leaving our camp set up for our return later in the day, we bounced on down the narrow dirt road to a town which flourished for many years as a major shipping point at the head of a railroad connecting with the port of Cordova. The growth of Chitna, the nearby towns of McCarthy and Kennicott,[1] and the building of the railroad itself was the result of one thing only—copper. This valley was known to contain extensive copper deposits long before the United States bought Alaska. In fact, the earliest Russian explorers heard about the red metal used by local Indians and tried to get at it. All their efforts ended in bloodshed, however; Copper River Indians were especially hostile and determined to keep strangers away.

Later, during the Klondike gold stampede, prospectors traveling through this area discovered rich copper veins, and the word began to spread to the "lower 48." The Bonanza Mine alone extracted twenty million dollars of the finest copper in one year, but the problem of transporting it to the sea two hundred miles away, with an impenetrable barrier of mountains and glaciers in between, was something else again. The only answer was a railroad, which would be worthwhile, considering the high grade and great quantities of copper.

In 1906 financiers Daniel Guggenheim and J. P. Morgan formed a syndicate, purchased the copper claims, and then completed the railroad by 1911. This construction job, while sounding easy, was actually an epic of early twentieth-century building. In fact the project faced so many obstacles of nature and man, including gun fights and a glacier which suddenly decided to advance two thousand feet, threatening already-laid tracks, that Rex Beach wove it all into his famous novel, *The Iron Trail*.

Once this C. R. and N. Line was completed, the Kennecott Copper Company began twenty-eight years of prosperity, gouging from the mountain side over a billion tons of copper worth more

---

[1] For some strange reason the town is spelled Kennicott, while the mining Co. is spelled Kennecott.

than two hundred million dollars. While the three mining towns grew, the port of Cordova also prospered, with at least a dozen ships a month sailing between there and Seattle.

The end came in 1938—totally and suddenly. Word was sent to the miners that they had twenty-four hours in which to pack their belongings and catch the last train out. Not only did operations instantly come to a halt, but the order was to leave everything behind except readily movable equipment. The story behind this move is long and complicated, involving new and questionable conservation laws, rising costs of operations, problems stemming from absentee ownership, and newer, far-cheaper company copper holdings in South America. It is a sad story for Alaska, a shattering blow to the economy of that area by "outside" interests who could care less. Cordova and Copper River mining have never recovered, although great amounts of the high-grade ore still remain.

Over the years the three little mining communities, so hastily abandoned, were a mecca for souvenir hunters. Anyone could walk into any of the buildings and help himself to early records of all kinds, belongings, equipment, and household effects. This is a tragic story, too: If the state had been able to preserve at least one of the towns, it would be a tremendous tourist attraction today. But better late than never—a few of the handful of people living in Chitna now have collected enough items to set up a museum, and together with the main street of early-vintage wooden buildings and rusting heavy equipment everywhere, Chitna is still a fascinating place to visit. Our children were especially interested in a twenty-four-hundred-pound copper nugget lying outside the Chitna bar (hauled in as payment for a few drinks?) and several abandoned 1920-vintage cars, which were not only amusing to them but also fun for a "play driving" game.

We grownups spent most of our time in the museum, greatly intrigued by early-day lanterns, phonographs, dishes, clothing, even a barber chair, all of which had been left behind in that mad twenty-four-hour scramble. We also talked with a young couple who are mining in the area and actually flying the ore out in a small airplane. While they did not go into successful production figures, they were most optimistic about what the future would hold.

Backtracking up the dirt road again, we spent one more quiet night at our lakeside retreat and then drove back to the Richardson Highway and turned south, toward the coast and Valdez. The drive was another of those scenic ones, with the Chugach range to the west of us and the Wrangells to the east. Obviously the only way we could reach the sea would be over a pass, and it would have to be a pretty spectacular one at that. As the road began climbing and we caught tantalizing whiffs of salty sea air, we were sidetracked temporarily by a tremendous glacier, the Worthington, which came down out of the Chugach almost to the road. Since the Pryor children had never seen snow, much less a glacier, we parked the car and scrambled down onto the ice to give them a romp.

Then on to 2700-foot Thompson Pass, where we had to stop once again while the kids all rolled in leftover patches of snow. It takes a lot of summer sun to melt down a thirty- to fifty-foot depth of snow! (The 1958 snowfall in Valdez itself was 184 inches, and during the 1928 winter, it was 517 inches.) While dodging snowballs as best we could, the rest of us simply gawked at the glorious panorama of sea, valleys, and mountains around us. Blue sky without a cloud helped tremendously, and it was impossible to convince Tap that this was an area with one of the highest precipitation figures in North America.

In addition to the view, the pass is rich in historical interest: As one of the few gateways to the interior it saw heavy traffic (all on foot) in early gold-rush days. We have often heard stories of the difficulties encountered as the men and women scrambled up the steep mountainside, frequently in deep snow and terrible weather. The hardship was great, and many lost their lives in the effort.

Now we glided effortlessly down to the coast, over a modern highway which once had been a footpath but later was widened for wagons. We could even see a few sections of the earlier trail, abandoned on the mountainside as the modern road builders cut out the sharper corners and steepest grades. And history pursued us all the way to the valley floor: As we wound through Keystone Canyon, an abandoned railroad tunnel reminded us that this was the site of that famous gun battle, all because two companies held the rights of way there for the railroad route. All the boys in the car were most awed by this story and insisted that we stop at every historical marker to "find out what happened next." I was only sorry I hadn't brought along the Rex Beach novel.

The town of Valdez, home to several thousand people, is also rich in history, which, as its name implies, goes all the way back to early Spanish explorers. Although Captain James Cook first sailed into the area in 1778, Spanish Lieutenant Salvador Fidalgo, leading a Spanish expedition in 1790, named the bay Puerto de Valdez, and this was the name chosen for a settlement when the first gold seekers arrived in 1898. With the departure of mining days, Valdez became another lazy little seaport town, a scenic gem for those few tourists willing to spare the extra time to reach a relatively inaccessible spot. This quiet serenity was rudely shattered, however, by the 1964 earthquake. Valdez was the closest community of any size to the earthquake's epicenter, and the disaster not only destroyed much of the town but also brought death to thirty people.

The day the earthquake struck started out as a festive one for Valdez—the Alaska Steamship freighter *Chena* was in port, and while many of the men residents were longshoring, their families went down to the dock to watch the activity so essential to their local economy. It was then that the first mighty jolt hit—buildings heaved, utility poles snapped like matchsticks, their hot lines showering sparks where they touched ground, streets cracked open, and the trees around town whipped violently back and forth.

Disaster and tragedy were greatest on the waterfront, out on the dock where the longshoring was in progress. The second mate of the *Chena* was standing on the deck of the ship when the wave struck, and he saw and felt the water come up beneath the ship, lifting it high in the air. Then the bottom seemed to drop out of the bay. The *Chena* fell, actually slamming against the ocean floor, and sent a huge wave of water up under the dock, where about twenty-eight people, including three children, were standing. The force of the water split the dock wide open, its two sections tumbling in opposite directions, spilling everyone into the churning depths.

Somehow the ship was able to survive the ensuing tidal waves which roared into the town: walls of water full of wreckage, logs, barrels, and oil. The oil-storage tanks had broken open, with the inevitable result—the oil which was coating everything burst into flames, and the people desperately fleeing from the water had to cope with fire as well.

The shivering survivors spent a cold, wet night huddled in cars at Thompson Pass high above the stricken town, and in the morning it was obvious that no one (other than those essential to recovery efforts) could go back—approximately 80 per cent of Valdez had been destroyed. The situation became even more tragic when a geology report revealed that glacial moraine on which the town had been built was now unsafe, highly susceptible to future quakes or landslides. With true Alaskan fortitude, the townspeople decided to abandon what was left of their homes and businesses and start a new Valdez on a safer location about four miles west, along the shoreline. With the assistance of federal agencies, a new town was carefully planned, and new roads, homes, schools, businesses, and a hospital followed.

This gigantic construction project was almost complete when we drove down the newly paved streets that July day of 1967. While we were impressed by the fact that we were driving past row after row of buildings that hadn't even existed three years earlier, our eyes were mostly on the magnificent natural surroundings. It would be a tough job to select one particular "most scenic town" in Alaska, but if I had to, my choice would be Valdez. Others must agree with me because its nickname is the "Little Switzerland of Alaska." The town sits by a large (over forty-five square miles), almost landlocked bay, and all of the shoreline is thickly forested with spruce, hemlock, and cedar. The deep blue water and rich dark green trees are totally encircled by a ring of mile-high mountains, their glaciers and slopes of snow dropping steeply to the coastline.

We drove out onto the new dock to wait for the ferry, which would take us on a twenty-hour trip south to Cordova and then west to Seward, and then we stood and gaped, totally absorbed by the view. So, of course, it was the kids who first spotted the ship, and there was great excitement as we all watched it steaming swiftly toward us, its blue and white hull barely causing a ripple on the calm waters. I knew the *Tustumena* was smaller than the three ferries on the main southeast system, so I was not prepared for the fact that it is really a large ship—238 feet long, with a capacity of forty cars and two hundred passengers. I was also pleasantly surprised in other ways: The word ferry had always meant to me a dumpy, run-down, strictly utilitarian boat (perhaps because of childhood rides on ancient tugboat types in New York harbor), but the *Tustumena* was sleek and trim, with a bright new look. Even the vehicle-loading platform (a necessity because of the high tides in this area) seemed to me a miracle in modern engineering techniques. Our kids were torn between watching the fascinating process of moving our car and trailer onto the ship and then down into the hold, or actually riding along with it. Some went and some stayed, all greatly awed by the large number of cars, campers, and huge van trucks which followed our trailer down into the seemingly bottomless depths. When we finally boarded the ship ourselves, we were as excited as if we were about to embark on a great ocean voyage!

By now I wasn't quite as amazed to find the interior just as modern and clean. While passengers can stay in the attractive lounge, which has comfortable pullman-style chairs, staterooms are also available, and after three nights in a tent we decided to splurge. The staterooms were similar to the sleeping accommodations on trains but brand new, with two bunks to a room. At this point, all of our highly excited youngsters wanted to see everything at once, so the first move on our part was to impose one rule: no running anywhere on the ship. After that everyone scattered (walking swiftly) in all directions, and we only met as a group for meals. (The food, incidentally, was delicious—well prepared and expertly served. This was another surprise to me: I guess because of my "Republican upbringing," I had always assumed that anything state-owned and -operated was likely to be a pretty shoddy operation!)

While we were only on the ferry for a period of twenty hours, every moment was memorable and was enjoyed by all of us to the fullest. Unfortunately, our one stop, at Cordova, came in the middle of the night, but not wanting to miss a thing, we sneaked out on deck in bathrobes and had a good look at the town bathed in the bright light of the 3 A.M. sun. Cordova, like many settlements in Southeast and coastal Southcentral Alaska, is a quiet little fishing town, a cluster of wooden buildings along a wooded shoreline, facing a number of small boats tied to docks and protected by a large man-made stone breakwater. The ever-present steep mountains effectively isolate the town from the interior.

Cordova is a little different in that it has fewer wooden build-ings now—after a major fire in 1963 which destroyed twenty-two businesses, more modern concrete structures were built along the main street. The town is also unique in the way it suffered from the 1964 earthquake. While other cities and villages were visibly damaged by the tremors, waves, land subsidence, and fire, the Cordova shoreline, being on the other side of the fault line, experienced an uplifting of anywhere from eight to fifty feet. Because there were no dramatic sights of destroyed or burned buildings, Cordova was lost in the great aftermath of publicity and recovery effort. But the town was almost as drastically af-fected for a community dependent on the sea and its resources. Because of the great upthrust of land, the Cordova harbor sud-denly became shallow, useless to ships until extensive dredging operations could be undertaken. Also, the town, often called the "Razor Clam Capital of the World" found all its clam beds high and dry, far above the new water line.

And these "hidden" twin blows to its economy were not all; Cordova had placed great emphasis for future progress on a new highway being built along the roadbed of the old Kennecott com-pany railway. This project would not only reopen the copper area but also for the first time would connect Cordova with the Alaska highway system. By 1964 about fifty miles of the highway had been completed, including a number of steel bridges. Within a few minutes' time the entire project was almost totally destroyed, yet because the highway "led to nowhere," it was completely overlooked during reconstruction planning. Only within the past year has work begun there again, and the people of Cordova are most hopeful that they will finally get their road link.

The greatest sign of land upthrust caused by the earthquake was around Montegue Island in Prince William Sound, almost on top of the epicenter, but as we cruised past its beaches and wooded hills early the next morning, try as we could, we were unable to see any signs of such catastrophic land movement. In fact, in view of the peaceful scene all around us, it was hard to believe such a thing ever happened. We were still blessed with clear skies and warm sunshine, and the waters of the sound were mirror calm.

We spent most of the time at the rail, watching the many large and small wooded islands slip by, for the most part uninhabited except for deer and other little animals. Occasionally we spotted deserted, decrepit wooden buildings along the shorelines, the ghostly remains of an earlier mine or cannery. We decided it would be most interesting to explore these relics sometime, perhaps reaching them by small boat from Seward. Beachcombing along those deserted beaches would also be great fun. But that day, on the speedy ferry, we had to be content to just look.

The most exciting sights that morning were the many glimpses of the marine and bird life all about us. My brother, who founded and runs Sea Life Park, the oceanarium in Hawaii, is a marine biologist, and Karen is his head porpoise trainer. So they both went wild over every dolphin or whale we spotted. They ran excitedly from port to starboard, using the long scientific names of everything we saw, and before the day was over, Tap was determined to do whatever he could to help build an aquarium on the shores of Prince William Sound. Knowing my visionary and determined brother, this is bound to come to pass!

It was with great regret that we finally had to leave the ferry at Seward (and part with the Pryor family, who had to return to Hawaii), but as I said earlier, it has really spurred us on toward planning a trip along the much larger Southeastern marine highway system next summer. In the past, my visits to that part of Alaska have been few, brief, and by airline. (The rugged coastline and frequently hazardous weather conditions preclude our using "Charlie.") It is a sad fact that most Alaskans seldom travel to the other sections of their state. Distances are so vast and air travel costs too great for a family to take a "weekend junket." This relative isolation inevitably breeds sectionalism, an ever-present factor in Alaskan politics, indeed, in many an Alaskan's thinking today. The Southeast is particularly isolated from the rest of the state because, other than taking a two-day drive to connect with the ferry at Haines, we can travel there only by airline. Even this link is not completely dependable because of difficult weather conditions. In fact, when planning a flight to the Southeast in the wintertime, it is good to be prepared to end up in Seattle or back in Anchorage again. Jokes are frequent about these abortive attempts and also the lengthy stays at the Annette Island airport, waiting for weather to clear at either Ketchikan or Juneau.

When the weather is good, however, the flight from Anchorage to Juneau is one of the most scenic that one can take anywhere in the world. After take-off, as the plane climbs out over the Chugach Mountains, it is easy to spot the Alyeska ski area and the large ice fields lying among the mountain peaks next to the coast. Once over Prince William Sound, which looks a lot smaller from a high-flying jet than from a ferry, the mountains of the Valdez area come into sight. And it isn't long before the plane is over the great piedmont glaciers of the St. Elias Range. The Malaspina Glacier alone is as large as the whole state of Rhode Island. (And in some places its ice is at least two thousand feet thick.) Directly behind it rise Mount Logan and Mount St. Elias, second and third highest mountains in North America. In fact, at this point on such a flight, it's easier to comprehend the startling fact that while fourteen-thousand-foot Mount Whitney was the tallest mountain in the United States before Alaska became a state, there are more than twenty-five peaks in the forty-ninth state which are higher.

Then, when one is already saturated with this exciting mountain panorama, the snowy summits and great ice fields of Glacier Bay appear beneath the plane's right wing. This thirty-six-hundred-square-mile national monument contains over twenty large glaciers, flowing from the twelve- to fifteen-thousand-foot peaks down to the water of the forty-mile-long bay. The famous Muir Glacier (named after naturalist John Muir, who first discovered the area in the late 1880s) has a sheer cliff face rising 265 feet above the water and is nearly two miles wide. When Lowell was sixteen, he made his first trip to Alaska, on a Bradford Washburn expedition to climb peaks in this area. He still talks of this Glacier Bay visit and says that it was then that he first made up his mind to come North some day to live. I suspect a boat trip into Glacier Bay (there is a regular run for tourists and even a comfortable place to stay overnight) might persuade a good many more visitors from "outside" in the same way.

Landing at the Juneau airport can be quite a mountain experience in itself. Fortunately for the peace of mind of the passengers, the airline captains on this run are well used to the situation and are undoubtedly among the most highly skilled pilots to be found anywhere. Also, the FAA insists on higher weather minimums, and as the jet slips down over Lynn Canal between the many steep mountain walls, it is easy to understand why. In bad weather, it is normal to see nothing until a high ridge suddenly looms up directly beneath the plane's wings, and only a few seconds later, the wheels are touching the runway. If the day is fairly clear, the wind is likely to be from the opposite direction, and the plane must make a steep bank between the mountain walls in order to land into the wind.

If the passenger is not too preoccupied with this "pursuit pilot" maneuver, the sharp turn provides a good glimpse of Juneau beneath—a town of seven thousand people (thirteen thousand in the area) clinging to steep green mountainsides, hugging the shore of Gastineau Channel. A large bridge spans the water to the town of Douglas across the way. Two other landmarks which can also be easily spotted are the Mendenhall Glacier, a giant ribbon of ice which spills down the mountainside near the airport, and on the other side of town, the large old wooden buildings of the abandoned Alaska-Juneau Gold Mine. Juneau, like so many other Alaskan towns, began as a mining settlement, and its namesake was the first prospector in the area, Joseph Juneau. In 1880 he and his partner, Richard Harris, discovered alluvial gold in the creek which now flows through the heart of the city and then staked claims to rich placer deposits higher up the mountainside. They also staked out a townsite (naming it Harrisburg —I wonder what the reason was behind the later switch—Joe must have had more friends), and the spot became home to thirty people within just a few months' time. The town grew fast but in a different way than the large tent cities of thousands of men in the Far North. The Juneau-Douglas area (and all of the Southeast) has a mild climate, with little severe cold or heavy snowfall, and is readily accessible by ships the year round. So incoming miners brought their families along, and schools and other community facilities (more than just bars!) were available as early as 1885.

Mining operations continued to develop on a large scale, as well as fishing and some lumbering, so by 1900 Juneau was a thriving town. It was then that Congress designated it as Alaska's capital, rather than Sitka, which had fallen into decline with the departure of the Russians. Because the legislature meets in the state capital each year from the end of January until April, Lowell, as a state senator, has seen much of Juneau, and the children and I have joined him on frequent visits. Actually, our many pleasant times there go all the way back to 1958 when Lowell was doing a television film on Alaska and we spent a month in Juneau in early summer. At that time of year all life is oriented toward the water—not only are the commercial fishermen busy, but everyone else is out on boats, usually with rod and reel. Families go camping via boat, the way we use our car or plane, and there are an endless variety of sheltered coves for them to visit and explore. Those without boats make the fullest use of the beaches in the Juneau area, either owning weekend cabins, or swimming and picnicking in public areas.

Summer or winter, hiking is another favorite pastime for residents and visitors, along the many trails up the steep mountainsides behind the town or out in the Mendenhall Glacier area. I much prefer the latter because the trails are not straight up! We also enjoy going to the Mendenhall for a day's outing because the glacier itself is a most intriguing and awe-inspiring sight. Only a small lake separates the sightseer from the great mass of deeply crevassed ice, and during the summer it is fun to sit on the warm gravel beach and watch great chunks fall from the icy wall. As little bergs they float about on the water until the warm sun finally melts them completely.

We were especially intrigued by the dark blue color of the ice deep in the great cracks, and at first I thought this was simply a reflection of the blue sky. But we later discovered that the blue is even more intense on cloudy days—apparently these crystals of glacial ice act like a prism, refracting the blue light and absorbing other colors. On an overcast day, blue, more than other colors, passes through the clouds. The more exposed ice is white because of the penetration of air bubbles, which refract all colors of light. At least this is the explanation given by the experts—while I find it hard to understand, I find it very easy to be constantly amazed at that deep, deep blue color within the cracks!

However, we don't just sit when we visit the Mendenhall: The children love to scramble up and down the many rocks and gravel piles left behind by the receding glacier, and two trails winding up the mountainside on either side of the ice are great fun for hiking. Neither is very steep, and the scenery is breathtaking. The west glacier trail is a good six-mile walk, and while this may seem like a fairly long afternoon's stroll, I suspect we have covered a lot more distance just hiking around the downtown area.

When we visit Lowell during the legislative session, we have no car, there are no public buses, and taxis are expensive. So we simply walk everywhere we want to go, and while we all enjoy it, I occasionally wonder why the capital had to be built on a mountainside. The city rises up in tiers, with many buildings perched on cliffs, almost vertical rickety wooden stairways connecting the various levels, and the streets are steeper and narrower than any in San Francisco, or anywhere else for that matter. In fact, Juneau has always reminded us of Darjeeling and Kalimpong, two hill towns built on mountain slopes in the Himalayas. There are two other strong similarities: the tremendous amount of rainfall and the many closely packed, rather run-down buildings in need of a good coat of paint. This "hill town" appearance gives Juneau a quaint and rustic atmosphere which is most appealing to tourists and undoubtedly to the residents themselves.

Of course, there are also some most attractive, well-kept homes and public buildings, and most notable among these is Alaska's White House, home to nine territorial and two state governors in the past fifty-five years. One of the oldest buildings in Juneau, dating back to 1913, the mansion is not a fancy grandiose type but a strikingly handsome three-story colonial structure. Painted a gleaming white, with green shutters, it has a stately pillared porch on the east side, which has a sweeping view of the town, the water, and the mountains. On the north, by the entrance way, stands a tall, equally handsome totem pole, a stark contrast to the colonial building behind.

The state capitol building, a few blocks farther uptown, is less pretentious and more hidden among school and office buildings. There the governor has his offices and the two houses of the legislature meet. I suppose I am the typical legislator's wife in that I always get a thrill out of watching my husband take part in the senate sessions. I also feel great pride as an Alaskan—I have attended legislative gatherings in other states (including the U. S. Congress) where members come and go at will, paying little attention to the speaker, talking, reading, even putting feet on desks. But all this is strictly out in Alaska: in the 1967–68 sessions Senate President John Butrovich, one of the most able men we've ever known, kept rigid order, allowing no senator to leave his desk without prior permission. And the atmosphere of silent attention and general dignity is most impressive. That is not to say there are never strong words or heated debate. On the contrary, since Alaska is the land of the individual, it goes without saying that the senate (and the house as well) is made up of twenty strong-minded, independent men: Voting is seldom along party lines, and violent arguments can be frequent but always subject to the ever-ready gavel of the president.

While I have attended a number of sessions in the last two years, there is one in particular that I will never forget and it all came about in a most sudden, surprising way. The children and I planned to join Lowell in Juneau over a long weekend in March of 1968. Then we learned that the governor's North Commission planned to meet there at the same time. This commission is composed of a group of men, Alaskans and non-Alaskans, who are studying the feasibility of building a railroad up to the arctic coast. My father is a member, and so we were all delighted at the prospect of at least a partial family reunion. When my dad called me from his home in Hawaii to tell me the good news, he also told me that General and Mrs. Charles Lindbergh were their house guests at that moment. (The two are old friends—Dad calls the general "Slim," a nickname known to only earliest St. Louis friends, and both have worked together in Pan American Airways for many years.) Dad indicated that he just might possibly persuade the general to come with him on the brief trip, while my mother would stay behind with Mrs. Lindbergh.

No sooner had I hung up the phone when a wild idea hit me. In fact, it hit me so hard that I instantly dialed long distance, undoubtedly to the tune of fifty dollars, and called Dad right

back. As persuasively as I could, I told him about the big conservation fight Lowell was leading in the senate at the moment,
seeking the passage of bills to wipe out bounties and sports hunting from airplanes. I told him that I knew that General Lindbergh
was vitally concerned with conservation all over the world and
that it would be of tremendous benefit to the Alaskan cause if
he would talk, even just briefly and informally, before a joint
session of the legislature.

Dad's reaction was less enthusiastic because he knew far too
well how the general feels about public appearances—he had not
given a speech of any kind in over ten years. But still, Dad said
he would pass along my message. I was crestfallen and spent the
rest of the day bemoaning that lost fifty dollars. That evening,
to my great surprise, I had another call from Hawaii: General
Lindbergh would agree to come and speak, provided there was
no fanfare—no television, interviews, and so forth. Despite his
dislike of publicity and any public acclaim, he would come simply
because he was so concerned about the future of Alaska's great
wildlife. Then the general and Dad would go on to Japan to
an international conservation meeting on the blue whale.

Of course I was elated, but now I realized I was also on a
spot. An ordinary citizen just doesn't go around inviting people
to speak before his legislature, and how in the world would we
ever get a man like General Lindbergh in and out of a small town
without public notice? I called Lowell in a grand panic (spending another six dollars) and breathlessly explained the situation.
He was obviously a bit stunned—from his brief words I could
sense that "there-you-go-off-the-deep-end-again" attitude. But he
said he would see what he could do, and that was that.

When the children and I arrived in Juneau the following day,
Lowell had obviously recovered from his initial surprise and had
everything all set up: A joint session would be held after the
general arrived; only the speaker of the house, the president of
the senate, and the governor knew about it, and all publicity
would be kept at a minimum. In fact, the secret was so perfectly
kept that when we met Dad and General Lindbergh at the plane
that Sunday, no one even recognized him. Word began to spread
on Monday, but despite the excitement felt by everyone, there

was also the great desire to grant the distinguished visitor the privacy he so fervently wished.

On Tuesday morning the large house chamber was packed long before the joint session began; once the galleries were jammed, visitors were allowed to stand along the walls of the chamber itself. From the moment the sergeant at arms announced, "Gentlemen, General Charles A. Lindbergh," to the brief introduction by President Butrovich and the resounding standing ovation, I kept wondering if it all could be a dream. Then when General Lindbergh began to speak extemporaneously for about ten minutes, naturally and quietly and with such total sincerity, it was immediately obvious why he had agreed to come, to tackle what he hated to do, breaking a ten-year public-address silence.

"I don't think there is anything more important than conservation," he said, "other than human survival, and the two are so closely intermixed that it's hard to separate one from the other. If we destroy our environment, our survival is not going to be very satisfactory."

The general went on to say that "we're in grave danger of losing the environment we inherited from all time past. Whether we lose it or not depends on laying plans now to preserve what is necessary to preserve." He talked of flying over Alaska years earlier and thinking that it would be impossible to destroy this country. "But, in view of what's happened elsewhere, and with the great improvement in transportation to out-of-the-way areas, it can happen with amazing rapidity. It is absolutely necessary that we take steps now to protect what to us at this time seems commonplace."

The general went on to talk about a few specific areas: the concern about the polar bear, the need for co-operation between hunters and conservationists, what a mistake it was to use ground vehicles or aircraft as "gun platforms," and the need to consider elimination of all bounties on predators. Then Lindbergh concluded by saying, "The action you take here is not simply for Alaska, it affects people all over the world because Alaskans hold stewardship over one of the last great wilderness regions on the planet."

With these profound thoughts still very much in mind, we flew home the next morning, out over the vast stretches of still-untouched, heavily forested land. Those many gigantic evergreens might look "commonplace" now, but unless future lumbering is carefully controlled, the land beneath us could become a denuded, man-made mess in a few years' time. And the many animal inhabitants, unseen from the air, could also vanish, just as they have in most other parts of the world.

Furthermore, this same forest wilderness is an all-important part of the great lure Southeast Alaska has for the tourist, an industry which, as General Lindbergh also pointed out, has just barely begun to develop. Enticed by the mild climate, the magnificent scenery, and the picturesque fishing villages, outsiders have been flocking in via the new ferry system.

Another popular way to travel in that area is on the seaplanes (Grumman amphibians) of Alaska Airlines. Our family visits, part of a campaign tour to Petersburg, Sitka, and Ketchikan, were in 1962, before the ferries had begun to run. So we flew and enjoyed every minute—except maybe the time when the cloud ceiling was only a few hundred feet and the plane seemed to skim just above the waves!

At other times, in perfect weather, we had spectacular views of the Juneau Ice Cap, a great flat sea of snow and ice lying among the mountain peaks behind the capital city, the source of giant glaciers such as the Mendenhall and the Taku. Flying on fifty miles south of Juneau, one sees some of the many spectacular fiords, which are so much a part of Southeast Alaska's scenic beauty. Tracy Arm, in particular, is most impressive: a fiord only half a mile wide, its water as deep as twenty-four hundred feet, its sheer rock walls rising to snowy mountain peaks over six thousand feet high. The very active Sawyer Glacier at the east end provides constant excitement—mammoth chunks of ice fall with a cannonlike roar from its towering mass, causing geysers of spray and creating icebergs as large as a full city block. Visiting boats always exercise caution, not only wary of the falling ice but also of the immense waves caused by their fall.

The towns of Petersburg and Wrangell are a few miles on to the south of this spectacular fiord area, on islands in the Alexander Archipelago. Both are basically fishing communities, but Wrangell is now home to a Japanese-owned sawmill, largest in Alaska. An "outsider" might wonder what Japan was doing in a small distant village like Wrangell, but Alaska is looking increasingly toward the Orient for trade. The ports of Asia are closer than our own East coast, and while Japan has the markets and factories, Alaska has the natural resources Japan lacks.

Although the children and I have not yet had an opportunity to visit Wrangell, we did see neighboring Petersburg on our campaign trip. Petersburg is often called the "Little Norway of Alaska." Not only was it originally settled by Norwegian fishermen, but the backdrop of water and mountains, and the neat, freshly painted white buildings clustered about a harbor containing over 150 fishing boats must continually remind the inhabitants of the home they left behind. Lowell and I enjoyed every moment of our all too brief stay in this little town, but Anne and Dave disagree. They hate to eat fish (I can't understand why), and when we toured several of the local canneries and processing plants (between sixteen and twenty million pounds of seafood are processed there each year), they had a fit over the strong fishy aroma, the slimy scales, entrails, and other gory details which completely escaped us. If they could just have kept their opinions to themselves—it was no help to Lowell when the kids held their noses and loudly proclaimed their distaste for anything fishy!

My own great love for any kind of seafood in no way made up for this behavior—even the fact that one of my great favorites is the tiny but delectable Petersburg shrimp. I also like halibut, another Petersburg specialty, but I had never seen the freshly caught fish before and was astounded by its bizarre looks—it is totally flat with one eye on top and the other on the bottom! While I was gaping at each large catch swung in by nets onto the cannery docks, Lowell was more concerned with the economics of this industry, vital to Petersburg and so many other communities in the state—the livelihood of thousands of Alaskans. In fact, Alaska has been and still is the nation's leading fishing state, annually turning in a larger catch than Massachusetts, Louisiana, Texas, or California. And the fishery has provided more money to the state treasury, more jobs and more opportunity in rural areas than any other single industry, including oil.

Another Southeast fishing town, but one with a sixty-million-dollar Japanese pulp mill as well, is Sitka, the former Russian capital. To the north and west of Petersburg, on the western shore of heavily wooded Baranof Island, Sitka looks out over the Pacific Ocean, numerous wind-swept little islets, and volcanic, snowcapped Mount Edgecumbe, whose shape closely resembles Japan's Mount Fuji. The Russians, led by Alexander Baranof, started a community there in 1802, one which grew into a thriving town, despite a tragic beginning when an Indian massacre wiped out all the first settlers. It was there that the Russian flag was officially lowered in 1867 after the United States purchased Alaska.

The flag ceremony took place high on Castle Hill, where Russian homes and Baranof Castle once stood. The only thing left today, after a tragic fire in 1894, is one solitary cannon. In fact, there is little left in Sitka now to remind one of those earliest days. St. Michael's Cathedral, a national historic landmark which dominated the town, its "onion-skin domes" providing a great deal of Russian atmosphere, burned to the ground in another tragic fire in 1966. Many of its irreplaceable icons, paintings, and furnishings were saved, however, and plans are now under way to rebuild an identical edifice. Another of the early landmarks, dating back to 1895, is an octagonal building, the museum on the Sheldon Jackson Junior High School campus. It is said to be the first concrete structure in Alaska, and Sheldon Jackson himself concocted the gravel and cement mixture to form the walls. The local Indians were most impressed and referred to the missionary as "the man who can make stone."

These Sitka Indian inhabitants lived in the area long before the arrival of the first Russians. They were a branch of the powerful Tlingit Indian peoples living in most parts of Southeast Alaska. The eighteenth-century European explorers visiting this area called them one of the strongest and most intelligent of any of the native peoples they had encountered anywhere. Unlike the Indians, Eskimos, and Aleuts farther north, the Tlingits did not have to expend all their energies battling a harsh climate; ample food was available to them at all seasons of the year, and there was no need to live in underground huts. Their houses were large and made of wooden planks, grouped together into villages usually placed along the beaches. Because their main livelihood came from the sea, Tlingits were skillful boatmen and used canoes hollowed from logs, some large enough to carry sixty people.

The Tlingits and Haidas, the other large group of Southeastern Indians, achieved a high degree of culture and placed great emphasis on family, rank, wealth, and prestige. The totems (monuments of sculptured cedar) became an important symbol in their lives. The Sitka Indians painted their family totems over the doors of their houses, indicating the Tlingit clan to which they belonged, but the Haidas of the far south actually carved their family and tribal symbols on cedar poles. Their carvings also recorded significant events and paid tribute to outstanding individuals. Some pole inscribers even went as far afield as telling the story of the earth's beginning and the creation of fish, birds, and animals.

Some of the most interesting hours during our visit to Sitka were spent at the national monument just south of the town, which contains one of the finest exhibits of totem poles in the world. It was a warm, sunny day, and it was a joy just to walk about the fifty-four acres of park. Footpaths, carpeted with fallen needles and fern, led us beneath thick stands of Sitka spruce and western hemlock. It was hard to believe that these giant trees were only second-growth timber—the original forest had been cut down by the Russians and the American soldiers who came to the area just after the United States purchase.

Here and there among the trees we would suddenly come upon a totem; there were eighteen altogether, a group which had originally been part of the Alaskan exhibit at the St. Louis Exposition in 1904. At one end of the park stands one of the tallest poles of all (fifty-nine feet), and it marks the site of the old Sitka fort. Only shallow depressions from the former foundations remain now, but it was there that the Indians made their last stand against European conquest.

From Sitka we flew farther south, deep into the heart of the totem pole country, to Ketchikan, Alaska's "Gateway City," first stop for ferries and cruise ships from Seattle and Prince Rupert. Since there is no large airport there, jets have to land at nearby Annette Island and passengers must switch to small seaplanes. Most Alaskan travelers are familiar with Annette and its airport because of the many hours spent there awaiting good weather in Juneau or Ketchikan. But by far the most interesting and unusual fact about Annette Island is that it is an eighty-six-thousand-acre reservation for the Tsimpsean Indian village of Metlakatla. Not only is this a model native community in every respect, but it also has a most unique history.

In the mid-nineteenth century, in response to an English sea captain's plea for help with the warring Tsimpsean Indians along the Canadian northwest coast, the Church Missionary Society of England advertised for someone to go as a missionary to this hostile people. William Duncan was a young English dry goods clerk, possessing no knowledge of theology but a deep religious conviction, and he volunteered to return with the captain on his next north Pacific trip. Duncan arrived at Fort Simpson (near present-day Prince Rupert) in 1857, and his first contact with the Indians was through Philip Clah, an Indian who played a large role in early mission work in Southeast Alaska. Clah taught Duncan the Tsimpsean language and helped him start a school at Fort Simpson.

Duncan eventually won many followers, and he and his Indian friends set up a special village, old Metlakatla, providing a school, church, large council house, a jail, a place to learn trades, and job opportunities for all. Each family owned a house, and all the structures looked alike, to avoid any boasting or jealousy. Each had a little smokehouse in the back yard for cooking or drying fish, a vegetable garden next to it, and flowers out front. The large white church, sitting in the middle of the village, rang its bell to wake everyone up in the morning and send them to bed at night. A native police force rigidly enforced the local laws and allowed no white man to camp within four miles of the settlement.

The town grew to include one thousand Indians and flourished for the next thirty years. Then high officials of the English Church Missionary Society began to insist on more worship formalities. Also, government officials began to seriously think about restricting Canadian Indians to reservations, and Duncan became increasingly unhappy about all this growing "outside" interference. In 1887, through his friendship with Dr. Henry Ward Beecher, eminent U.S. Congregational clergyman, and Episcopal Bishop Phillips Brooks of Massachusetts, Duncan obtained a hearing with President Cleveland and congressional leaders. As a result, the Metlakatla Indians were officially granted refuge on any nearby American island they chose. The Tsimpseans scouted the adjacent Alaska territory and picked Annette Island for their future home. There they found plenty of trees for houses and fuel, lakes for water, a good harbor, and an ample amount of fish for food supply and a profitable industry.

In 1887 over eight hundred people moved from the old Metlakatla to the new, crossing the border from Canada to the United States. They had support from no one mission but from many friends, and with the help of Duncan's continued inspiring leadership and tremendous faith, modern Metlakatla grew into an even stronger community. The new church was large and beautiful, often called "Alaska's Cathedral"; two schools were built, one for boys and one for girls; salmon canning and boat building kept everyone busy and still does today; and the people continue to learn about self-government and life under law and order. They themselves earn and spend about one hundred thousand dollars a year. They keep up their town and make their own improvements, operate their own schools, and care for their sick. Metlakatla could be no greater monument to William Duncan, who died there in 1918, after sixty years of work among the Tsimpsean Indians.

The flight from Annette Island north to Ketchikan takes only fifteen minutes, and as the plane (an ancient, creaking PB-Y at the time of our visit in 1962) settled down on the waters of the Tongass narrows, it was obvious why there is no large airport at Ketchikan—no room! The city clings to a narrow coast-line shelf, some of the buildings edging up the steep mountainside behind, and the scenery is dominated in all directions by thick evergreen forests. While some mining played a role in the early days of this town, too, the emphasis has mostly been on fishing, with many canneries located in or near town, all kept busy by a fishing fleet of over two thousand boats.

The economy of present-day Ketchikan also includes timber—the large Ketchikan pulp mill employs one thousand people and produces more than six hundred tons of pulp a day. It was hard for me to believe, during a visit to the mill, that such gigantic logs could be reduced to pools of tan liquid within a few minutes' time and finally wind up in large rolls of paperlike Tongacell. Of course, this operation was far more appealing to our children than the canneries we had visited, but it appealed to me far less

—I had to spend the time frantically clutching their coats as they leaned way out over the catwalks to watch those sharp, gleaming blades cut the logs to ribbons in seconds flat.

Campaigning with children in tow can have its drawbacks, and one further incident in a Ketchikan store was the final blow (at least for David). He was misbehaving terribly, as any four-year-old boy can, and I decided it was time for a showdown right then and there, regardless of the number of votes I might lose for Lowell. But before beginning the paddling, I did take off my "Thomas for Congress" button!

VIII

Earthquake!

The people of Anchorage live in widely scattered areas surrounding the compact business district. The strong individual, who would rather die than live anyplace even remotely resembling a suburb but must still work in town, can be located as far away as fifty miles from the heart of the city. Despite a one-hour commute, many Anchorage area residents live on 160-acre homesteads or beautiful wooded tracts of land northeast into the Matanuska Valley. Others choose to live in relative isolation to the south along Turnagain Arm, enjoying mountainous scenery of spectacular beauty. Still hardier souls have built homes high on the slopes of the Chugach Mountains behind the city. Their snow stays through April and comes again in early October, but they enjoy a view which is probably unrivaled anywhere else in the world.

The other residents of the city do live in suburban areas similar to those found in any other state. A number of lovely homes are within easy walking distance of the heart of town. For the most part, these are the older homes of early Anchorage, before the rapid post-World War II expansion. Many of the city's first families still live in this area and, I suspect, occasionally groan over the sprawling new appendages of their once small, friendly town.

In the last eighteen years thousands of homes have been built in a five-mile area between the heart of town and the mountains to the east and southeast. To the southwest, high on the bluffs along the shores of Cook Inlet, developers promoted the exclusiveness of Turnagain-by-the-Sea and built fifty-, seventy-, and one-hundred-thousand-dollar houses which made the most of sweeping views of the water, three great mountain ranges, and mighty Mount McKinley, rising like a lone white cloud over 240 miles away.

During our first year in Anchorage, while renting one of the smaller homes in Turnagain, we spent many hours engaged in what is probably one of America's most time-consuming pastimes —house hunting. We were looking for what would be our first really permanent home in ten years of married life. At that time I frequently remarked that once we found our dream home, it would take bulldozers to ever make me move again. Well, bulldozers played a part in our subsequent forced removal, and in the process my ideas about a permanent home have drastically changed!

We had almost given up, in the spring of '61, when we found Chilligan Drive. Technically, it is the southernmost street in Turnagain, but the fifteen families who lived there looked on Chilligan as something special, not just another part of suburbia. In fact, the dead-end dirt road was off quite by itself, separated from the clean, paved streets and manicured lawns of Turnagain by a wooded gully. It was the trees we noticed first—a profusion of spruce, birch, and aspen, unusually large for this northern area. And the families obviously had placed their homes in among the trees with the greatest care, cutting down only the minimum necessary for space. The houses themselves blended in well with the woods—all were one-story frame buildings, stained shades of brown or gray.

Our home, for which we had looked for so long, was at the end of the street, still in the woods, but closer to the bluff, high over the water, facing that spectacular view. In fact, the entire setting was more perfect than anything we had ever seen in our travels, and we both knew immediately that here was our "shangri-la." We bought the house and moved in right away.

From a mother's point of view I was delighted with the two acres of woods, which the children could play in, and I was especially pleased to discover such compatible Chilligan Drive neighbors, including many children of all ages. Sharing the bluff next to us, Wanda and Perry Mead had owned their lot for five years before they could go ahead and build on it. They had dreamed and planned and carefully marked many of the great old trees which would just have to stay, regardless. The house they had looked forward to for so long was finally completed in the summer of '63, and energetic, tomboyish Wanda and all five children spent most of the warm days working hard out-of-doors. The girls, Pam and Penny, took on the project of transplanting wild flowers, while Perry, the oldest at twelve, divided his time between hauling rocks and helping his mother chase the two little boys. Paul, at three, had an astounding way of disappearing within a few seconds' time and then quickly reappearing on a Turnagain street over a mile away. Merrill, the baby, with blue eyes and golden curls, could do no wrong, even after pulling up all the flowers the girls had just planted.

Vee and Cal Bashaw and their two children lived across the street from us, their home overlooking the thickly wooded gully. Vee was the irate lady who chased the moose away from her beautiful shrubbery! Her lovely flowers provided us with a delightful view away from the water.

The Ted Shohls, also on the ravine side of the street, chose to plant their yard with wild strawberry and dogwood plants rather than grass—both were busy doctors and had four small children, so it was a practical matter, as well as an aesthetic one. They loved to see the bright red berries beneath the trees, and they transplanted wild ferns and irises to complete the woodland scene. Even the children's swing, gathering place for twenty-odd Chilligan little ones (I never could get an accurate count—it was certainly one of the most prolific streets in the city), was made of rough wood rather than the usual green and red metal department-store variety. Across the road, with over three hundred yards of woods between their homes and the bluff, the Ken Johnsons and Dave Evansons provided most of the flowers: gigantic begonias, delphiniums, and pansies. Dave Evanson had a most enviable green thumb, and when he wasn't working at the weather bureau or helping Clara with their two children under two, he was working hard outside. Dick and Barbara Sutherland and Donna and Bud Schultz had just moved in on either side of the Evansons and had exciting plans for their yard areas.

And so it was for everyone on Chilligan—a special feeling of pride for their street and a lot of thought and care for their yards and homes. The Ingrams did more than that—they built their house by themselves. It took several years of a lot of hard work on weekends and evenings, living in the basement until they could finish the upstairs. March 20, 1964, was the big day when it was finally completed and they moved up.

Before we had signed the final papers on our new home, Lowell, aware that there was an erosion problem along the sandy cliffs of the bluff, called on a well-known local geologist. He was told that the erosion was caused by strong tidal action in the inlet and by seepage of water through the layers of sand and clay. This blue clay is a relatively unstable substance, and it is found in great quantity throughout the Turnagain area. In fact, at one time a few years back, a small clay products factory had been started and later abandoned on a bluff area to the southwest of Chilligan, on what was now called Clay Products Road.

Lowell and the geologist decided that in view of the gentle slope of our bluff line, compared to the more prevalent steep, abrupt areas, our erosion rate would not exceed a foot a year. At that rate we would not have to begin to worry for another fifty years. If we had been even more thorough and had looked up a 1959 geology report in the city library, we would have read that not only is this moist and plastic blue clay highly susceptible to erosion, but it is also so unstable that under certain conditions, such as the violent shaking of a strong earthquake, it could be set into motion. Even then I doubt that we would have hesitated long in buying—we knew Alaska had frequent mild quakes, but simply because we had so many slight ones, we were told there was no danger of a strong one. Earthquakes in 1936 and 1954, which had been strong enough to knock down chimneys and cause landslides along Turnagain Arm bluffs, had either been virtually forgotten or just were never mentioned to new-comers like us.

And because Anchorage was born as late as 1914, no one knew of any strong quakes in the area before that. I remember now, in my walks through the woods around our house, coming upon three- and four-foot-wide depressions: some long, some short, zigzagging at random but roughly parallel to the bluff. I didn't think they could be stream beds, and the thought of earthquake fissures did come to mind. But when I looked at the large old trees growing in the depressions themselves, I dismissed them as being too far in the past to worry about. I'm glad that at that time I did not have even a premonition of the disaster facing us—that within three years (almost to the day) of finding our dream house, we would be at the very center of the worst earthquake ever to hit North America.

I'll start from the grim beginning.[1] On that bad Good Friday of March 27, 1964, Lowell left for Fairbanks in our plane about 3 P.M. We had had a snow storm for two days, and it was just letting up enough for Lowell to take off.

About five o'clock I went upstairs with the children to watch TV. Dave and I sat on Anne's bed for a while with her—she had a headache. Of course, we all took off our shoes.

Dave was six and Anne eight. They both were in cotton shirts and pants, and I wore a red wool dress and nylon stockings.

It was a little after 5:30 that I heard a rumble. I had heard one before, just preceding a mild earthquake last summer, but we also heard frequent rumbles from the big guns firing at the army base.

Something instantly told me that this was another earthquake. I leaped off the bed, yelling, "Earthquake!" I grabbed Anne and called to David. They both moved with lightning speed. We had reached the front hall when the house began to shake.

We rushed out the front door with David protesting, "But, Mommy, I'm in bare feet . . ." Bozie must have slipped out with us.

We were about ten feet beyond the front door when it suddenly seemed that the world was coming to an end. We were

[1] The following account of the author's earthquake experience first appeared in the *National Geographic Magazine* of July 1964.

flung violently to the ground, which was shaking up and down with the sharpest jolting I've ever felt. It seemed an eternity that we lay there in the snow.

Within a few seconds the entire house started to fall apart, splitting first right at the hallway we had just come through. We heard the crashing metallic noise of breaking glass, then that horrible sound of wood being broken apart. The trees were crashing all about us, adding to the terrible din.

I looked toward the car to see if it was shaking as much as during the last quake, and as I watched, the garage collapsed on top of it!

Now the earth began breaking up and buckling all about us. A great crack started to open in the snow between Anne and me, and I quickly pulled her across it toward me.

This was the only moment during the entire quake when I felt any panic. Seeing that fissure widen next to me was the exact picture I'd always had in my mind of what happened in a violent earthquake. And the fact that it opened between Anne and me, threatening to separate the three of us, truly frightened me for a moment.

Then our whole lawn broke up into chunks of dirt, rock, snow, and ice. We were left on a wildly bucking slab; suddenly it tilted sharply, and we had to hang on to keep from slipping into a yawning chasm. I held David, but Anne had the strength and presence of mind to hang on by herself. Although crying, she was still able to obey commands—thank God, because poor Dave was hysterical, and I could only hold him tightly.

Now the earth seemed to be rising just ahead of us. I had the weird feeling that we were riding backward on a Ferris wheel, going down. I always hated riding on them anyway. And I also had the brief fearful thought that we were falling down into the sea.

The worst of the rocking stopped, and as I looked around, I realized that we and our entire property had fallen down to sea level. I could see nothing left of the house, except part of the roof, and it looked terribly close to the water.

I remember noticing the kids' bright yellow and red swing set perched on a cake of ice of its own, but all I could think of was that the water would probably rise and we would be trapped.

The cliffs above us were sheer, with great sections of sand and clay constantly falling. The jumbles of earth all about us had stopped moving, but large hunks were breaking apart everywhere.

The children were both hysterical, crying and saying over and over, "What will we do? We'll die . . ." I knew we'd have to move now, carefully but fast. I had to find a way up that cliff, and we would have to climb over the great chunks of earth without falling into holes and crevasses.

I knew I couldn't carry both children or even one—Dave weighed a chunky seventy-five pounds and Anne was a husky eight-year-old. So my first job was to calm them down and explain what to do. I told them that we would get out all right but that we had to stay calm. (It's still an awesome thought to me that I never felt calmer—I had often heard that this happened to people at times of great crisis.)

I suggested that first we say a prayer asking Jesus to take care of us and guide us, and both children stopped crying, closed their eyes, and fervently pleaded with Him to take care of them.

This had an extraordinary effect on them and on me. Anne was ready now to climb on her own, and although David was still worrying about his bare feet and frostbite, he had stopped crying.

The next fifteen or twenty minutes were one great nightmare as we clambered up and down the great slabs of earth and snow. I found one large tree leaning against the cliff and thought for a few moments that we might be able to shinny up it.

Anne made a brave attempt but climbed only a few feet. I knew Dave could never do it, so I looked for another way up. We started walking to the right, staying far enough away from the cliff to avoid the still-falling sand.

It was then that I first noticed Dr. Perry Mead's house—nothing showed but the flat roof. I could see two of their children standing on top of a car but could not tell which of the five they were. They were crying and yelling, so I called to them to stay right there, that I'd bring help.

I was terribly torn between going over there to try to get them and moving on up the cliff. But I was literally carrying David at this point and hauling Anne up and down the steep areas, and since I couldn't possibly handle two more small children, they would probably be safer standing on that car roof, I thought, than scrambling among the rocks and crevasses.

Suddenly a man appeared on the cliffs above. All three of us immediately yelled, "Help, help, come get us!" and he shouted down that he would find some rope, then disappeared.

He was an unbelievably welcome sight, but the kids became hysterical again when he disappeared. I tried to assure them that help was on the way, and we found an extra-large mound of snow-free earth to wait on. Our feet were really in bad shape by now; none of us had any feeling left in them at all.

As we stood waiting for what was probably only five to ten minutes but seemed an hour, I realized that there were many more houses flattened along the cliff in the direction we were heading—not just the two homes on the bluff side of Chilligan Drive.

The Bashaw house, originally across the street from us, was now sitting right on the cliff just above us. Broken water pipes stuck out beneath it, and electric wires were strewn down the cliff and across the rocks near us. This alarmed me, and without scaring the kids any further, I tried to warn them not to touch any wires.

On the water side I recognized what was left of the Evanson home, and it was another heartening sight to see Dave Evanson standing by it. The children started calling to him for help, but I quickly hushed them because it looked as if he was having plenty of troubles of his own.

I was puzzled by the position of the Evanson home. It had been quite a distance down the street from us, and now it appeared to be right next to the Meads'. With a shock I realized that I could not even see the Schultz home, which had been between the Evansons' and the Meads'. I wondered if little Julie Schultz, Anne's best friend, had been home at the time of the quake.

All these thoughts whirled through my mind as we waited for what seemed an eternity. I kept glancing back to the sea, concerned that it might be moving in. For the first time I began to feel the cold and started to shiver. Poor David, in blue jeans and cotton shirt, was shaking now, his lips blue.

Suddenly six or eight men appeared at the top of the cliff. One, whom I cannot identify (a great pity because we feel eternally grateful to him), started down the cliff toward us.

Both the children hugged our rescuer, and I could feel their sense of relief as they told him how cold they were. He put his black wool jacket around Anne. (For a week she wore it almost constantly. It is dirty and worn and much too big, but it will be her most prized possession for a long time to come.)

She was all set for the climb now and started right out on her own while our friend picked up David and carried him the rest of the way. With the children taken care of, I turned to poor Bozie. He was whimpering and shivering, and I tried to coax him up the cliff, but he wouldn't come. I had to leave him, and it hurt, but there was nothing else to do. We still had a treacherous climb ahead ourselves.

At the top there was a steep, sheer rim which I really don't think I could have scaled by myself. But many willing hands hauled us up quickly. I remember thinking, why, I don't even have to help, they can just lift me as if I were an inert bundle.

Once over the top of what was left of our street I saw Wanda Mead, her face strained and white, and told her about her two children. Then we were hurried to a car, and before I could look around at what was left of our lovely street, we were whisked away. The man driving, Harold Rhett, took us to his home a few blocks east. There we were rushed inside and wrapped in many blankets.

We must have lain on the Rhetts' couch for about an hour. The biggest job was trying to warm up. We were shaking, but there was no heat or electricity, so we were unable to make anything hot to drink.

I had the children rub their feet, and the feeling seemed to come back fast, much to David's relief. My own remained numb, and I began to think that I might have a real frostbite problem.

Suddenly there was another strong earth tremor, and we all ran out of the house. I had taken off David's wet pants and my soaked dress, so we were just wrapped in blankets. The wife of our host suggested we get into their pickup truck to stay warm.

We sat there another half hour, feeling the earth continue to tremble and seeing the trees wave above us. The people from the houses around us were standing in the street in small groups—

no panic, no emotion showing—calmly discussing what to do next. Their calmness helped me.

Another great help was the radio in the pickup. Station KFQD was broadcasting, and the announcer was matter-of-factly discussing the quake, including the aftershocks, and saying that there was no need for alarm.

"Stay in your homes or cars and wait for further word," he kept repeating, saying that so far as he knew there was little actual damage anywhere.

This bothered the kids. "Wait till he sees our street," they said.

People now began bringing armloads of blankets and food from their homes, loading their cars to move farther away from the inlet. This was fine with me. I became very impatient to move on, especially when the announcer began to broadcast warnings of possible tidal waves.

I suddenly felt overwhelmingly alone without Lowell there to make decisions, and wondered where we should go. Then I remembered that our church and the minister's home were both well back toward the mountains and would be the perfect place to head for. It was now, too, that it first dawned on me that we had nothing left of our personal belongings—not even the clothes on our backs, because we had shed most of them for our neighbors' blankets.

Lowell and I have always been the sentimental kind. We had collected albums of family pictures which we treasured. And we had boxes and boxes of slides and movies which we had gathered all over the world. Lowell's office had been in our home, and he kept all his valuable camera equipment there, all his papers and manuscripts.

But we were also collectors of other things—antique furniture, china, and silver, and curios from our travels. We had Tibetan religious paintings, straw beads from Timbuktu, petrified wood from the Saudi Arabian desert, and brass from India.

They had all meant a great deal to us, partly reminding us of our pleasant travels, I guess. But at this moment of realizing that all was gone, it just didn't seem to matter. I was too overcome with thankfulness that we had escaped unharmed, and I could sense that both children felt the same.

They did not talk about Bozie, perhaps because he had been

suffering from a crippling hip disease and we knew his days were numbered. But David cried over our two cats. He was especially attached to the impish black kitten, Sylvester.

Another thought I had while waiting in the pickup truck was what extraordinarily calm, cool-headed people these Alaskans are. The men made plans, the women and children went on carrying armloads to cars—while everything around us shook with aftertremors.

We had often thought that Alaskans were a special breed of people, made from the same strong mold as early American pioneers. Now the community reaction to this sudden catastrophe was dramatic proof of it.

I'm afraid I was feeling less and less calm with every passing moment. I was greatly relieved when the Rhett family, who had given us shelter, were ready to move out to a safer area. The wife drove the station wagon, loaded with their children and overnight supplies; the husband led the way in the pickup with the three of us. He had just made another quick trip over to Chilligan Drive, and reported that everyone was accounted for except two of the Mead children.

My heart sank. Could these be the two I had left standing on the car? This horrible thought tormented me for many hours that night and the next day. Did I make the right decision? Should I have tried to return to collect those children?

As we drove down the familiar streets of Turnagain, I was appalled at the wide cracks in the roads—gaping, jagged fissures that looked bottomless. I began to think we would inevitably find some too wide to cross, that we might have to remain in the area after all.

We made our way, surprisingly quickly, to the Seward Highway—the main artery out of the city. Traffic was amazingly light. Ambulances and police cars with flashing red lights sped past us, and soldiers directed traffic. The world was inky black, pierced only by car headlights and—surprisingly to me—the brilliant flashing of the railroad crossing lights. The bells were clanging, too, and I wondered where the train was: I realized later that the quake must have triggered the warning mechanism, and it probably clanged needlessly for hours.

Soon we were climbing the hill to St. Mary's Episcopal Church

and its rectory. Both buildings were dark, and for a moment I
was terribly afraid that no one was there. Now what would I do?
I had forgotten that all electricity was off, and when our minister,
Alexander "Sandy" Zabriskie, greeted us at the door, I felt another tremendous wave of relief.

But once in the doorway we found a cold, dark, thoroughly
messed-up house. Sandy's family had gone to a less damaged
home for the night, and he had returned only briefly to check on
his own house.

The moment Sandy closed the door and turned to tell me what
to do next, I felt better. First he lit candles and then brought us
a platter of cold roast beef and a carving knife.

This was all the kids needed. Candles meant a party, and they
forgot fear and became excited over a greasy platter of cold, almost raw meat. It was food, and they were starved—it was now
about 8:30. They needed no forks, plates, or napkins. We knelt
around the table, and I whacked off big chunks of the rare meat,
which the kids gobbled up.

Their spirit was contagious, and I began to eat some myself.
No beef ever tasted better!

While we ate, Sandy collected clothes for us. His four children
were much younger than Anne and David, which made the task
more difficult. Wool socks were the most welcome find for all of
us, oversized boots for Anne, pants for David—which came only
to his hips and couldn't be buttoned—and pants and a shirt of
Sandy's for me. His wife Margy wore a smaller size, I found
regretfully.

Just when the warmth was returning to our bodies and spirits,
we heard another slight rumble and the house began to shake.
There was no need to yell to the children. They rushed ahead of
me to the front door. I did stop to blow out the candles, to avoid
danger of fire. Then in the darkness, I fell right over the
Zabriskies' great brown dog, who was running in the same direction. The two big bruises from this mishap were virtually the
only injuries suffered by the three of us during the entire quake.

By the time I had picked myself up, the tremor had stopped
and Sandy was assuring us that we needn't worry about any more
strong jolts and that we shouldn't try to run outside each time.
We tried to accept this, but during that long night ahead, when

the area was almost constantly shaken with afterquakes, the kids and I rushed toward the door almost every time.

While Sandy was talking of moving us down to join his family, the Warren Twiggses came to the door. He was the senior warden of the church and had come by to see if there was any damage or something he could do to help. Since they had plenty of space at their home, it was quickly decided that we should join them for the night.

I noticed no more cracks in the pavement, but it was snowing heavily and the street was a sheet of ice. Ordinarily I worry about such driving conditions, but at this point they didn't concern me in the least.

My thoughts, now that we were assured of a place for the night, were about Lowell. Surely he must be worrying terribly about us. How could I possibly get word to him? I was concerned that he might try to fly right back, and the weather at that moment couldn't have been worse. I also wondered if Fairbanks could have suffered from the quake.

Warren Twiggs was due at his Federal Aviation Agency communications job at midnight, so I asked him to try to get word through to Fairbanks. I had not heard a radio since leaving the pickup, and I did not know what the communications problem might be.

The Twiggses' home looked normal, except for no heat or electricity. Margaret Twiggs and I decided our first move would be to bed the children down for the night.

This was easier said than done; they refused to consider leaving me to go into one of the bedrooms, and the couch right by the front door looked the most inviting to me. So we made a bed on the living-room floor with all the blankets we'd collected that evening, topping them off with two of the Twiggses' sleeping bags. Soon the children were warm and comfortable. They slept for a few hours after midnight, but both frequently awoke in terror from nightmares.

I lay on the couch under blankets, still not really warm. We were lucky that the temperature outside did not drop below 20 degrees that night. Sleep was out of the question because I wanted desperately to get in touch with Lowell. A constant monitoring of the radio seemed wisest. The Twiggses had a portable, and I perched it on the arm of the couch and lay listening all night long.

By midnight, communications were beginning to filter in from communities around us, and we heard terrible stories of sea-wave destruction in Kodiak, Seward, and Valdez. It was an eternity to me before contact was re-established with Fairbanks, and I heard with relief that it had felt merely a strong jolt.

The broadcasters began to relay messages from local families to relatives in other Alaskan towns. There was no hope of getting any word out to the "lower 48" yet. The Twiggses' phone was not working properly, and I could only listen to, "Please tell my husband, John Smith, that his wife and children are fine," and, "To my mother, Mrs. James in Fairbanks, all is well."

Locally, there was a continuous stream of, "Tell John his father and mother are at the Stewarts," or, "The Johnson family wants to know the whereabouts of daughter Ann." I heard many of our friends asking about family members, and as the night wore on, reports poured in locating the lost.

It was several hours later that I first heard that a Wien Consolidated prop-jet was en route from Fairbanks to Anchorage, bringing doctors and supplies. I just knew Lowell would be on that plane.

I knew that the pilot would be Merrill Wien, the airline's head pilot and one of our closest friends. The weather was still grim—snow and fog—but Lowell and I had both flown with Merrill under many tough conditions. We knew he was just about the best there is, and I had no fears for them that night.

Suddenly the radio announcer said, "If anyone knows the whereabouts of Mrs. Lowell Thomas and family, please contact us immediately." I ran to the telephone and was so overwhelmed to find it working that I could hardly talk to the person who answered. But I got the essentials through, and just half an hour later, in the first light of dawn, I watched our Travelall roar up the street.

I practically laughed out loud at the sight of this great, muddy station wagon—I thought it had disappeared with the house! —completely forgetting that Lowell had taken it to the airport. It was like receiving an unusually exciting Christmas present to realize that one material possession was left.

Words cannot describe our reunion. The kids and I were tremendously relieved, but Lowell's emotions were those of a man who had not known for many hours whether his family was dead or alive.

All I wanted to do now was cling to him and talk. But he felt he should return to Chilligan Drive immediately to see if there was anything he could salvage and if he could find the dog, to whom he was greatly attached.

We tried to keep occupied during his absence with the practical necessity of cooking breakfast for six people over one tiny Coleman stove. Margaret Twiggs did a remarkable job of producing eggs, bacon, and coffee for all. But the children! They jumped and rolled and ran all over the small living room, their leaping and laughter shaking the house. I was distressed at such behavior, but Margaret assured me that it was a very good sign of return to normalcy.

I was beginning to wonder how much of this new development I could put up with, when the kids screamed that Daddy was back. They were out the door like a shot—and no wonder.

Lowell was coming up the walk with little black Sylvester in his arms and Bozie trotting along beside him. That kitten and the big German shepherd were never so overwhelmed with lavish affection.

When the excitement died down slightly, Lowell told us of making his way down the cliff—to find a thoroughly subdued and shaking Bozie lying by the still-intact bedroom wing.

The bedroom stairs were exposed, and he walked up them and into the rooms. Pictures were still on the walls and some furniture still standing. But other belongings were everywhere. Lowell realized that much of this could be salvaged if the water did not rise any farther. Waves were lapping at the garage, and the sea had virtually covered the Mead home. At David's bedroom door he pushed the bed back to get inside and out popped a little black head. Lowell had never been overly fond of cats, but at this moment he said he was highly pleased to find little Sylvester.

Next day, friends digging among our debris picked up a box of clothing and out walked mama cat—unhurt but probably having run through seven of her nine lives. Now the whole family had been reunited, and we were overwhelmingly thankful to God for having spared our lives during one of the world's worst earthquakes.

Easter Sunday 1964 will always have a special place in my memories—and it won't be visions of Easter bonnets or a leisurely holiday dinner. The church was cold at 8 A.M. without heat, and we and many of our friends who were homeless, too, clumped down the aisles in borrowed boots and weird assortments of misfit clothing. Anne was still wearing her rescuer's coat, far more meaningful to her than a new Easter bonnet; David was still holding up his pants; and I was still wearing Sandy Zabriskie's corduroy pants and wool shirt.

The singing had never sounded so enthusiastic, nor had the spiritual warmth been so noticeable, although it was so cold in the building that people's breath showed as they sang. Prayers of thanksgiving have never had more meaning, and the Epistle for Easter Day is indelibly etched on my mind: "If ye then be risen with Christ, seek those things which are above . . . Set your affection on things above, not on things of the earth. . . ."

It was many weeks before we heard the full stories of our neighbors on Chilligan—we had all become totally scattered about the city, living temporarily in unfurnished apartments or crowded in with friends. We were all too busy with efforts to salvage belongings and pick up the pieces of our lives to think about social gatherings of any sort. (In fact, it was several months before most women were willing to leave their homes and families at all for fear of a second such disaster.) But Memorial Day was a time each year when all the families of Chilligan gathered for a neighborhood picnic, and so we met together for the first time since the tragedy, crowding into the Johnsons' four-plex apartment, eating from paper plates on the floor while we listened to each other's experiences on that bad Good Friday.

Vee Bashaw, her energy and vitality gone for a moment, told of how thankful she was to have been at home that afternoon with both her sixteen-year-old daughter, Jill, and twelve-year-old son, Win. After having lived in Alaska for many years, mild quakes were an old story to her. So her first reaction, when the house began to shake, was to run to her china closet and throw all her weight against the door.

"Once I had done that," she explained, "I couldn't have let go of that tall dancing giant even if I had wanted to. Jill was trying to keep her balance and hold onto her chipmunk's cage at the same time, and Win was just trying to stand up. It got more intense until the lighting fixtures were hitting the ceiling on both sides, doors swung open, and dishes were literally flying across the floor. Instead of looking toward the inlet, we looked toward the creek at the trees, which were simply dancing like crazy, huge giants going every direction. I kept saying, 'It will stop,' and Jill cried, 'It's the bomb, the bomb,' when all of a sudden Win yelled, 'Oh, no, Mom, the road is gone . . . we gotta get out of here.' One glance in that direction, and the horror was unbelievable. I shouted, 'Tay's house is gone . . . and, oh! so is the Meads',' and with that we took off out onto the balcony, down the stairs, and flew across the creek through swaying trees and screaming children who ran right along with us."

The children were more reticent, their stories brief and matter-of-fact, lacking emotion, or at least effectively concealing it. Donna Mae and Bud Schultz were still at work Friday at 5:30, while nine-year-old Julie was home with their new housekeeper, an older woman who had just recently arrived from Germany and was finding life on the American frontier a totally new experience in every way. An earthquake of any magnitude was entirely beyond her comprehension, and so she remained rooted to the living-room floor when the Schultz home began to shake. When objects started flying about, Julie became alarmed and finally persuaded the frightened lady to leave the house with her. Julie simply states that just as she reached the edge of her driveway, her home and yard broke apart and fell away toward the water. Clara Evanson, who happened to glance out her window at just that moment, said she had never seen a young child run faster, while pulling the housekeeper along, and the ground was literally breaking up at her heels as she ran.

Dave Evanson was home with Clara and the two babies that afternoon, and Dave said, "When I first noticed the tremors, I glanced at my watch to see how long they would last. This is habit, being in the weather bureau here. The time was 5:36 and 10 seconds by my watch.

"My own impression when the first tremors began was that it provided an opportunity to point out to our youngsters a new experience. 'Look, Janie Lou, an earthquake,' I said. As the little girl looked, the clock fell off the mantel. We heard a glass fall out of a kitchen cupboard. I went in to close the cupboard door to save the others and returned saying, 'It can't get any worse.'

"But this quake kept going. Out the back window I noticed the children's swings swinging out to the horizontal. The big window near Clara shattered. The earthquake was getting rather severe, so a poor place to sit was near the windows. I told Clara to move, but she was already on her way.

"The first destructive earthquake for Anchorage, I thought. Of course, other quakes had broken glassware and cracked masonry, but when my own window breaks, that makes it *destructive*. A painting we prize fell off the wall and hit me. A part of our front porch broke and fell down. My thought was that with the broken windows, and now the porch, this earthquake was getting expensive. It had made its impression. Now I hoped it would stop. It kept going.

"The house tilted sharply downward, and the refrigerator slid to the opposite wall of the kitchen. The top door of the refrigerator came off and rested temporarily against a cabinet as oranges rolled out after it. The kitchen floor became more level, but the walls twisted terribly and most of the rest of the windows broke. I could no longer look outside. Anyway, we were kept busy inside."

Clara said: "The hallway walls next began to close in on us, so David ordered, 'Get under the kitchen doorway.' While we were moving from the hallway entrance to the doorway between the living room and the kitchen, plasterboard broke and fell from the ceiling in chunks, hitting us and showering us with loose vermiculite insulation. We stood with our bodies arched over the children.

" 'Well, we're all together,' David said, trying to be cheerful. The floor broke, and sand came up from below into the living room until it covered some furniture. Part of the roof then broke away above us. It was immediately apparent that the sand might provide an escape route through the ceiling timbers and out the roof.

" 'Come on,' David said. 'My foot is stuck,' I said. It was the first thing I had said since the shaking began.

"David took my baby from me, put both babies on the sand upheaval, and gave a terrific pull on my arm which freed me. He picked up both babies, one under each arm, said, 'Hurry up,' and we climbed through the ceiling timbers, through the hole in the roof, over some still-moving debris, and up on a ridge of sand quite above the roof of our house."

Dave said, "After the dust had settled and we were talking about getting some clothing out of the wreckage to protect us, Janie Lou and Ted [the children] looked around. Ted was just then beginning to whimper.

" 'House broken,' Janie said.

" 'We'll buy Mommie a new house,' said I, although I didn't know how this would be done at the moment."

Barbara Sutherland doubts that she can ever again be a disciplinarian. She had told her two little daughters, four and two, that they could go out and play again before dinner, but under no condition could they leave the back yard. She was in the kitchen when the quake struck, and she ran out to join the girls. They were nowhere in sight, and just as she reached the road, her house and grounds disappeared. The next few moments were frantic for her until she found the children playing in the gully, safe and relatively unafraid. To this day, she shudders to think of what might have happened if they had obeyed her and remained in the back yard.

Grace Johnson's daughter, Nancy, had been playing in the gully, too. In what seems to be typical nine-year-old fashion, she said, "The kids all thought the waving of the trees and shaking of the ground was kind of fun, like being on a boat." When the worst of the motion was over, Nancy ran up to the street, saw the great hole where her neighbors' homes had stood and her own house teetering on the edge of the new cliff. Her one thought was to rescue the five new silver dollars her father had just given her, and before her mother, who was standing nearby, could intercept her, the child had run up the driveway and into the precariously balanced house. She came right back out, happily clutching her treasure, much to the relief of her mother.

In the following days, the Johnson house fell down the cliff slowly but surely. The back walls went during the quake, and the rest caved in as the ground beneath it thawed and sloughed off.

In the meantime, Ken Johnson and his two teen-age sons braved the slanting floors and teetering walls to salvage as many belongings as they could. On Easter Sunday, Mike Johnson was collecting the laundry, which had been hung in the basement. He was dangling from some upright beams, facing the great open space of what had once been the back wall. Suddenly there came a loud roar, and a helicopter was hovering there, the pilot urgently signaling him to get the h—— out. Mike obeyed, but only after he had collected the rest of the clothes.

It is difficult to describe the feelings of these families as they watched their homes and land break up into bits and pieces within a few minutes. It is even harder to talk of the thoughts and emotions felt by Thelma and Del Ingram as they stood on the street and watched the home they had built with their own hands being torn and wrenched apart as the ground beneath it moved swiftly and steadily, like a volcanic flow, hundreds of yards out and down to the sea. Thelma had been working in the basement at 5:30, and at first thought the shaking was the result of Del's carpentry work upstairs. She quickly changed her mind and ran up to join him. He was still carrying a hammer as they ran outside.

Although these people were in the midst of the disaster, many others far removed from the area were experiencing equally strong feelings of fear and frustration as they thought of their loved ones in the midst of the catastrophe. Rosalie and Ted Shohl were taking their first vacation away from the children since the eldest was born. They had flown to Hawaii on March 24, leaving the four little ones at home with loving, jovial Sara, their competent Negro housekeeper. On Friday night, March 27, Hawaiians were routed out of bed by air-raid sirens signaling a tidal-wave alert. What was causing the tidal wave, the Shohls asked. A dreadful earthquake in Alaska, was the reply, and they rushed for the telephone. Unable to get through, they turned to the radio and heard those first exaggerated and distorted accounts of the city of Anchorage in flames, the entire Turnagain area fallen into the sea, and hundreds of lives lost. Then the Shohls could do nothing but wait for available transportation, with no further word of their family until they reached Chilligan Drive on Sunday noon. Rosalie ran down the street toward a group of neighbors salvaging belongings. "Are my children dead or alive?" she cried.

They were alive and unharmed, and their home, along with the other houses on the gully side of Chilligan, had come through unscathed. At the time of the quake, the four children were in the basement watching television. Big, slow-moving Sara was upstairs cooking supper. When the shaking grew intense, she raced down the heaving steps with the speed and agility of an athlete, gathered all four into her ample arms, and prayed and sang hymns until the worst was over. When a neighbor looked in on them a short time later, he found them all calm and unafraid.

There was sadness on Chilligan Drive, with the loss of so many homes and possessions, and at the coming to an end of a neighborhood we all loved so well. But real tragedy struck at the end of the street. On Good Friday afternoon, the Meads' oldest daughter, Pam, went to visit a friend in Turnagain. Wanda decided to run over to a nearby shopping center to pick up a few Easter gifts for the children. Perry, Alaska's only neurosurgeon, was still hard at work. Young Perry, a most reliable and level-headed twelve-year-old, was left in charge of little Paul and Merrill. Nine-year-old Penny, self-reliant since a toddler, was his able assistant.

During the year in which we shared the bluff with the Meads, we saw a great deal of the Mead children and came to love them almost as our own. Because Penny is just our Anne's age, she became virtually a part of our household, and the two were inseparable companions. David was much younger than Perry and a good deal older than Paul and Merrill, but the two little boys were fascinated with David's sand pile, his trucks and cars strewn all over it. Paul spent many hours there, but we were often unaware of his presence because he was the shy and quiet one. Gay and impish Merrill, at two years of age, remained closer to home. But during the warmer months, when Wanda worked on her garden, Merrill often toddled up our driveway to join the rest of the gang. The youngest of five, although with the appearance and disposition of an angel, he could be as determined and stubborn as any of the older boys.

His brother Perry was the same in many ways—although there was no Thomas his age to play with, he often joined the younger boys and was unusually gentle and patient while playing with them. He was also a strong, active twelve-year-old, ever ready for rough cowboy-Indian games in our woods during the summers and, when winter came, was one of the best of Alaska's young ski racers.

The story of the tragedy was difficult to piece together, as it had to come from Penny alone. She said that the four of them were sitting at their kitchen table, eating some fried chicken, when the violent shaking began. When it quickly worsened, she ran down the back steps and outside, with Perry just behind her, leading little Paul. Penny said that Perry then left them and ran back inside to get Merrill. At this point the house and land began to break up, and Penny says that she saw Perry, while holding Merrill, fall into one of the many crevasses and disappear from sight. Then she and Paul clambered to the top of a car parked in the driveway. She gives no reason as to why she did this, a move which probably saved their lives, and I think it amazing that Paul was able to join her, when I recall the strength of the shaking which flung me to the ground.

Just a few moments after we passed the two standing on the car, Paul Crews, a good friend from a nearby street, clambered down the cliff and picked up the thoroughly frightened children. Then, although he and other members of the Alaska Mountaineering Club spent most of the night searching the ruins of the Mead home, no trace was ever found of Perry and little Merrill.

Perry died a hero, and his father also lived through the days following the disaster as a truly heroic individual. All through the first grim night of terror the radio frequently broadcast pleas of, "Urgent—Dr. Mead needed immediately at Providence Hospital." For the next twenty-four hours, and for many days afterward, he went from bed to bed at the hospital, tending to the needs of his patients, tears streaming down his face from the sorrow of losing his two children.

Those of us who lived in the Turnagain area were, for the most part, so concerned with our own safety and loss that for a long while we were unaware of the terrible damage inflicted on downtown Anchorage. Then, as we listened to the radio during the long night afterward, sparse reports from all parts of the city began to piece together a picture of great and almost unbelievable destruction. Many homes, stores, and apartment houses crumpled or sank due to more earth slides, and other tall buildings were extensively damaged or totally destroyed simply because of the severe shaking of more solid ground.

One downtown area—mostly residential and covering about fifteen blocks between L Street and the bluff, slipped toward the water, leaving large holes and long, jagged cracks in the snow-covered ground. Many homes sank down into deep pits—the frame buildings usually remaining intact but incongruously peeking above ground at second-floor level. People in these homes at the time of the quake said they felt as if they were riding down an elevator. A steady downward sinking until they were looking out windows at dirt walls instead of trees and sky.

The six-story Four Seasons building just off L Street didn't fare as well—destined to become the luxury apartment house of Anchorage, with commanding views of the city to the east and the Alaska Range to the west, it was structurally completed at the time of the quake, but workmen were busy with interior finish work. Fortunately, the entire crew of forty-eight men left the building minutes before 5:36 P.M., headed for their homes and the Easter weekend. At 5:36 witnesses watched the luxury apartment house rock back and forth for the first few minutes and then crash to the ground—one large rubble pile of cement and steel. At first it was thought that fissures or holes in the ground were the cause for such total collapse, but later studies by engineers revealed structural failures in the building itself.

Just across the street, the new four-story Presbyterian Hospital withstood the violent shaking with no structural damage. But as soon as the quake was over, doctors and administrators within the building realized they would have to evacuate. They were without electricity or heat, supplies and medicines were strewn all over the floors, and a three-story chimney crumpled on tanks of oxygen and nitrous oxide, releasing the gases throughout the building. Mrs. Elizabeth Trigge, director of nurses, vividly described the chaos in the hospital pharmacy: "The broken glass and drugs were this high on the floor," she explained, holding a hand about two and a half feet above the floor. "The syrup and liquids were this deep," holding fingers four inches apart. "Mixed in all this were pills and packages," she said. "But on the floor of the central supply room is a great stain in violent red. A gallon bottle of tincture of zephiran crashed in the quake. I paint and have always wanted to try surrealism," Mrs. Trigge said, pointing to the wild design on the tile floor. "I call this one *Friday's Fury.*"[2]

The moment the earthquake was over, Dr. Harvey Zartman, a pediatrician with offices on the second floor, rushed up to the hospital's nursery and, after many trips up and down the three flights of unlit stairs, collected all the new-born babies in his car and drove them out to Anchorage's other hospital. The twenty-two other patients were evacuated just as rapidly and safely.

Another slippage of ground on the north side of the city caused a large section of the main street, Fourth Avenue, to sink ten to twenty feet below ground level. Fortunately for the people crowded into the bars and stores in the two-block-long section, the sinking movement was similar to the L Street area—fairly slow and steady. The buildings remained intact, and everyone was able to get out without injury.

On Fourth Avenue at 5:36, a gas-station attendant gave up trying to pump gas into a car as it lurched and bounced about. He ran out into the street, where the asphalt was rolling like ocean waves. (Many people, experiencing the quake while on the streets or sidewalks, commented on this extraordinary motion of the ground—others, standing or lying on the concrete floors of buildings said that the concrete rolled in waves, too.)

The attendant, while having a great deal of trouble standing, watched all the buildings in front of him sink slowly beneath ground level. People were running out onto the street, falling down, grabbing hold of lampposts or cars for support. Parked cars were being slammed together, and many slid down into the gigantic hole formed by the sinking ground. One witness said that nobody yelled or screamed, that the only sounds were the breaking of the glass windows, the clanging of the cars, and the groaning of the wood buildings.

A bartender in one of the bars said that although the first tremor was greeted with jovial flippancy, when it gathered force and bottles and glasses began to fly about, panic took over.

[2] *The Anchorage Daily News,* Monday, March 30, 1964.

Women screamed and remained rooted to the spot, while men rushed headlong for the doors.

The Denali movie theater, in that same two-block-area, also sank slowly until its marquee was resting at ground level. Hundreds of children were crowded into the other theater farther uptown, enjoying a special holiday matinee, while the Denali was closed until evening. A switch in theater schedules could have ended in great tragedy. (One of the mothers in the uptown Fourth Avenue Theater reported that although the building shook violently, there was no damage and no panic among the many, largely unattended, children. Once the quake was over, the manager kept them all at the theater until frantic parents came to pick them up.)

One of the oddities of earthquake behavior was clearly apparent along Fourth Avenue—while the buildings on the north side sustained heavy damage and large sections of the street were ripped apart, the stores lining the south side of Fourth Avenue came through unscathed, not even a crack in their large plate-glass windows. The whimsey of the quake passed over them, but on the next block to the south, along Fifth Avenue, the handsome new First Federal Savings and Loan building, three stories of mostly glass walls, was extensively damaged. Strangely enough, almost all the glass remained intact, but the interior partitions and the back brick wall looked as though they had been slapped by a giant hand.

Just a few blocks away, on the south side of Fifth Avenue, stood Anchorage's newest and largest department store—J. C. Penney's. The five-story building had opened just a year earlier and was the largest of the J. C. Penney's chain west of the Mississippi. Bill Tobin, managing editor of the *Anchorage Daily Times,* was parking his car in front of the store at 5:36. When the shaking began, Bill says, "I leaped from my car, with the engine still running, and ran into the street. A woman there was about to fall, and I grabbed her. As we stood supporting each other, the Penney's building waved and rocked.

"The building was windowless above the first floor, and sheathing on the outside (large four-inch-thick precast concrete panels) began to peel off and fall in the street. As I watched, my car was smashed flat. But the engine still ran."[8] His engine continued running until it ran out of gas three hours later. Other cars parked along that curb were smashed, and one of the nine people killed during the quake in Anchorage was Mrs. Mary Louise Rustigan, crushed in her car there. Eighteen-year-old Lee Styer was killed on the sidewalk nearby. Another woman was trapped in her car while waiting for a red light in front of Penney's, and when rescuers finally dug her out she was alive but badly injured.

Two other smaller buildings in downtown Anchorage, both auto-sales stores, collapsed completely, but the three tallest structures remained standing. However, of the three, two fourteen-story apartment houses, 1200 L Street and the Mount McKinley Apartments, took such a beating as they whipped back and forth that the structures were severely damaged, and it was three years before they were repaired enough for occupancy again. Large X-shaped cracks appeared beneath the windows on almost all floors, and the interiors were just as badly damaged.

The third downtown "skyscraper" to remain standing was the Anchorage Westward Hotel. The fourteen-story building now has the distinction of being the tallest structure to come through a quake of such great magnitude without major damage. The relatively small amount of damage that did occur was a result of the fourteen-story section banging against the two lower wings of the luxurious hotel.

One hotel guest was standing just outside the entrance at 5:36. He ran down the hill to the safety of a parking lot, then turned to watch the building sway from ten to fifteen feet to the north and south. His main thought was one of distress that his movie camera was still up in his hotel room! (Most of the tall buildings in town moved primarily in a north–south direction, but also showed evidence of east–west displacement. The downtown Cordova office building revealed damage primarily from east–west movement.)

Many others on streets nearby watched the swaying of the Westward with mixed feelings of amazement and horror. Our dentist, whose office was just across the street from the hotel, told us he could see it from his window. Dr. Joshua Wright had

[8] The Indianapolis *Star* (Indianapolis, Indiana), March 29, 1964.

a patient in his chair at 5:36, and while the dentist was all set to run downstairs and away from his antiquated building, his patient remained glued to the chair, staring out the window at the hotel, almost hypnotized by the great swaying of the building.

Bob Reeve, famous Alaskan bush pilot and head of Reeve Aleutian Airways, was celebrating his sixty-second birthday with a group of friends in a newly opened restaurant at the very top of the hotel. After a lifetime of exciting and hair-raising experiences, Bob talks of being knocked back and forth from wall to wall, along with chairs, tables, plates, silverware, and glasses, in a most matter-of-fact way. About halfway through the ordeal he did wonder where all his guests had gone. When the quake was over, he calmly picked up his hat and coat and walked down the fourteen flights of stairs, finding a thoroughly shook-up group of friends waiting on the sidewalk outside.

Clifford Cooper, bartender of the top-story restaurant, described how he and the other guests managed such a hasty retreat down to street level: Cooper said he was caught in a hail of flying glassware, broken bottles, and other bar equipment. Six guests caromed off overturning tables and chairs. "The building was rocking," Cooper related. "Plaster fell. As we crawled and ran, the hallways buckled and rose as much as forty-five degrees." In the confusion, Cooper had found a flashlight behind the bar to lead the guests out of the building down pitch-dark hallways and fifteen flights of stairs. "The flashlight saved us,"[4] Cooper declared.

Other parts of town received damage to varying degrees. The Government Hill area, a section of stores and homes on higher ground directly north of downtown Anchorage and separated from the city by low-lying Ship Creek, sustained damage from another ground slide. The new Government Hill elementary school was torn in two, half of the one-story modern structure falling crazily down the hillside. If it had not been for the Good Friday school holiday, many children would have been involved in a tragic experience.

Located in the Ship Creek area between Government Hill and downtown Anchorage are the railroad terminal buildings and

[4] *The Anchorage Daily News,* Monday, March 30, 1964.

yards, the port of Anchorage, numerous fuel storage tanks, and many warehouses. Several of the latter collapsed, and the newly opened port sustained some damage but, fortunately for the city, was able to receive ships within four days after the quake. And most fortunately for the port authorities, this facility was one among the very few businesses or individuals to carry earthquake insurance. (It is hard to explain why more people didn't have this coverage, other than that it was an added expense and seemingly unnecessary, in view of the frequent mild quakes and the very slight amount of damage suffered by the city over the fifty years of its existence.)

It is also hard to explain, after mentioning the fuel storage tanks, why Anchorage was spared from fire, the terrifying result of the San Francisco earthquake in 1908. Fires could have devastated the entire city because firemen would have been helpless without water. One explanation often given for the absence of fire was the almost immediate cutting out of electricity in all areas of the city. The Anchorage International Airport probably had the closest call with a fire possibility. The shaking of the quake caused over a million gallons of aviation fuel to spill all over the area. Jim Moody, an engineer at the field, was high in his praise of the airport police: "They had the gas turned off in a matter of minutes, which undoubtedly prevented a major fire." Urgent warnings were also broadcast to all residents, telling them to stay away from the entire runway area. One cigarette from one sightseer could have set all of Anchorage afire.

Aside from the spillage of fuel, the airport escaped with less damage than was first thought. The runways were cracked in a few places, but it was not extensive, and they were ready for use three days later. The terminal building was thoroughly "messed up" but structurally safe, with the exception of the control tower, which collapsed, killing William G. Taylor, an air-traffic operator.

Fortunately for Anchorage, Elmendorf Air Force Base on the north side of town sustained relatively little damage (as did Fort Richardson, the large army base), and the jet-sized runways were available for incoming and outgoing flights as soon as electricity was restored a few hours later. The Elmendorf hospital had to be evacuated due to structural damage, and one man was killed on the army base . . . Pfc. Gary Kletarek was struck by falling debris and died three days later of severe head injuries.

Anchorage's Providence Hospital fared better structurewise and became a local point for recovery operations immediately following the quake. Providence is a general hospital of 155 beds and is owned and operated by the Sisters of Charity of Providence. The building is practically new, first opening in 1962—a six-million-dollar, five-story steel structure.

Sister Barbara Ellen, hospital administrator, and four of her sister aids were attending Good Friday services at St. Anthony's Catholic Church. Although services continued, as soon as the quake ended, Sister Barbara Ellen and her four assistants left immediately. They had the state's largest private hospital to worry about.

Ed Fortier, public-relations director for the hospital, was in his first-floor office at 5:36. When the shaking became intense, he decided to head for the main lobby but slipped and fell three times along the way. He met the switchboard operator in the hall, and the two made their way back to the switchboard with great difficulty. Ed says, "The internal broadcast system was operative, and I told Mrs. West (the operator) to broadcast: 'Please remain calm. Stay in your rooms. The building will stand.' She did this first while the quake was at its peak and repeated the entire message at least once before the shaking stopped."

One of the patients said later that he would always remember the calmness that unknown voice brought to them—"You might call it 'verbal sedation!'" he said. Other patients talked of the harrowing experience of rolling helplessly in their beds from wall to wall, while objects fell all about them. Yet, Ed Fortier said later that he did not see one person, patient or personnel, leave any of the upper floors during the quake. Nor was there any panic afterward, and no patients were injured.

The moment the shaking stopped, personnel began to assess their situation. As Sister Barbara Ellen later stated in a report: "All internal communications were dead except the broadcast system. All phone links with Anchorage were dead. Water mains and pipes within the hospital were intact, but outside mains had been broken and the regular supply was lost. Power was off, and the hospital was operating on an auxiliary power plant that supplied a few key areas, leaving much of the building in darkness. Falling cables had rendered both elevators useless. Throughout the hospital, essential supplies had been tumbled to the floor. Much of the critical pharmacy area was a mixture of broken glass and medicines."[5]

If Sister Barbara Ellen had any doubts as to whether Providence could operate, not one of her staff sensed them. Her determined confidence had an uplifting effect on all personnel. During the difficult hours ahead, she set an example of calm, constructive action.

"The hospital is standing. God has spared all our patients and personnel from injury and death. We are needed now and will get to work,"[6] she told a lay worker who expressed doubts that the hospital could function.

As of 6 P.M., Providence personnel were unaware of the loss of the other two hospitals and of the extent of damage in Anchorage and other areas. By 7 P.M., volunteers, the injured, and dazed and homeless persons began streaming through the entrances, and personnel proceeded as fast as possible to prepare the hospital for all-out emergency operation. Engineers had already arrived and determined that the building was structurally safe. A spring at the rear of the hospital was tapped by the portable pump and sent water to the boilers and sanitary system. Drums of treated drinking water were quickly made available. Mattresses were placed in the main-floor halls for the first surge of casualties. Volunteers worked fast to clean up spillage and debris, and the pharmacist and storekeeper determined that despite breakage there were sufficient essential supplies on hand. The emergency and surgical rooms were quickly made operational, and doctors organized themselves into emergency teams to handle large numbers of casualties.

One of the most difficult aspects of the emergency facing the hospital was the total disruption of communications, which made accurate assessments of the situation almost impossible. (Radio

[5] Ed Fortier, "Alaska Medicine," Vol. 6, no. 2, June, 1964, Anchorage Printing Co.

[6] Ed Fortier, "Providence Hospital and the Alaskan Quake," "The Providence Sister," Vol. 1, no. IV, Summer, 1964, published by the Central Development Office of the Sisters of Charity of Providence, Seattle, Wash.

communication, via mobile radio units set up outside the building, provided a link with city emergency headquarters by 9 P.M.) The other, equally difficult aspect which a hospital usually doesn't face was that so many of the medical, nursing, and nonprofessional staff members themselves were victims of the earthquake. And yet they all showed up for duty and did not leave, despite terrible problems facing their own families, until the immediate emergency was over. The entire performance by these dedicated people was truly heroic, and there were as many heroes among the countless volunteers: the three newsboys, at the hospital to deliver papers, who volunteered to climb into a narrow storage area to retrieve a working supply of blood substitutes; the men volunteers who carried patients on stretchers, heavy oxygen bottles, and water tanks up the stairs to higher floors; a doctor's wife who volunteered to set up a nursery for the homeless children and children of hospital workers (mattresses were placed in the lobby and physical-therapy room for scores of the homeless).

Many other volunteers helped to provide coffee and sandwiches all during the long night (a local bakery brought five cases of bread), a difficult feat because the kitchen was inoperative for hours. An unidentified minister carried down the supper trays from upper floors, all dishes were washed by hand, and a Saturday morning breakfast was delivered on schedule to all patients. Infant formula water was sterilized by heating it in the doctors' coffee urn. With the electric ice machine inoperative, a central supply worker made urgently needed surgical cold packs with snow.

By Sunday night, forty-eight hours after the quake, all facilities at Providence were operating normally again. A check on records showed that 108 persons passed through the emergency-room treatment area from 6 P.M. Friday to noon on Saturday, with eight casualties admitted. From Saturday noon until midnight Sunday, March 29, an additional eighty-nine persons were processed through the emergency room, with seven more casualties admitted. By Saturday noon it was obvious that quake injuries were far less than first expected, and the biggest medical headache during the rest of the weekend was respiratory infections among children due to homes without heat.

While the hospital coped with the enormous task of treating

the sick and injured, the city was facing many, almost overwhelming problems seldom faced by any other municipal government. Within five minutes on that Friday evening, Anchorage suffered municipal damage to the extent of $43,745,000 and private-property damage around $155,218,000. 215 homes were destroyed, over twelve hundred were damaged, and 157 commercial buildings were rendered unusable. Nine people were killed in the quake, and over two hundred were injured. The city was also without power, heat, or water, and many areas had no sewer or telephone service.

Of course, most of these facts were not known to city officials immediately after the disaster. With darkness falling, bringing freezing temperatures and bad weather, and virtually all communication disrupted, one of the biggest problems was to assess the casualties and damage. The city and civil-defense personnel immediately set up an emergency headquarters in the Public Safety Building. The four radio stations went back on the air on a public-service basis, using emergency power. Volunteers were quickly dispatched as emergency police troops to guard and seal off stricken areas, and rescue teams were organized. The military immediately offered all possible aid. The Alaska Army National Guard, on its last day of two weeks' active duty in Anchorage, was ordered to remain and assist. Businesses throughout the area offered needed supplies and equipment, emergency shelters were set up to care for the homeless, and agencies such as the Salvation Army and the Red Cross swung into emergency operations.

All city departments went into action the moment the quake was over and worked tirelessly around the clock to restore facilities. We were all truly astonished at how fast electricity was restored to some areas. By 7 P.M. that same night the city's gas turbine was back at work but running on oil, as the natural-gas line feeding the plant was ruptured. The system went out again for part of the night when the oil supply was depleted, but by three o'clock Saturday afternoon most of the Anchorage area was receiving steady, reliable power—less than twenty-four hours after the disaster!

Public-works crews were moving just as fast, repairing the many cracks and breaks in the main roads, tackling the almost insurmountable water and sewer breakage problems (over 60 per cent of the lines were broken). And fourteen inspection teams of architects and engineers immediately began the job of checking all public buildings for damage.

As the city officials moved fast and efficiently, there was no panic in any area, no looting of darkened or damaged shops, no hoarding of food supplies when stores reopened (we never had a shortage of any commodities, despite the great distance our supplies must travel). In short, the tremendous effort exerted by everyone, officials and private citizens, to get back on their feet and help their fallen neighbors do as well, was a truly heroic and selfless endeavor which has few equals in the annals of modern American history.

While city departments tackled the restoration of facilities, emergency headquarters sent rescue teams to search downtown and Turnagain debris. Jim Scott, an Anchorage veterinarian and outdoors enthusiast, was one of the leaders of recovery operations and reports, "Along the Turnagain bluff I met a number of members of the mountaineering rescue group. We organized three teams of men, with three per team, and with the aid of climbing ropes and flashlights we went through the area looking for dead or injured. The destruction was beyond description. A mass of land on a bluff some sixty feet above the level of the Cook Inlet waters had dropped about forty feet down into and out into the inlet. It had been an area of beautiful homes with nice lawns, trees, and lovely gardens—now it was heaved and broken with jagged, grotesque spires of clay and sand and sharp pressure ridges lancing the entire area. Shaped like a large dipper —the handle section two hundred to four hundred yards wide and a mile long, and the bowl a huge circle going about a half mile into the center of a birch forest. Now the trees were wracked at every angle.

"We searched for four hours, crawling, slipping, sliding, cussing, praying not to find anything bad, poking, prying, combing the houses, the ground, looking for injured or dead. That clay was wet—there were about eight inches of snow on the areas of ground not ripped apart—we were wet, muddy, and thankful that we found no one. Reporting to the Public Safety Building, we were asked to get a little sleep and meet back there early in the morning to take rescue teams—men with mountain-climbing experience—into the multiple-story buildings to check again for injured or dead.

"At 6 A.M., the new Penney's store was the first building to check. In teams of two we covered each floor—it was dark, spooky, with the floors heaved and cement pillars broken, the shelves a shambles, items strewn everywhere. As we moved across the floors, each team of two on a separate floor, the building creaked and the floors trembled. Each of us gasped as our flashlights encountered his first partially visible mannequin. Once out, we laughed a bit about it—it eased our nerves, yet made me feel strangely guilty in doing so.

"We went on to the other buildings, all masses of destruction. Thank God for no fires—there was no functional fire control other than tank trucks—like trying to boil the ocean with a match, only in reverse. We moved on to Fourth Avenue; a large section on the north side of the street had dropped into a deep hole, the marquee on the Denali theater was level with the street. Rumor had it there were three bodies near this area—one without a head. We were not happy about looking; also, the buildings were still settling. With every tremor we would jump—walls swayed and creaked. We went into the B & B Bar, a shock hit us, there was a man sitting at the bar, bottle in one hand and glass in the other. Silence. Then, 'There's no one, nope, thersh no one here.' We laughed—then asked him to move out. He left without comment. We were so stunned, we didn't ask him his name. The bar itself was on a 50–20-degree angle—some of the beer glasses upright and still full, bottles behind on the shelf angled but still standing. Another day and place and we might have been in an amusement-park fun house—but then a tremor hit; we moved out in a hurry.

"Thus, Saturday morning went; in the theater we had taken a couple of candy bars each—there were plenty all over the counter-area floor—couldn't help feeling guilty about it, but we knew they would be lunch and supper. The flashlights were dimming, so we replenished them from the Anchorage Hardware. One of the crew walked in and out a broken window—slipped down the angled floor to get them, then climbed out of the building. Again, we all commented on feeling badly about not being able to tell the owners—but I felt sure they wouldn't mind. By noon we were nearly done—no injured, no dead left in the downtown area."

When Jim Scott and the rescue crews had finished their grim task of looking for the injured and dead, they returned to Turnagain to help homeowners salvage belongings. The mountaineer and mountain rescue groups were joined by local Rotary Club members, and within the next few days Jim found himself in charge of over two hundred volunteers (over 70 per cent were boys under twenty). With the order to take out anything of value, the men and boys, working along with the homeowners, spent long backbreaking hours hauling heavy loads up the steep, sandy banks. By Tuesday this big salvage effort was aided by donated equipment—tractors and trucks to lighten the loads and level the banks (hot food was supplied by the Salvation Army and Rotarian wives)—but during the first few days the volunteers frequently climbed out with washing machines or heavy chests or large rugs strapped on their backs.

Those of us who lost our homes were at first overwhelmed by such spontaneous help and asked only for articles of clothing or items of sentimental value, such as pictures. But as we dug among the ruins and found more and more belongings and as the initial shock of the tragedy began to wear off and we faced the practical necessity of starting another household from scratch, we came to realize the importance of saving as much as we could. And time was of the essence, too—a constant rain was damaging possessions strewn on the ground, and high tides were further destroying some of the wreckage.

When Lowell first decided to join Jim Scott in salvage efforts, on Sunday morning after Easter church service, he wanted me to go, too. I had no desire to return to the ruins, to see my lovely home in such a grim state, but Lowell felt I had to go. Only I would know what feminine things would be most important and where to look. So within an hour after the church service a large group of Lowell's friends had gathered by the bluff, including many members of the mountaineering club.

The house was one horrible twisted mass of wreckage—with only the bedroom section fairly intact. As I crawled up the stairs after the mountaineers, I had the silliest thought—all those muddy feet on my carpet! But then I made myself think practically and helped pick out the items for first priority: all clothing, the pictures on the walls, which could never be replaced, my jewel box containing little of value but many sentimental mementos, Anne's dolls, some medicines, and a few books. Our large library was in the destroyed section.

Then I wandered about the debris for a while, finding the oddest items in the most unlikely places. Boxes of Lowell's precious film were scattered all over the sand. One of my Steuben-glass vases perched on a mound of clay, without a crack or chip, looking as if on display in a store window. The men pulled away one of the kitchen walls, revealing the refrigerator, almost intact. When Lowell opened the door, he found two-dozen eggs, all unbroken! I had purchased them just a few hours before the quake for the children to dye for Easter.

During the week after the quake we spent long hours digging among the debris, hauling out bundles of sodden books and papers, pieces of broken antique furniture, wet, muddy clothing, and curtains. It was a treasure hunt which we could not enjoy, but we were amazed and amused by some of the things that survived. For instance, one of the first armloads to be brought up contained all of March's still unpaid bills—and we were not anxious to find them!

One of our greatest treasures, a flag of free Tibet, had hung over the living-room fireplace. So with the help of several boys, Lowell dug around under the mound of bricks from the collapsed chimney. He commented that Lord Buddha would have to perform a miracle to save that flag, and he certainly did. At the bottom of the pile they found a crumpled and torn piece of silk—no sign of its frame or mounting.

Despite our preoccupation with salvaging possessions, we felt, as did everyone else involved in the disaster, a tremendous sense of thankfulness at just being alive—nothing material had importance any longer. One woman, whose home was not damaged but who decided to move toward the hills after the broadcast of the tidal-wave alert, wrote later: "There was nothing in the house that looked of any value—just the children."

In the weeks and months after the quake no one paid any heed to the almost total loss of china and glassware—for any entertaining, assorted jelly glasses were fine, and camping gear was greatly appreciated. The only furniture we salvaged was from our bedrooms, so anything old and unneeded from neighborhood basements was accepted with pleasure. This included clothing until we were able to salvage our own. (For a few days the children were forced to play indoors because they were without shoes or warm clothes. And although I felt sorry for them at the time, the benefits derived from such an experience were all too obvious the following winter: not one lost mitten or boot from November until March!)

Much has already been said of the wonderful spirit of co-operation within the community—from the moment the quake was over. It was truly one of the greatest experiences to come out of the disaster. Everyone wanted to help everyone else, regardless of the loss suffered personally. It would be impossible to ever record even a small portion of the unsolicited and selfless aid so readily contributed by so many. One simple example—on Easter Sunday our minister, Sandy Zabriskie, put up two lists at the back of the church, one for the "haves"—all those who had clothing and household goods to contribute—and one where those who had lost everything could write down what they needed. At least twenty of St. Mary's 150 families were homeless, and many more had lost their china and glassware. Yet at the end of the three services that Sunday the "have" list was more than three pages long, and only two names stood on the "have not" list, put there by Sandy himself!

To add to the spirit of neighborliness, many of us suddenly realized just how much our friends had really meant to us. As we scattered about the city, resettling in any available apartment or house, we lost contact with those closest to us, and a common sight in Anchorage during the weeks after the quake was the chance emotional encounter between friends. When we might ordinarily have waved or called out, "Hi, how are you," we now kissed and embraced, unashamed of tears or showing how over-joyed we were just to see one another alive.

And contact with friends meant even more because few mothers of young children wanted to leave home at all for two or three months afterward. There were none of the usual social gatherings—we did not even relish the thought of leaving little ones with sitters while we went out to dinner. This was partly because we had come so close to losing loved ones, and the natural reaction was to remain with one another. (During the first few days after the quake, after we moved from the Twiggses' home to the Zabriskies', we four slept in one small room, with both cats and the one-hundred-pound shepherd! We didn't have to—we all wanted to, deriving great comfort from just being close together.)

To be with one another was also especially important in view of the aftershocks continually shaking the whole area. We, who had felt calm in the midst of the big quake, now reacted as total cowards at the slightest tremor. Whenever we had one at night, which was frequently, Lowell accused me of reaching the hallway within a second's time. And the newest pastime in Anchorage could aptly be called "Watch for Quaking." Eyes turned to hanging lamps or chandeliers. One friend, whose lights are more firmly fixed, hung a rubber ball on a string from her ceiling—the slightest motion and she headed for the door.

We all quickly discovered that heavy tractors or trucks could easily shake a house, and whenever we had a strong wind we were in for a miserable night. In fact, it was months before our David could sleep through a windstorm without waking in great fright. Just the sound of rattling windows was enough to bring back those few moments of terror.

Turnagain residents were especially aware of ground motion— they felt they were sitting on top of a bowl of jelly, partly psychological perhaps, but geologists did label this residential area unstable for a period because of the thick amounts of blue clay beneath the top soil. The land just behind the slide area was marred by many fissures, large and small. The cracks ran across yards, straight across paved roads, asphalt driveways, and concrete basements. Most of the houses there suffered damage of varying degrees, and underground sewage and water pipes were out of commission for weeks afterward.

Almost all of the aftershocks were extremely mild, compared to the "big one," but we couldn't be sure when one might suddenly increase in severity. Experts in other parts of the United States all hastened to assure us that never in the history of earthquakes had one place been hit by two devastating quakes within a short time. But it didn't take long for Alaskans to dig up the fact that Chile had been rocked by two corkers only a year apart!

Our strongest aftershock came just one week after the big jolt. Seismographs registered it at seven on the Richter scale, which is stronger than the average earthquake. Quake-conscious residents streamed from swaying downtown buildings and homes, but no damage was reported, and once we had recovered from our initial fear, we were quick to note that a tremor with a magnitude of seven was extremely mild compared to 8.6!

Normal living returned surprisingly fast in the weeks and months ahead. Facilities within the city were functioning as usual within a few days, although Turnagain residents had to put up with portable toilets and barrels of water for a good while longer. As to be expected, children were the first to bounce back to normal, thoroughly enjoying the unexpected school holiday and playing for long hours at a favorite new game—"earthquake!" While watching them, I was fascinated at how detached they could be as they knocked down toy homes or upended their trucks and cars. This type of play went on for months, and during the summer dirt piles were a great favorite because the children could cause great land upheavals. I have heard psychiatrists say that these games were the best therapy of all for the kids and it was just too bad the grownups didn't play them, too!

The city moved rapidly to put schools back into operation, and the holiday did not last long. Within a few hours of the quake, school personnel were checking buildings, and on Saturday morning an "Operation Back to School" was set up at the school-district administration building. Teams of engineers began to survey all school buildings, and Monday, April 6, ten days after the disaster, ten of the eighteen elementary schools in the district reopened. All junior and senior high schools went into operation two days later, and by the following Tuesday, just twelve school days after the quake, all schools were back in service—a few double-shifting with others because of building damage.

Most of the families who had to be evacuated from Turnagain decided to return their young children to the undamaged Turnagain school for the remainder of the year. It created complicated transportation problems for many of us, but we felt it would help the children return to normal living faster if they remained with the same teachers and students. The kids were delighted to be back with all their old friends and in a familiar routine, but many mothers were facing another trying period—their first separation from their children and the realization that the youngsters would be facing aftershocks of varying magnitudes by themselves. Actually, most of the children were never even aware of the slight tremors that spring, and I remember that their reaction to one strong one (when many teachers ordered students to take shelter under desks) was one of total indifference. I can't say the same for the parents!

Epilogue

I always add P.S.s and P.P.S.s to my letters, a sign of lack of organization, I suppose. But postscripts can also be meaningful afterthoughts, and in any story about Alaska I would not want to take leave of the reader on tones of tragedy and natural disaster. While the 1964 earthquake had a profound effect on Alaska and Alaskans, it is still only a small part of the story of the Great Land.

Five years have gone by since the big quake. The memories are dimmed, but feelings of terror lie just beneath the surface. All it takes is a slight tremor or a swaying fixture to arouse them again. Yet to Anne and Dave the date no longer means anything. They shrug it off, as only youngsters can, far more interested in other activities of the present March 27. As I went about town the other day, I asked a number of people if they knew what anniversary was coming up this spring. No one remembered or really seemed to care—many had not even been here at the time. (The latest census shows that 46 per cent of Alaskans have lived in the forty-ninth state no longer than five years.) Aside from brief comments in the press and on the radio, the community is going about its usual daily business in an optimistic, busy, boom-town atmosphere.

There are few visual signs left to remind people, in this area or in any of the other towns hit by the natural catastrophe. I'm sure this is a disappointment to the tourist, who for some reason or other remembers far better than the Alaskan. Fortunately for the visitor trade, our city government used foresight in the midst of early clean-up operations and designated the slide area on the south side of Chilligan Drive as Earthquake Park. While those of us who had lived there dread returning to see the still broken-up chunks of ground, the mounds of now dried-up blue clay, and the trees (some still living) at weird, topsy-turvy angles, the visitors flock to the park the moment they arrive in town.

While tourists gape at what nature tore down, Alaskans are ever busy building up. The growth in the Anchorage area particularly has been truly unbelievable, and all signs indicate that it will move even faster in the next five years. Plans for a gigantic causeway to span Turnagain Arm are moving swiftly toward the construction stage; a four-lane expressway connecting the Anchorage downtown area with the airport will be completed soon; a number of new high-rise buildings and large shopping centers have just been finished or are on the drawing boards; a large new junior high-high school complex will be started in 1969, with another due a year later; at least three new elementary schools will be built this year; the giant Community College branch of the University of Alaska will be opened shortly, and as far as private homes are concerned, every time I drive around town I discover a new subdivision—they seem to sprout from the ground overnight!

The Alaskan is an eternal optimist, a determined individual, and a hard worker, and it is this combination that makes dreams come true. Most residents of the forty-ninth state are also aware of standing at the threshold of a period of sweeping change—not only economically but culturally and socially as well. With the tools of modern technology available today, it is possible to conquer our vast wilderness and overcome the harsh climate now more than ever before. Untold natural resources, so far not even explored, can be developed to their fullest capacity. More roads, better airfields, harbors, and even a railroad into the arctic will open up areas greatly isolated for so long. The Alaskan native peoples, the largest aboriginal group within any state of the union, face the greatest change of all, hopefully toward a living standard and opportunities far better than the conditions which have held them down for so long.

Change must be faced—it can be for the good and beneficial to all, but at the same time it must be held in its proper perspective. As General Lindbergh told us, the eyes of the world are upon Alaskans—can we, as we develop, still maintain that which is so dear to us? We must always keep in mind why we came to live here in the first place and why others like to come visit—we want no part of overcrowded cities, suburbs, and freeways; or of smog, water pollution, and a swiftly vanishing countryside, where the only wild life can be found in zoos. And we must be especially aware that these great changes which have taken place in the "lower 48" can creep in almost unnoticed at first: the cutting down of a stand of trees leaves others open to the ravages of wind and the soil susceptible to erosion; the moving of dirt can kill vegetation and change water courses; the dumping of oil by one ship in an inlet or gulf not only kills present marine life but can greatly affect future inhabitants as well; a faulty sewer system has already contaminated the streams closest to Anchorage, and pollution could hit our air just as quickly.

Surely there is enough land in this enormous state, almost large enough to be a country of its own, so that through careful planning and vigilant control, the development which is inevitable can go hand in hand with preservation of wilderness areas. It is so imperative to Alaskans, and to all Americans as well, that we can continue to fly over or drive or walk through our towering mountain ranges with their perpetual snow slopes and glaciers, our seemingless endless forests and tundra plains, all unpeopled except for the ever-abundant wild life, and to enjoy to the fullest our rivers, lakes, and streams. At times when I do fly over this wild terrain, as on our January trip to Fort Yukon, I am at such a loss for words that I always turn to my favorite poet, Robert Service, who so effectively caught the spirit of the northern wilds. In describing that midwinter flight, I quoted two lines from his *Spell of the Yukon:*

From the big, dizzy mountains that screen it
To the deep, deathlike valleys below.

The next four lines mean even more to me in that they simply sum up all my strongest feelings for Alaska:

Some say God was tired when He made it;
Some say it's a fine land to shun.
Maybe! but there's some as would trade it
For no land on earth—and I'm one.[1]

[1] *Collected Poems of Robert Service*, Dodd, Mead & Company, New York, 1958, p. 3.

Index